STAYING AFLOAT WHEN THE WATER GETS ROUGH

Praise for David Posen's bestselling *Always Change a Losing Game*, now in its sixth printing!

Here's what reviewers have said:

"Everyone can relate to this book! Dr. Posen teaches us, through practical and entertaining stories, how to make our lives better in every way—and inspires us to take action!"

—Jack Canfield, co-author of *Chicken Soup for the Soul*

"This book makes change seem fun rather than a chore. Dr. Posen shows you how to turn dreams into reality. Begin reading any page—you'll not want to put this wonderful book down."

—Christine A. Padesky, Ph.D., co-author of *Mind Over Mood* and Director, Center for Cognitive Therapy, Newport Beach, CA

"The book reveals a healer's insights, wit, compassion and a comforting degree of common sense."

—Peter Trueman, *Pathways Magazine*

"For a change: a practical book full of the clinical wisdom of an experienced physician."

—Dr. Stanley E. Greben, Professor Emeritus of Psychiatry, University of Toronto

"This book is perceptive, instructive, productive and written in an entertaining fashion. It is a valuable addition to any growing person's library."

—Dr. Ron Taylor, Toronto Blue Jays Team Physician and former major league baseball player

"Overall rating: excellent; weaknesses: none. A flowing, comfortable, easy-to-read tool."

—Laura Heraty, *Canadian Medical Association Journal*

"The book is enjoyable, amusing and easy to read, and a must-buy for the multitudes of people who live with far too much stress."

—Wendy Peters, *The Business Executive*

STAYING AFLOAT WHEN THE WATER GETS ROUGH

How to live in a rapidly changing world

DAVID POSEN, MD

JAICO PUBLISHING HOUSE

Ahmedabad Bangalore Bhopal Chennai
Delhi Hyderabad Kolkata Lucknow Mumbai

Published by Jaico Publishing House
A-2 Jash Chambers, 7-A Sir Phirozshah Mehta Road
Fort, Mumbai - 400 001
jaicopub@jaicobooks.com
www.jaicobooks.com

Published in arrangement with
Key Porter Books Limited
6 Adelaide Street East, 10th floor
Toronto, Ontario
M5C 1H6, Canada

STAYING AFLOAT WHEN THE WATER GETS ROUGH
ISBN 978-81-8495-249-0

First Jaico Impression: 2011

Printed by
Saurabh Printers Pvt. Ltd., Noida

To my remarkable mother, Ida Yudashkin Posen,
a woman well ahead of her time but who died much too soon.

Contents

Acknowledgments 11
Have You Been Affected by Change? 13
Introduction: Does Anyone Know What's Going on Here? 15

PART ONE: Thinking about Change

1. **Why Can't Things Stay the Way They Are?**
Understanding the Need for Change 24

2. **Why Is Change So Hard?**
Why Change Is Difficult/Stressful/Threatening 34

3. **Is There Any Good News about Change?**
Seeing the Benefits of Change 47

4. **We're All Change Agents**
Belief in Your Ability to Deal with Change 68

5. **What's So Funny about Change?**
Keeping, and Using, Your Sense of Humor 77

6. **Where Am I?**
Stages in the Change and Change-Adjustment Process 87

PART TWO: Taking Action

7. **When the Going Gets Tough, the Tough Get Strategic**
Starting to Deal with Change 104

8. **Don't Just Jump In**
Planning, Practicing and Preparing for Change 125

9. Change Is So Exhausting!
Generating and Maintaining Energy for Change 136

10. I Can't Go That Fast!
Pacing the Rate of Change—and Pacing Yourself 156

11. You're Not Alone
The Need for a Support System 167

12. Living in the Question
Dealing with Uncertainty—Questions Without Answers 182

13. How the Masters Do It
The Ingredients of Change-Hardiness 197

14. You Have More Control than You Think
You Can Do This!—Conclusion 215

Appendix: We Have More Control than We Think 223
Suggested Readings 225
Index 227

Acknowledgments

MANY PEOPLE WERE WILLING AND EVEN EAGER to help me in the preparation of this book. I am touched by their generosity and kindness and wish to thank them by name:

Dr. Peter Norlin, who gave me the title of Chapter 7, numerous pieces of wisdom on the subject of change and many detailed suggestions about my manuscript.

Dr. Erica Fischer, Judy Knapp, Sue Hanna, Dr. Robbie Campbell, Tony McLean, Dr. Alan Brown and Rick Maurer, who critiqued the manuscript in detail and gave many helpful recommendations.

Joanne Riley, Dr. Terry Riley and Dr. Carl Robinson, who reviewed my manuscript, commented on it and gave me early positive feedback.

Doris Burns, who helped me significantly with Chapter 6 and taught me a great deal about the process of grieving.

Beverley Slopen, my agent and mentor, who kept telling me I'd write another book and whose guidance and encouragement have been invaluable to me for years.

Susan Renouf and the team at Key Porter Books for their confidence in both my books and for their unfailing and ongoing support of both projects.

Clare McKeon at Key Porter Books, who shepherded me through the editorial process with great patience, understanding and generosity of spirit.

Doris Cowan, my editor, who carefully pruned, tightened and punched up my manuscript.

Carol McCarthy, who helped me get organized for the final push and who tracked down a lot of little details with her sleuthing.

Olga Perkovic, at McMaster University Social Services Library, for going the extra mile to ferret out information on the Yerkes-Dodson Law.

My patients and seminar participants, who, through sharing their thoughts and experiences with me, have taught me at least as much as I hope I've taught them.

And my wonderful family, Susan, Jaime and Andrew, who fill our home with love and laughter, for their great support and encouragement during the writing of this book.

Have You Been Affected by Change?

CHANGE COMES AT US FROM MANY DIRECTIONS, often all at once. Think of your own recent experiences. Which of these changes have affected you?

- Has your work environment changed significantly? Are you now working from home? Has your office been computerized? Have you started shift work?
- Have you started your own business, alone or in partnership with others?
- Have you changed jobs, lost a job or had your job description altered considerably?
- Has your company downsized, merged or relocated?
- Has your workload increased significantly? Are you being asked to do more with less?
- Has your company expanded rapidly? Do you have increased responsibility and/or decreased resources?
- Are you currently unemployed (perhaps for the first time)?
- Have you just completed your education and aren't sure what to do next?
- Have you moved to a new city or a different part of town?
- Have you experienced financial setbacks or problems? Have you had to dip into your savings to tide you over periods of low income or unemployment?
- Have you had to liquidate a business or declare personal bankruptcy?
- Have you retired from the paid workforce (voluntarily or involuntarily)?

- Have you experienced serious illness that has caused you to change your lifestyle?
- Have you sustained a serious injury or become disabled?
- Have you suffered the loss of a spouse or close relative?
- Have you married, or remarried, or entered a common-law relationship?
- Have you become a parent for the first time?
- Have you acquired children by entering into a blended-family relationship?
- Have you separated, divorced or ended a long-term relationship?
- Have your grown children left home (the empty-nest syndrome)?
- Have your adult children moved back in (the boomerang-kids syndrome)?
- Have you moved from an apartment into a house or vice versa?

These are the kinds of changes that can turn our lives upside down. Learning how to manage these changes can lead us to a better life. That's what this book is about.

INTRODUCTION

Does Anyone Know What's Going on Here?

> ***"Change is inevitable, except from vending machines."***
> **ANONYMOUS**

MY FATHER USED TO TELL ME, "YOU DON'T TAKE kindly to change." And even though my life has had its share of adventures and new directions, I've come to realize that he was right. I've often resisted change and had trouble letting go of what was familiar, comfortable and secure. Here's a simple example.

In 1984 my wife and I moved from a condominium to our first house. I was faced with many new pleasures that apartment dwellers don't have to bother with, like shoveling snow and cutting grass. I decided to use a manual lawn mower, because it was what I was used to—and I was a little intimidated by the motorized ones, having seen numerous finger injuries over the years. Besides, its pleasant, rhythmic sound reminded me of spring. I'd also be making an environmental statement (no noise or air pollution from our house)! Things went well for a while until the grass got thicker in July... until the first time I had to mow after a rain, when the grass was still wet... and until I discovered that pushing the mower uphill wasn't nearly as pleasant as pushing it downhill. The second year, my neighbor smiled over the fence one day and said to his son, "C'mere, Matt, here's a history lesson for you! This is how people *used* to cut the grass. Take a good look. You'll never see anything like it again." We both laughed, but it was one of those moments of clarity. I finally acknowledged I was making the job harder than it needed to be, given the technology so readily available. That afternoon I visited my local hardware store (to make the leap from the fifties into the eighties) and heard myself thinking, "You see, Dad, I'm not afraid of change!"

My first book, *Always Change a Losing Game*, was about making positive personal changes to improve health, productivity, relationships and self-esteem, and to reduce stress. In other words, change was seen as internal, voluntary and a *solution* to many problems (the "losing games" we play). In this new book I am looking at the kinds of change that are external, uninvited and often *cause* problems. I want to explore ways for us, as individuals, to better manage the change and uncertainty in our rapidly changing world. Many of the changes we're confronting these days are imposed on us by circumstances, or by other people. For example, I remember scrambling to find office space in 1986 because the building I'd been in for fourteen years was sold and they wanted my office for another tenant.

Change happens to us all. A neighbor called me recently to say goodbye; she was moving to the United States, because her husband had just been offered a promotion that meant relocating. She was thrilled for him, but she loved living in our town. They'd only been here a few years, but she'd put down roots, made friends and established a pleasant life. Now she had to uproot herself again, a change she had neither asked for nor wanted. Her husband didn't have much choice in the matter, either—his job was being eliminated in a reorganization. They had nowhere else to put him, so it was either accept the move or start looking for new employment.

We're living in a time of unprecedented change. It affects every area of our lives, and the rate of change is accelerating. But even though change is a fact of life, most of us find it difficult and stressful—especially when it's rapid, extensive and imposed on us. This book is about managing change and the effect it has on us. And my message is:

You're not alone.
There are things you can do to make it easier.
And you're going to be OK.

We've Come a Long Way in Fifty Years

In 1996 I attended a retirement dinner for a popular doctor at our hospital. One of the nurses prefaced her tribute by reading this playful reflection (author unknown) on the changes that have occurred in the lives of those born before 1940:

In our lifetime, consider the changes we have witnessed: most of us were born before television, penicillin, polio shots, frozen foods, plastic, contact lenses, Frisbees and the Pill. Before radar, credit cards, laser, ballpoint pens, panty hose, dishwashers, electric blankets, air conditioners—and before man walked on the moon.

We got married first and then lived together.

We were before househusbands, computer dating, group therapy, FM radio, tape decks, electric typewriters, artificial hearts, word processors and yogurt. For us "time-sharing" meant togetherness, not condominiums; a "chip" meant a piece of wood, "hardware" meant hardware and "software" wasn't even a word!

In 1940 "made in Japan" meant junk and "making out" referred to how you did on your exam. Pizza, McDonald's and instant coffee were unheard of.

We were here for the five-and-dime stores—for a nickel you could buy an ice cream cone, ride a streetcar, make a phone call, buy a Pepsi. You could buy a Chevy for $600 and gas was eleven cents a gallon.

Back then cigarette smoking was fashionable, grass was mowed, Coke was a cold drink and pot was something you cooked in. And we were the last generation to think you needed a husband to have a baby!

No wonder we're sometimes resistant to change.

Confusion: A Sign of the Times

With the scope of change so wide and the rate of change accelerating, we can all be excused for feeling confused. Some of the changes have been truly breathtaking. Who would have thought that communism would collapse, apartheid would end and a Middle East Peace Accord would be signed, all within five years? Suddenly old enemies are allies and everyone has to make a huge mental shift to get used to the idea. Other changes, like the Internet, still seem like science fiction (I exchanged three E-mail messages with a man I didn't know before I thought to ask him what city he lived in—the answer was Hong Kong). Yet many changes seem to make no sense at all. Consider the following:

- Company X launches a new initiative with great fanfare and at huge expense. Then eight months later they scrap the whole idea and jump on a totally different bandwagon.

- Company Y wants to downsize, so they offer buyout packages to their employees. Result? Only the best people take the severance, leaving the ranks depleted of skill and leadership.

- Company Z downsizes by a third, struggles for six months and then hires back half as many workers as they let go.

Business is filled with a whole new vocabulary: mission statements, outsourcing, reengineering, downsizing, TQM, ISO 9000, just-in-time inventory, flex time, doing more with less, outplacement services, running lean and mean.

Banks are now selling insurance, insurance companies offer financial advice, deregulation has come to the airline industry, mergers and megamergers abound, hotel names go from Hyatt to Sheraton to Holiday Inn at warp speed and free-trade zones are obscuring traditional national boundaries.

And change is not just confined to the workplace. After years of huge government spending and massive debt accumulation, administrations are now into cost-cutting—often passing the buck from one level to another. In Canada the federal government cut transfer payments to the provinces, who then did the same to their municipalities and sectors such as health and education. Then *those* officials cut budgets to hospitals and schools leaving *their* administrators to cut staff and services. Everyone's having to learn on the fly how to do with less—*much* less. One of the biggest changes of all is the growing disinclination of governments to take care of people—the end of "entitlement."

The Internet's growing so fast that legislators can't decide what it means or how to control it—or if it *can* be controlled. In addition, information overload has become overwhelming even to speed readers.

Two articles of faith and dependability have fallen on uncertain times: Job security is now a thing of the past, and real estate, as a secure investment and appreciating asset, has become neither.

Sports teams change personnel to improve performance, filling the roster with strangers with whom the fans feel no connection whatsoever (the Dallas Mavericks basketball team cleaned house so thoroughly in early 1997 that by late February not one player remained from the 1996 season). Other teams keep the same mediocre players but change the logo and uniforms (to give the *impression* of change)—and then raise ticket prices! Then there's expansion and moving of franchises to different cities. In football this led to an interesting game of musical chairs. The Oakland Raiders moved to Los Angeles, the home of the Rams. Then the St. Louis Cardinals moved to Phoenix, the L.A. Rams moved to St. Louis, and the Raiders moved back to Oakland. So now we have the Arizona Cardinals, the St. Louis Rams and *no one* left in the City of Angels. No wonder so many people are having an identity crisis these days!

We also have two-career families, blended families, latchkey kids, DINKs (double income, no kids) and TINS (two incomes, no sex—everyone's too exhausted).

As a result we're feeling confused, stressed out and often scared. No one seems to know what's going on, which changes to make or how to implement them. We look to our leaders for guidance and direction only to find them either as confused as we are, fighting among themselves or no longer relevant. Whether in business, government, sports and entertainment, family life, economics or religion, great change is afoot—not just in technology but in the very way we live our lives.

The premise I want to present is that *no one* really knows what's going on or how we should best proceed. These are uncharted waters for all of us. No one's ever been through the information revolution before, nor massive deregulation. None of us has ever dealt with technology that changes so fast. Moore's Law, devised by Intel founder Gordon Moore in 1965, states that computing power will double every eighteen months—which means there will be a hundredfold increase over the next ten years! We're all flying by the seat of our pants and learning as we go—along with our leaders and policy-makers, both political and corporate.

"Education is what you get from reading the small print. Experience is what you get from not reading it."

UNKNOWN

This is what a learning curve looks like:

At the beginning we learn by trial and error. It's the only way we can discover how to read, ski, drive a car, use a computer or master any new skill. No one is instantly proficient. Watch little kids learn to walk. We captured this wonderful moment on video with our second son and it's a riot to watch. He chose the moment himself, found his balance for a few seconds, fell, got up, took a few more wide-based jerky steps, fell again. But he persisted, never got discouraged and laughed all the way (I'm sure the cheering section of two parents and a three-year-old brother helped make it a thrilling moment for him). But this is how we all learn—by *doing*. And mistakes are part of the process.

I believe that what we're experiencing now, at the close of the twentieth century, is a collective learning curve. We are all trying to figure out what to make of the new technology and the new economic realities. Which leaders should we follow? Which gurus are just flash-in-the-pan, flavor-of-the-month hucksters? It's all very confusing right now, but it will eventually sort itself out.

The Need for Resilience

With all the changes going on, especially in the realms of work and economics, two life skills in particular have become essential in today's world. They are **resilience**, by which I mean a sense of buoyancy, elasticity, the ability to bounce back from adversity or setbacks, and **adaptability**, the capacity to adjust, accommodate or conform to new situations or different circumstances.

Here's a playful story that illustrates what happens when you do things the same way all the time, regardless of the circumstances. It seems an enterprising young man in Australia had the novel idea of teaching a kangaroo to play golf. He worked with his protégé until he felt ready to share his amazing pupil's talents with the public. With TV cameras whirring, he introduced his student to the journalists and correspondents who'd gathered in droves from all over the world to watch the kangaroo tee off on the 450-yard first hole. The kangaroo hopped up to the tee and swung. *Whack!* He sent the ball sailing three hundred yards straight down the middle of the fairway—a perfect shot. Everyone followed eagerly as the kangaroo hopped down the fairway in pursuit of the ball. Again the gallery members took their places as the kangaroo got set for his next shot. *Whack!* And it was another terrific drive. But there was a problem—it, too, went three hundred yards, soaring past the hole and onto the next fairway. The kangaroo had been well trained—but only to do one thing, no matter what the situation.

We need to be open-minded and flexible.

Purpose of the Book

Change is happening on many different levels simultaneously. There is **global change** (like the last recession, the gradual dismantling of world trade barriers and the Internet), **regional change** (such as the fall of communism in Eastern Europe), **national change** (for example, the managed health-care system in the United States), **local change** (like the amalgamation of Toronto's municipalities) and **personal change** (what's happening specifically in your own life). Observing this phenomenon is like looking at an object under a microscope, using ever-stronger lenses to focus more deeply and in more detail. Many books about change have emerged in recent years, but I am struck by how few of them deal with change on an individual level, discussing the impact of change on each of us personally and what we can do to manage it. That is the purpose and focus of this book.

I have another goal, as well: to soften the message about change. Much of what's been said and written about change is alarmist and confrontational, filled with dire warnings: "Wake up and smell the coffee! Change is here. *You have no choice*"; "Get with the program and stop complaining"; "You think *this* is bad? You ain't seen nothin' yet!" These tidings lack compassion and understanding. People are anxious and confused enough already. What we need is a message that says, "Yes, change is a reality. And the pace of change *is* accelerating. It's normal to feel some apprehension. But it may not be as difficult as you fear. And here are some things that will help you adjust." That's the note I want to sound in this book.

Given that change is happening whether we like it or not, the questions I want to address in these pages include the following:

What will increase our comfort with change?
What will make it easier for us?
What tools will we need to handle it?
What will give us the resilience and adaptability we require?

I've divided the book into two main sections. First, *Thinking about Change,* which deals with getting our minds and moods in shape (our attitudes about change and about our ability to deal with it), that is, how we *think* and *feel* (Chapters 1–6). Second, *Taking Action,* which discusses specific strategies to help us manage change, that is, things we can *do* (Chapters 7–14).

Even though this book was written primarily to address the megachanges in the workplace, the economy, technology and politics, the ideas and principles apply equally well to other kinds of change: moving to a new town; adjusting to marriage or parenthood; dealing with aging, retirement, illness or injury; coping with marriage breakdown, the death of a spouse or the empty-nest syndrome. There are a multitude of changes to which we all have to adjust in the course of a lifetime. But I do believe that we have what it takes to handle these events or to learn the skills necessary to do so. We're living in a time of turmoil and upheaval, but it's also a fascinating time to be alive. Let's explore how to stay afloat in the rough waters in which we now find ourselves.

PART ONE

Thinking about Change

CHAPTER ONE

Why Can't Things Stay the Way They Are?

Understanding the Need for Change

HERE WE GO AGAIN! ANOTHER CHANGE OUT of the blue. What's it about *this* time?" Sound familiar? How many times have you heard about a new initiative in your workplace and wondered, "What's the point?" or, "Weren't we doing just fine the way we were?" It's hard to feel enthusiastic about changes when you can't see the logic behind them. Even if you don't agree with the reasons that certain changes are being made, it helps if you understand what those reasons are. You'll feel more comfortable when you know that decisions have some underlying rationale and are not just some arbitrary whim or harebrained scheme someone thought up this morning in the shower.

"Understanding is always a good lubricant for change."
CHARLES HANDY

Here's an example. Nobody likes it when hospitals are closed. Patients lose their familiar surroundings, people lose the convenience of a local facility, and staff members lose their jobs. No wonder protest movements emerge to save particular community hospitals. Very credible arguments are put forward to prove that these hospitals are unique and should be spared.

In 1996 the Ontario government announced it was closing ten of the forty-four hospitals in Metropolitan Toronto. There was great resistance to this idea, but the politicians were determined. They explained the logic behind their radical decision: government debt had mushroomed and annual deficits were deemed out of control. Over the preceding several years of hospital downsizing (again for fiscal reasons) 4000 beds had been closed across the city. This was equivalent to ten 400-bed hospitals. This meant that they had forty-four *partially* filled hospitals, for which they were paying *all* the costs for heat, lighting, maintenance and administration. Why not close ten hospitals, redistribute the beds to the remaining facilities and save the cost of running the equivalent of ten empty buildings? Whatever your view about the role of hospitals in a community—or your opinion about the bed closures in the previous years—the economic logic of these hospital shutdowns is hard to refute. In addition, the demographics of Toronto had changed over the years such that eighty percent of the hospitals were south of Bloor Street, a major east-west artery (pardon the pun), but eighty percent of the population lived north of Bloor. The politicians also pledged to allocate some of the financial savings to an expanded home-care program. Even folks who are unhappy with the decision admit that it makes sense and that the changes are necessary.

Here's another illustration. A company for whom I did a change-management seminar introduced a retraining program, which they called "flex-trade," to increase the skill set of their employees. For example, a pipefitter would learn to do welding, or a welder would be trained as a millwright. Some of the workers resisted, feeling it was an unnecessary and unfair imposition on them to have to take more courses; but others understood why the company wanted a more versatile workforce. It had advantages for them, too—they could get on with a job instead of waiting for, say, a fitter to come and do his part of the work (which produced delays and downtime). The intent of the program was to create more efficiency and a smoother operation. (It also reduced the boredom and frustration that often results from waiting around on the job.) Understanding the rationale behind the initiative made the program more acceptable to the workers.

Goodbye, Hello

Several of my patients have had changes in their employment status lately. They have taken retirement packages (some quite generous) only to be rehired by their companies to do the same job—but as a consultant. On the face of it, this trend seems a little goofy, but there's a sensible reason for it: it's cheaper for corporations to pay their workers as independent contractors than as salaried employees. The same logic underlies the practice of hiring part-timers to replace full-time staff. From the employers' perspective this makes sense on several levels. First, they're not required to pay benefits such as vacation, sick time, extended medical and dental insurance, and so on. Second, they can book staff hours to meet work demand, thus eliminating downtime and saving money if the workload is uneven. Third, it often provides a larger talent pool from which to draw trained workers.

Many companies introduce changes to increase efficiency (computers, fax machines), give better service (more front-line staff) and improve cash flow (just-in-time parts delivery). The goal is to increase competitiveness, enhance profits and, in some cases, just stay in business. Lee Iacocca's massive restructuring at Chrysler years ago is an example of how disaster can be averted by making bold changes. As the business world evolves, companies have to change to keep up with the times, new technology, different consumer demands and/or new government regulations.

The old ways aren't working anymore. The old services aren't in the same demand. Typewriter ribbons don't sell in today's market. Neither do phonograph-record players. The skiing industry has been transformed by the exploding popularity of snowboards. Phone companies and airlines are scrambling for market share, the result of deregulation. Sports teams that didn't want to enter the free-agent market have been eclipsed by big-spending clubs. New arenas and stadiums are being built to appeal to the new sports fan: big companies who want to sit in luxury boxes and are prepared to pay megabucks for the pleasure.

The message is clear: If you don't change, you'll be left behind. Pat Gillick was the genius general manager of the Toronto Blue Jays who built two World Series teams in 1992 and 1993. But in the late eighties, when the team was really starting to roll, they stalled for a year because Gillick decided to keep essentially the same players as he'd had the year before. When the Jays faltered, the GM picked up the derisive nickname "Stand Pat" Gillick, for failing to keep improving the club.

It's Everywhere, It's Everywhere

Radical change is not just happening to you or your company—you're not alone! It's a global phenomenon. When I prepare seminars for various companies and professional groups, I hear about the specific changes (or upheavals) they're going through. I speak to nurses facing massive layoffs as hospitals downsize or close; teachers dealing with shrinking budgets, larger classes and integration of special-needs kids in mainstream classes; retailers fighting to keep market share and ward off creditors; accountants looking for new areas of activity as technology has taken over most of their auditing function; factory workers and bank employees relearning their jobs as their companies modernize and automate.

And remember—this isn't only in North America. Former communist countries are coming to grips with democracy and capitalism; control of Hong Kong has reverted to China; the black majority has won power in South Africa; free-trade zones are developing in various parts of the globe; the marketplace and stock markets have become global and interdependent; computers are everywhere, with the Internet close behind, connecting us all just as communications professor Marshall McLuhan predicted. We're living through the most dramatic period of change since the Industrial Revolution, and it's not over yet. Baseball's Yogi Berra was right when he said, "The future ain't what it used to be."

The S-Curve

It's helpful to know why change is necessary (to solve problems, contain costs or stay competitive), and it's comforting to know that it's not happening just to you. But there's another fact about change that makes it even more understandable: it's an ongoing, natural, inevitable process. Everything has a beginning, a middle and an end. This fact of life can be appreciated visually using the "sigmoid," or S-shaped, curve shown below.

As Charles Handy noted in his book *The Age of Unreason*, this shape depicts the life cycle of empires, political systems, careers, product lines, sports teams,

The Sigmoid Curve

relationships and all living things. There is a beginning, a rise, a crest and an inevitable decline. Think of the British Empire, which began in the eighteenth century, held sway in the nineteenth century and has been largely dismantled in the twentieth. The Greek, Roman and Turkish empires—all have come, dominated and gone. The Russian Empire under the communists lasted only seventy years from start to finish. The same in sports: dynasties were established by the New York Yankees in baseball, Montreal Canadiens in hockey, Boston Celtics in basketball, Cleveland Browns in football. All were dominant when I was a teenager. They had their day in the sun, then faded away. Where are hula hoops, eight-track tape decks, 3-D movies and other products? They were all the rage for a while.

"Everything that has a beginning has an end. Make your peace with that and all will be well."
THE BUDDHA

When I was a kid, we listened to 78 rpm monaural records and thought they were just swell. Then the 331⁄3 "long-play albums" came along, and what a breakthrough that was! Then there were those little 45s that we took to parties, and soon stereophonic replaced monaural sound. Cassette tapes replaced reel-to-reel recorders; Sony came out with the Walkman, which meant you could be wired for sound when out for a stroll. But it wasn't long before CDs revolutionized the sound industry again—smaller than LPs, they had better-quality sound and were more resistant to damage. Every one of these products had a start, a heyday and an eventual decline. It goes with the territory. Each represented an improvement at the time, but the overarching feature is constant change.

Romantic relationships also follow the sigmoid curve. The cycle begins with great enthusiasm and preoccupation with another person. We call this period when you're enthralled with this attractive, delightful, charming and near-perfect creature "infatuation" (a.k.a. "falling in love"), and it can last weeks or months, occasionally years. But sooner or later the novelty wears off. You become more comfortable with the other person. You also start to see the imperfections. Then you either accept that this person's still pretty wonderful and settle into a deeper association, or you lose interest and drift apart. Either way, the relationship changes. The stages can be represented as follows:

> Euphoria→excitement→enjoyment→taking for granted→losing interest→time to leave *or* time to reinvest energy and make a commitment

In a marriage, too, there are stages as people mature and circumstances shift. Again the one feature that is constant is evolution and change.

Even in the natural world, the S-curve is continually demonstrated. Life is dynamic. Nothing is static. As Heraclitus said, "You can never step into the same river twice," because it's forever flowing and changing. The cycles of a single life follow the curve: birth, growth and development as we follow the line upward toward adulthood and the height of our physical and mental prowess. In later years our energy, health and faculties start to decline, and inevitably we all die. Plants and animals go through the same cycle. Trees go through yearly cycles starting with buds in late winter that turn to leaves in the spring and summer, only to change color and wither in the autumn, finally dying and falling to the ground as winter sets in. Throughout nature the pattern is all there in this simple geometric shape. Years ago, in an article by an eminent biologist, I came upon a statement that leapt off the page at me. It was the most dramatic illustration of the constant state of change and evolution in nature I've ever read. He noted that more than ninety percent of all the species of life that have ever existed in the world are now extinct. That certainly puts a lot of things in perspective.

Change has always happened according to this pattern. The only difference is that today's changes are more rapid and wider in scope. What used to take a generation now takes only a few years. Remember those huge mainframe computers that filled an entire room? They had less computing power than the calculators you can now hold in your hand. The Industrial Revolution took generations to evolve; the Information Age is coming at us much faster. But the shape of the process is the same. And the principle of change, the rhythm driving the music, is as old as time itself.

Rethinking the "Stable" 1950s

Life used to be stable, constant, enduring—or so we imagine. Some ask, "Why can't we go back to the fifties? Life was simpler then, less hectic." But was it as tranquil as we remember? Sure, the chaos and calamity of the Second World War was over, the Allies had won, life settled back to normal and economic prosperity abounded. In retrospect, it seems to have been a mix of "Father Knows Best" and a day at the beach. But the reality was very different. Remember the Cold War, the nuclear-arms race, the Korean War, McCarthyism (with its witch hunts for "communists" and Hollywood black lists), the polio epidemics, bomb shelters, the launching of Sputnik and the Space Race, the Hungarian Revolution and the Suez crisis? In 1955 Rosa Parks's courageous refusal to sit at the back of a bus in Birmingham led to boycotts and sit-ins, while *Brown vs. the State of Arkansas* led to school integration in Little Rock in 1957. Net result? The birth of the civil rights movement in America. Meanwhile, in 1955, an obscure musical group called Bill Haley and the Comets released a song called "Rock Around the Clock" and a new form of music, "rock-and-roll," was officially born, changing the face of pop music forever (and shocking my parents' generation along the way).

In fact, the decade that many of us look back on as quiet and uneventful turns out to have been a time of radical and far-reaching change. Change is part of the fabric of our lives and always has been.

Why Is This Happening?

Three facts about change can help increase our comfort with what's happening now.

1. **Change is inevitable.** In August of 1971 I moved to a beautiful town of 50,000 people on the shores of Lake Ontario and west of Toronto. I thought I'd stay a few years and then move on, but Oakville has been my home ever since. However, it's not the same place it was back then. I would have liked the local government to close the gate the day after I arrived and keep the place small and folksy. But nothing stands still. We now have 120,000 citizens and the town is growing yearly. Our pleasant community hospital has had two major expansions and I sometimes get lost in the new wings. Our house is in a new part of town that was forest and farmland fifteen years ago. Change happens! It's just the way it is. Actually, Oakville has controlled its growth to a great extent. It's been

done thoughtfully and tastefully, and the main street has lost none of its charm. But nothing stays the same.

2. **Change is necessary.** In the 1970s inflation in Canada topped twenty percent and wreaked havoc on the national economy. The government brought in wage and price controls to try to stabilize the situation. In the 1990s runaway debt threatened to bankrupt the country. Enter huge cutbacks in government spending to staunch the fiscal bleeding. The cost of oil and gas in America was laughably low until the OPEC price rises started in 1973. So enterprising scientists started looking for alternative energy sources. Solar power emerged as one option, and electric cars are now being tested in California (an innovation that could solve two problems: the current levels of dangerous pollution and the eventual depletion of fossil fuels). Staggering health-care costs led to bed closures and downsizing, but also spawned the concept of day surgery: patients arrive at hospital in the morning and sleep in their own beds that same night. Necessity is the mother of invention, and many changes are instituted simply to solve new problems.

3. **Change makes things better.** Plenty of changes are not strictly necessary—but they are definite improvements. I remember my mother doing laundry in an old washing machine that had a wringer attached for squeezing excess water out of the clothes. Then she hung everything, from sheets to underwear, outside on the line to dry. Later she'd have to bring in the dried clothes. If it rained partway through the process, she'd have to quickly haul in all the wet stuff and wait for the weather to clear so she could start all over again. What a marvel it was when washers and dryers came along to reduce the time and drudgery of doing laundry! The same for dishwashers and other labor-saving appliances. We could all live without them—and many people still do—but changes like these do make our lives easier.

> **"Things don't get better by chance–they get better by change."**
> ANTHONY ROBBINS

More recent innovations include computers that are ever smaller and faster. There's no pressing need for this except to satisfy our growing impatience for portability and speed ("You've only got a 14.4 modem? What do you do to fill the waiting time?"), and manufacturers put huge efforts into staying ahead of the competition. The miracle of computers is recent, but already we're blasé about them in our frenzied quest for more/better/faster. The Internet itself was not *necessary*—in fact, its users are only now beginning to figure out what it's good for—but nobody doubts its incredible potential for learning and the rapid sharing of ideas. Change really can make life better.

What About Tradition?

Sometimes I'm troubled by changes that seem to have no compelling reason and appear to destroy things of value. But maybe I'm just hanging on to the sentimental past. I was one of those people who was shocked and upset at the prospect of tearing down Maple Leaf Gardens, the venerated hockey arena built in Toronto in 1931. I'd had dozens of thrilling moments in that place as a kid and it held a very special place in my memory bank. Then I went to the Gardens twice in two months in early 1997 after an absence of many years, once for a Toronto Raptors basketball game and once for the Ice Capades. It was a real eye opener. I realized how tired and run-down the building was, how uncomfortable the seats were, how little leg room there was, how dull the lighting and unattractive the lobbies were. After that I joined with the chorus favoring a new complex. In April of 1997 I read that MLG was the oldest arena in the National Hockey League—by three decades. Even the fabled Madison Square Garden had been replaced with an up-to-date facility.

In Great Britain the debate over the relevance of the monarchy has been going on for years. But the death of Diana, Princess of Wales, sparked a different kind of debate—and a royal crisis. Diana's warm and informal way with the public stood in stark contrast to the formal, reserved, cool behavior of the Royal Family. In the week following her death there was a public outcry for more openness and less tradition-bound aloofness from the Queen. In the months that followed, she and her family responded by doing away with a number of customs that distanced the British monarch from the public.

Obviously the answer is balance. We need to preserve the best of the past, but we also have to move forward.

In summary, everything runs in cycles. Nothing is static. We can't freeze-frame our kids, our neighborhoods or ourselves; we're all a work in progress, so to speak. There's a process called "maturational readiness," which determines when we will walk, talk, ride a bicycle, get married and so on. It's inescapable and it keeps our lives dynamic and colorful and interesting. Other changes are made out of necessity, to deal with new realities. Finally change results from our insatiable appetite for progress and making things easier and/or better.

Even if we dislike certain changes or find them uncomfortable, it helps if we can understand the need or rationale behind them. This makes it easier to accept the changes and adjust to them.

Change can also feel unwelcome, difficult or downright threatening. In the next chapter we'll look at some of the reasons.

CHAPTER TWO

Why Is Change So Hard?

Why Change Is Difficult/Stressful/Threatening

IN MY FINAL YEAR OF MEDICAL SCHOOL I had to decide where to serve my internship. I had just returned from a four-month externship at the Veterans Administration Hospital in San Francisco and I didn't want to stay in Toronto. I was eager to strike out into the world. This desire grew stronger through the year and I started to become critical of life in my hometown. I began expressing my intention to leave more vocally and forcefully. Many of my classmates were also looking elsewhere but doing so more quietly.

All the graduating medical students applied to several teaching hospitals, listing their choices in order of preference. The program was coordinated by the Canadian Intern Placement Service (CIPS). The hospitals also ranked the applicants, in *their* order of preference. Then the two lists were matched up with priority going to the students (that is, the student got his/her highest choice; the hospital's wishes were secondary). I put the University Hospital in Edmonton, Alberta, first; the Vancouver General second; and two Toronto hospitals third and fourth, just to fill out my list—I was sure I'd get my first or second choice.

"Going from worse to better is always inconvenient."
BENJAMIN FRANKLIN

The night before the filing deadline I suddenly panicked. I'd only been to Edmonton for one day and knew almost no one there. It was 2000 miles from home and got darn cold in the winter. Suddenly the allure of adventure faded, and instead of itchy feet, I got cold feet. At the last moment I reversed the order and put the Toronto hospitals first and second, Edmonton and Vancouver third and fourth. I mailed the application to the CIPS and went to bed.

During the next few weeks I was pretty quiet about my decision. Internships were constantly being discussed around the student lounge, but I no longer joined in the conversations. One day someone mentioned that he was fed up with Toronto, too, and he was going to do what Dave Posen was doing: leave town. I felt like Gary Cooper in *High Noon*. Here was the moment of truth and I had sand in my mouth. When the others pressed me for details about my supposed plan for revolt and adventure, I started to squirm, but finally I had to admit that I, one of the bigmouthed leaders of the exodus, had caved in and was staying put. The resulting surprise and mockery were muted and good-natured, but I still felt like a coward and a cop-out.

Then someone asked, "Why don't you change your application?" (the announcement of final placements was still two months off). "How can I do that?" I said. "I sent my application to the CIPS weeks ago." He asked, "Do you know who the CIPS is?" I hadn't a clue. "Mike Wyman!" he exclaimed. Mike was a student in the year behind us (later to be president of the Ontario Medical Association). Where I'd always thought the CIPS was some big bureaucracy, it turned out to be just one guy—and someone I knew and liked. "Just call him. It's not that complicated." Now, of course, I was on the spot. Would I renew my very public stance of rebellion against the status quo? But I was also re-energized in my resolve to leave and encouraged to see that many others were making similar plans. The best part came next. Timidly I called Mike Wyman to explain my self-created fiasco and was greeted with, "Hi, Dave, I've been expecting your call. In fact, I set aside your application when it arrived. It's sitting right here on my desk. So, what do you want first, Edmonton or Vancouver?"

Funny how little twists of fate can change your life. I had a wonderful year in Edmonton, and even met the man who later married my sister!

This story, which I've used as a touchstone whenever I balk at taking new directions, illustrates the difficulty so many of us have with the idea of change. In this case I wavered and external factors played a role, but in the end the decision was my choice. Most of us find change (especially when it's imposed) uncomfortable, unpleasant, stressful or even threatening. Why? What is it about change that we find difficult? Why do people resist change? There are many answers to these questions, but they can be summed up in two words: **loss** and **fear**.

Letting Go and Looking Ahead: They're Both Hard

It can be very difficult to let go of the past. You may have strong feelings of loss. And starting something new is often associated with fears. Let's look first at loss.

Change means **loss of what is familiar and predictable, comfortable and secure**. Even if a situation isn't ideal, or perhaps even pleasant, we have a feeling of control because it's known to us—and because we've found ways to adjust to it. With change comes the loss of whatever control we had or at least felt, and that can be uncomfortable or even threatening, especially if you're someone who has a great need for control or likes to be in charge.

Loss of control: One of the biggest drawbacks of change for many people is the loss of control, real or perceived. Control, of course, is a relative thing. It is a fact, but it is also a feeling. For example, we can't control the weather, but if we can buffer its effects (with, for example, the proper clothing and shelter) we feel a measure of control in dealing with it. If you're out in a fierce electrical storm, it can be terrifying. But the same storm can be exciting or even enjoyable when viewed from the safety of a screened-in porch or through a large bay window. Extreme cold became an adventure for me when I lived in the Canadian Arctic, largely because of my incredibly warm, three-layer parka.

Business executives who leave their jobs lose a real measure of control. These people were decision-makers who had a lot of choice in their work lives, often deciding when they worked, at what tasks, with what staff and equipment to support them and so on. Losing that kind of autonomy and independence can be very troubling. Sickness or injury can also lead to a loss of control. Anyone who's ever been a hospital patient knows how little input they have into their environment, their daily routine and even in the decisions that directly affect them. Normally we choose when to wake up, what to wear, and when and what to eat. Losing control of such basic issues is always stressful.

Loss of your comfort zone: I always prided myself on being able to give subcutaneous vaccine injections relatively painlessly. The procedure involves a small, sharp needle and a smooth but quick thrust just under the patient's skin (*sub*: under, *cutaneous*: skin). Even little kids were surprised when they didn't feel a thing. Then in 1984 the province of Ontario started a new program that involved a different vaccine. The good news was that the new vaccine would be better absorbed and more effective (the rationale behind the change, as discussed in the previous chapter). The bad news was that the new vaccine had to be given directly into a muscle (*intramuscular* injection). That required a bigger needle and was more likely to cause pain to the patient. I had no choice about the changeover, although it meant giving up a technique I'd learned to do quickly and well (which was less stressful for *me*, as well as my patients). I had to leave my comfort zone and I found it unpleasant to do so. However, I eventually became proficient at the new skill, establishing a new (or expanded) comfort zone.

Loss of competence, confidence and self-esteem: When change requires us to learn new skills, we lose the feeling of competence we had when we were performing tasks we'd already mastered. When we're good at something (competent), we also feel self-assured (confident) and good about ourselves (we have high self-esteem). Change often moves us into areas where we are neither skilled nor certain, and that undermines our self-concept. A young man I know has just graduated from university and landed a job in a rapidly growing company. He's in their two-year management-training program, learning from the bottom up. It's his first real job, offers a lot of opportunity for advancement and pays a decent salary. The problem is that he's at the start of the learning curve (not just for this job but for all the basic management skills to which he's never been previously exposed). His mother told me he's working long hours without complaint, seems to be enjoying the challenge, but "doesn't like feeling stupid." We can all relate to that! The good news is that this stage passes as we learn and develop abilities. But in the short run we lose our feelings of competence, confidence and self-esteem, and that loss, although temporary, can be very unsettling.

Loss of identity: Some changes require a shift in roles, and we often lose our sense of who we are or where we fit. The young man I just mentioned was a popular college senior just a few months ago. He had a place in the university community and knew who he was. His identity included being a student, editor of the college newspaper and a "big man on campus." Now he's a rookie, a freshman, a neophyte in the business world. Not only have his surroundings, routine and responsibilities changed, but so has his entire self-concept. He has lost, albeit only temporarily, the sense of who he is and where he fits in the world.

When people change jobs, move to a different city, become unemployed, get a promotion or get married or separated, they lose their previous identity for a time. This can be dislocating and uncomfortable, especially if your self-esteem is tightly connected to that identity. Sometimes it can also be amusing. Lester Bowles Pearson was Canada's prime minister from 1963 until he resigned in 1968. He told this story about the transition in a radio interview. After the ceremony in which the official leadership of the Liberal Party was turned over to his successor, Pierre Elliott Trudeau, Pearson got into his limousine to be driven home. It was late and he was drifting toward sleep when he noticed that the car had just driven past 24 Sussex Drive, the official residence of the prime minister in Ottawa. He said to his driver, "You've just missed the driveway," to which the man gently replied, "I'm sorry, Mr. Pearson, but you don't live there anymore."

Loss of power, authority, status: Sometimes change means more than a loss of identity. It might mean a real loss of status or even power. Demotions, firings, electoral defeat or resignations from positions of authority can be quite a jolt after a period of entitlement or influence. The same occurs when wealthy people lose their money. They not only lose their significant financial resources, but they lose the power and status that this wealth conferred on them. Whether deposed by others or voluntarily stepping down, going from *Who's Who* to "Who's that?" can be a big loss.

Loss of relationships: I changed careers in 1985, giving up family practice after seventeen years to work full-time in the field of stress management and lifestyle counseling. I also gave up my active staff privileges at our local hospital. When asked over the years what I missed about my days as a GP, the answer was always the same: the people. I sure didn't miss the stress or the long hours, and I certainly didn't miss the nights and weekends on call. But I missed the relationships: with my patients, the nurses and staff at the hospital and my medical colleagues, although I still run into various folks on occasion. When people leave jobs or neighborhoods, when companies downsize or shut down, when students graduate and move on to other endeavors, they leave friends and acquaintances behind—people with whom they've developed important bonds. This is an area of loss that's especially significant for me, so I keep in touch with people, but it's not the same and often we slowly drift apart. In the past fifteen years my two best friends in Oakville moved away. I'm still here but *their* leaving created a change in *my* world. However, we still visit and stay connected—and both assured me their leaving had nothing to do with me!

Loss of physical places: When we talk about roots, we usually mean two things: people and places. Both give us a sense of belonging and security. Geographical roots include your house, street, neighborhood, town and even country. Familiar landmarks are touchstones for us. When we leave a place, there's often a great sense of loss. Everything that is customary and therefore comforting is suddenly gone. This is a major loss for many people when change requires them to move from a place they've called home.

Loss of a dream: Ending a relationship is a painful experience. So many emotions surface and the feeling of loss is profound. But one of the losses that's often not identified is loss of the "dream." This was once explained to me by a woman after her engagement was called off. She said she'd not only lost the person and the companionship in the here and now, but also lost her hopes and fantasies about the future: getting married, having children, building a home, growing old together. One of the clear mental pictures she had was of sitting on the front porch as her husband returned home at the end of the day, strolling around the white picket fence and coming through the gate. In a way she felt the loss of things she'd never had. But in another sense, the dream itself (and the pictures she'd created in her mind's eye) was already a real entity—and having to let it go produced an added dimension of loss. This woman kept a friendship with her former fiancé and eventually married another man with whom she created a different, but equally compelling, set of dreams.

Loss of physical faculties: When change results from illness, injury or advancing age, there is a loss of physical ability. Whether it's eyesight or hearing, mobility or strength, losing certain faculties is a major blow. Loss of hearing can be devastating to a music lover, just as failing eyesight would be especially hard on an avid reader. One of my patients became ill and had to give up two of her most treasured activities, golf and her daily walk. The former was one of her great pleasures, the latter was crucial to her feeling of vitality. Their loss left a significant void in her life.

From Loss of the Past to Fear of the Future

Letting go of the past is hard enough. But the pain of loss can be compounded by **fear** of what lies ahead. What are we afraid of? Even when the change appears positive (a new house, new job, promotion), there is apprehension. What will it be like? How will I manage? What unexpected things may arise as a result? A striking example of fear (in this case, anxiety) in response to a positive change is contained in this story about a former patient of mine. Here's the scene: she's a single mother, working two jobs to make ends meet, perilously close to needing welfare. A legal letter arrives, announcing an inheritance. Problem solved? Relief at last? You might think so, but actually this woman began worrying about money more than she ever had before. Would it be enough? Should she quit one of her jobs? How should she use it? (Pay off debt? Move to a nicer apartment? Take a much-needed vacation? Invest it? Who should she consult to advise her?) She was also feeling some guilt (did she really deserve this money?). Although the money was a welcome windfall, allowing her to climb out of a desperate financial situation, it was also a shock. Her daily decisions had been familiar and straightforward, if sometimes unpleasant, and she'd gotten used to the way things were. Now she was disoriented, jolted out of her comfort zone, with all kinds of new problems to face for which she'd had no prior preparation. Over time, however, she was able to adjust. She got a financial adviser, gave up one of her jobs and even treated herself to some creature comforts she'd long done without.

So even positive changes can be stressful and difficult. Consider the number of people who die within one or two years of winning a lottery. The money throws their lives totally out of whack and is often far less of a blessing than they could ever have imagined.

What are the fears that make change difficult?

Fear of the unknown: Our minds are very good at working overtime to conjure up worrisome scenarios, scary outcomes and perplexing "what if's" in new situations. Most people feel more secure when life is predictable. Knowing what's going to happen next confers a feeling of control that is very reassuring. Ambiguity, uncertainty and unpredictability are stressful for most people, especially if some of the possible consequences are dangerous or threatening. If there's a reorganization at work, the first question we are likely to ask is, "How will this affect *me?* Will I be demoted? Will I be given more work than I can handle?" And, of course, the biggie: "Will I lose my job?"—an even greater fear in today's economy because other jobs may be in short supply. In fact, fear of job loss is close to number one in most people's minds, and anything that poses a threat is stressful indeed. One of my patients noted that middle managers were most resistant to change and fearful of its outcome. As it turned out, they had good reason to be fearful during the recessionary downsizing of the early nineties.

Uncertainty has a fascinating effect on people. We fear it so much we'll go to great lengths to avoid it. Take the phenomenon of political elections. There are endless polls that tell us what is likely to happen, exit polls during the voting to detect trends and then those tedious hour-by-hour, minute-by-minute media extravaganzas after the polls close, analyzing results and trying to predict the outcome.

The uncertainty of nine months of pregnancy is also hard for us to take. Women and their families are often so anxious to know the sex of their unborn child that they seek this information from amniocentesis results, X-rays and ultrasounds. They can't wait until the baby is born. Even buying lottery tickets creates a time delay that some folks can't stand. The lottery organizers were quick to relieve customers of this vexing inconvenience by introducing scratch-and-win tickets. Now you can know within five seconds if you've won. (Of course, the fact that losers will usually buy another ticket on the spot had *nothing* to do with this marketing decision!)

In my thirty years of medical practice I have observed another amazing thing about uncertainty: patients often find that getting no news is more stressful than getting bad news. Biopsies for cancer are the most dramatic example. From the moment a suspicious lesion is recognized, the fear of cancer can be overwhelming. Usually a biopsy is taken as quickly as possible, but the stress continues at a high level until the results are known. If the growth is malignant, one might expect the stress to escalate even further, but in fact the fear and worry actually *diminish*. Of course, the stress doesn't disappear, but **people can usually handle a difficult "known" better than a frightening "unknown."** If the lesion is cancerous, patients will often say things like "Well, at least now I know what I'm dealing with," or "OK, what's the next step?" During the time the outcome is undetermined, they're caught in limbo, where all they can do is wait (with their worries and fears). No action can yet be taken. Waiting for the other shoe to drop is often more stressful than when it drops, even if it lands with a thud.

So, change is stressful because of the ambiguities involved. We leave the known present for the unknown future. And **uncertainty is always associated with a loss of control**. Some people have higher control needs than others and therefore less tolerance for uncertainty. A man once told me, "I don't like surprises. I like order and predictability. I want to know what's going to happen next." (Imagine throwing a surprise party for this guy. Instead of feeling touched and delighted, he'd probably seek out the organizer and spend the whole evening blaming him or her!) Uncertainty and ambiguity are also difficult for perfectionists, who like everything to be neat and tidy.

Fear of failure: Change, especially in the work world, often moves us into new roles. We have new responsibilities and different skills to learn. This raises concerns about whether we can handle it—and if we can't, what that will that mean for our job, our career and (especially) our self-esteem. Like uncertainty, the fear of failure is particularly unpleasant for cautious people, who tend to avoid risk-taking, and for perfectionists. People who have never experienced significant failure are also likely to fear it more than people who *have* failed (and have realized that the world doesn't immediately fall apart). Change is usually less threatening if you know you'll survive.

Peter Vaill points out in his book *Managing as a Performing Art* that adults have difficulty with new learning because they're averse to making mistakes. Even tiny errors upset them, undermining their confidence and self-esteem, causing them to be intimidated and resistant. New technology can be particularly frightening to older people. For example, Jim Harris notes in his book *The Learning Paradox* that those born before 1950 use automated banking machines far less than younger people do.

Here's a true story about a struggle with technology that had a laughable but fortunate outcome. An employee at the Seattle Kingdome was arrested in 1997 for setting up a video camera in the locker room of the Sea Gals (cheerleaders for the Seattle Mariners baseball team) to tape them while they changed. He was caught—because the only footage he got was of *himself* setting up the camera (looking at the ceiling, the room, adjusting the camera and so on). He was obviously unaware that the camera was *on* at the time. Later, when he pressed the remote control to *start* the camera, he in fact turned it *off* and ejected the tape (all without realizing what he was doing). It was lucky for the Sea Gals that he had never learned how to program his VCR.

Fear of embarrassment: Failure is one thing, embarrassment quite another. Learning new skills involves going through a phase of decreased ability (or plain incompetence) in which we feel inept and conspicuous. If others are watching, we may suffer embarrassment, humiliation, even loss of self-esteem. Anyone who's ever been in a tennis class or practiced public speaking at Toastmasters knows what it's like to learn new skills in a public forum. It keeps you humble. But "humble" for some people is the same as "humiliating." They reproach themselves for not succeeding right away, allowing their self-esteem to ride on their halting first efforts, instead of commending themselves for accepting challenges and taking risks. Another group who find change threatening in this way are folks with high needs for approval. They hate for anyone to see them in situations where they appear less than competent. (These people should avoid trying to make a career on the concert stage or in standup comedy.)

Fear of new people: Any athlete who's been traded to a new team knows that some adjustment to a new coach and teammates is inevitable. It can be especially stressful if he has preconceived ideas along the lines of "That coach is a real taskmaster" or "Their captain is a jerk." The same apprehensions are common (and probably quite normal) in mergers, takeovers or changes of boss. The fear can be general ("What will they be like?" or "What if I don't get along with them?") or specific ("I've heard about that guy" or "I never liked her when she was with XYZ Company"). So change not only involves the *loss* of people we like but *fear* about the new folks we'll be surrounded with after the changeover.

A Few Other Reasons Change Is Difficult

Aside from losses and fears, change can be unpleasant because:

Change requires effort and time. The implementation of change can be inconvenient for this reason. There are new skills and new procedures to be learned, new people and responsibilities to get used to. Every time I get a new piece of electronic gadgetry, I'm amazed at how long it takes to work through the glitches or simply to program the new machine. Then there's the hassle factor when things don't work immediately.

Say your department is being reorganized at work, with new teams and reporting systems. As if your job isn't demanding enough, you now have to take time to work through the adjustment period of a different structure, learn a new job description or familiarize yourself with a new software package. It's also a lot of trouble to teach procedures to a co-worker; this is one of the reasons people don't delegate well. It's quicker and easier in the short run to do it themselves—but the short run eventually becomes the long run and they never get around to passing on the chore.

Change can result in value conflicts. Many corporate mergers or buyouts bring together different business cultures that have the potential to clash. For example, what if one group is young, dynamic and ambitious, used to technological innovation and change and eager to move forward, and the other organization is peopled with older, more conservative types who value tradition and service to customers and find the other gang loud and aggressive? There's bound to be conflict.

In the health-care field, where downsizing has left hospitals understaffed, nurses complain that they can no longer give patients the level and quality of care they used to give and took immense pride in. It offends them to have to rush around, giving patients short shrift and spending more time on paperwork and documentation than at the bedside. Morale has been a problem among nurses for years for many reasons, but the undermining of their professional pride and integrity is understandably near the top of their list of grievances.

Blended families are becoming increasingly common in our society. This is where social interaction gets really up close and personal. The merging families always have different traditions, routines and dynamics, but if there are big conflicts about values (in the areas, for example, of money, discipline and religion) the change can be bumpy and bruising unless serious attempts are made to acknowledge and resolve these issues.

Change can make you feel besieged. The fast pace of change in today's society has left a lot of folks feeling overloaded, weary, put upon and, at times, overwhelmed. Workers feel they're being exploited or taken for granted if changes are not implemented sensitively and carefully. It's particularly important to elicit, listen to and respond to employees' concerns. People are especially threatened by change—and likely to resist it—when it is imposed harshly (for example, with the in-your-face attitude that says things like "This is the way it's going to be, get with the drill, stop whining, don't be such a wuss").

In summary, change is usually stressful, even when it's positive change. It's especially difficult when it's rapid, extensive or imposed on us by others.

Change is hard because it means letting go of the past and moving forward into an uncertain future. It's normal to feel the loss of what was and to fear what is to come. Some of our losses are profound, and a time for mourning is necessary and appropriate. Some of our fears are justified and need to be addressed. Feelings of apprehension, confusion, anger and demoralization are not uncommon. They need to be worked through and shared with others.

There's no doubt that change is difficult for most of us, although it's important to note that some people are quite comfortable with change and even welcome it. (We'll learn from these change-hardy folks in Chapter 13.) Whether we're creatures of habit or just prefer what's familiar and secure, we usually approach change with trepidation and concern. Perhaps our natural caution is a protective mechanism to keep us from jumping too quickly into potential danger. I think it's crucial that our feelings about change be acknowledged, understood and respected, not ignored or demeaned. However, we can't stay stuck in the status quo. Change is a fact of life, and we have to learn to move on, despite our natural resistance to things that are outside our comfort zone or are potentially threatening. How we can do that is the subject matter of the rest of this book.

CHAPTER THREE

Is There Any Good News about Change?

Seeing the Benefits of Change

MOST SITUATIONS IN LIFE CAN BE looked upon in different ways, depending on circumstances and your own point of view. The same is true about change—as illustrated by the following story:

In July of 1997 I was in Texas to give a presentation. On my way back to Toronto (via Chicago) I encountered a problem at the San Antonio airport. Despite the glorious weather in Texas, there was a storm in Illinois, and O'Hare was backing up. Flights were being canceled all over the country, and the beleaguered but wonderfully pleasant airline agent was patiently working with each passenger to set up alternative travel arrangements. Of course, she was using a computer to survey the situation and quickly book new flights, operations that would have been painstakingly slow before the advent of information technology.

"An adventure is only an inconvenience rightly understood. An inconvenience is only an adventure wrongly understood."
G.K. CHESTERTON

Finally it was my turn. She told me my only chance to head north that evening was to take a charter to Minneapolis and fly on to Toronto the next day. What a coincidence! My twin sister lives in Minneapolis. But I wanted to be sure she was in town (I knew that she and her husband were on vacation). I would have been really popular with the people waiting behind me if I'd slowed everything down by going and using a pay phone. So I pulled out my little cell phone and called her on the spot. Then I thought "What if the line's busy or no one's home?" No problem. Their answering machine would take my message if they were out, and they also have call-waiting. My sister was on the phone, but sure enough, her line clicked twice and she switched over to my call. I quickly told her I was coming in that night, gave her the flight number and time, hung up and completed my arrangements at the airline counter. Life in the nineties, with all its electronic gadgets, does have its benefits! The same new technology, which can be so irritating and intimidating, can also be extremely convenient.

I marvel at the miracle of airline travel. The whole idea of this multi-ton machine lifting off dazzles me. But my little episode in San Antonio is just as impressive in its way, and it couldn't have happened twenty years ago. Technology allowed me to make a cumbersome, if not impossible, set of communications within minutes. Computers, cell phones, call-waiting and other recent inventions simplify our lives immensely and represent huge progress.

The world has seen more change in the past fifty years than in the entire history of humankind. From television to antibiotics to air-conditioning to space travel, new systems have astonished our imaginations and enriched our lives. And now, with the microchip and digital technology, we're about to be transformed all over again.

Water, Stress and Interest Rates: Lessons in Perspective

Is **water** good or bad? Odd question, isn't it? But if you think about it you'd probably conclude that there's no single answer. You'd say, "It depends on the circumstances." If the water quenches your thirst or sprinkles your lawn, it's good. If it floods your basement, it's bad. If you're a good swimmer, water becomes a recreational playground. If you can't swim, it poses a threat—if not a terror.

What about **stress?** Some people cringe when they hear the word. They can't think of one good thing to say about it. But actually stress can be positive when it protects us from danger. The "fight or flight" response pumps adrenaline into our bodies when we're threatened, giving us the energy to fight or run away from an attacker, to jump out of the way of a swerving car or a falling object. Stress also gives us energy and focus to perform tasks well (for example, when you're working against a deadline, playing a sport or studying for a test). The good news about stress is that we need a certain amount of it to motivate and stimulate us. Dr. Hans Selye (the father of stress theory) called it "*eu*stress," from the Greek root *eu*, which means "well" (from the same root as in the word "euphoria").

What about the other side of stress, the side we don't like? Dr. Selye called this "distress," because it's unpleasant or harmful. This includes all the times we're scared, worried, angry or feeling under pressure. This can be not only disagreeable but damaging to our health, causing everything from headaches to heart attacks.

So, just as with water, stress can be positive or negative, beneficial or injurious. Despite its bad press, stress is neither good nor bad in itself. Again it depends on the circumstances.

As I write this book **interest rates** are near an all-time low. Is that good or bad? Again there's no single answer. If you owe money, it's great. But if your money is invested in fixed-income assets like bank accounts or GICs, you get a lousy return on your funds. Interest on bank accounts today barely covers inflation. Retired people living on savings see their incomes fall when rates are low. Here again deciding whether low interest rates are good or bad depends on who you are and what your situation is.

Change: Both Good and Bad, Take Your Pick

Now let's apply this lesson to our views about **change**. There's no question that change can be positive. For instance, I think we'd all agree that indoor plumbing is a good thing! Ditto for public education, the automobile and heart-lung machines. All represented radical change when they were introduced, and all have been enormously beneficial. Progress can have a downside, however. Historically it has often put people out of work. When they introduced the diesel engine, did anyone consider the impact it would have on the coal man who showed up for work the next day only to be told his coal-stoking job had become obsolete?

I heard an interesting discussion in the 1970s about the difficulty certain immigrant women, from countries like Portugal and Italy, had integrating into North American society in the 1950s. These women often became isolated and depressed. One theory blamed the problem on refrigerators! It turns out that in the Old Country women had to go to market every day to buy food because, in their small villages, they didn't have refrigerators.

Perishables like milk and vegetables had to be bought fresh. Despite the inconvenience, there was an important benefit to this activity: the women met daily in the marketplace and visited with each other. They'd exchange news and pleasantries and enjoy a regular flow of social interaction. In America, with modern refrigeration, daily trips to the market were unnecessary. This was a plus for busy people. But it removed an important opportunity for immigrant women who spoke no English to socialize with their European sisters.

Some thirty-odd years ago a friend sent me a short article from *Reader's Digest* describing a mythological conversation between a Greek god and the mortals of Athens. The god was offering a tool of incredible benefit to the populace. It would simplify their lives, make travel fast, expeditious and comfortable, and allow them to visit distant lands that would otherwise be out of reach. In exchange, however, the god required the random blood sacrifice of hundreds of humans each year. He was turned down immediately by an indignant citizenry who were appalled that such an offer would even be made. Then the author of the article noted that Americans had struck exactly that bargain when they embraced the motorcar. In return for the benefits of the automobile, 50,000 lives are lost randomly in the United States each year, to say nothing of the hundreds of thousands of injuries. It is a sobering perspective on the cost of progress. Yet none of us would consider giving up cars to return to the horse and buggy.

All of which brings us back to the question: Is change good or bad? The answer, clearly, is BOTH. Virtually every change brings benefits and drawbacks, and we usually consider it a good change when the positives outweigh the negatives. But too often, when we resist the very idea of shaking up the status quo, we focus on the negatives to support our argument and justify our opposition. It is this negative thinking that increases the stressfulness of change and makes adjusting more difficult. This is not to suggest that every change is wonderful. But we'd make change much easier for ourselves if we learned to identify and focus on the *benefits*—especially if the change is going to happen anyway.

This leads to some important principles:

1. We can't always choose what happens. But we can always choose how we look at what happens.

In 1974 I broke my arm playing football. It required immediate surgery to repair the damage and another operation six months later to remove the screws. For half a year I couldn't participate in sports, couldn't play my trombone in our local orchestra and wasn't allowed to skate or ride my bicycle. Needless to say, my activities were cut back considerably. Can there be anything good in this story? Well, yes. My life in those days was pretty frenetic. I was a busy family doctor, played sports and music and did some community work. I was also a bachelor with a busy social life—once every two weeks I'd stay home to do my laundry, but otherwise I was mostly out and about. It was too hectic and I knew I should ease up. When I broke my arm, one of my first thoughts was, "Well, this is going to slow me down. I might even learn how to relax." I purchased my first color TV set and finally bought some nice furniture for my apartment (I'd been renting basic furnishings for three years). I started reading and listening to music again, activities I loved but rarely made time for. My accident actually enriched my life.

Did I have to break my arm to moderate my frantic pace? No. But that negative event was the impetus. Even at the time I was able to see that unwanted change in my life as a positive experience with a host of benefits. I couldn't "unhappen" my accident or "unbreak" my arm, but I had a choice in how I looked at it. By choosing to see the beneficial side I was less upset and more motivated to make the best of things.

2. Almost every situation has some benefit, if you look for it.

One of my patients developed a chronic illness. It was not life-threatening, but it did mean she had to take considerable time off work, and she lost her job. So here she was with a health problem and out of work—hardly welcome changes in her life! One day I asked if anything positive had come out of her situation. She immediately listed the following:

- "It's made me a stronger person because I've had to deal with it (the illness) for so long."

- "It's made my marriage stronger because of all the stuff we had to go through. Now I feel we can go through anything."
- "I was always close to my family, but this has brought me even closer to them. I'm not going through it *alone*."
- "We've had to learn how to handle money wisely since I stopped working. We never had to do that before."
- "I never liked the work I was doing. This gives me the opportunity to do what I really want to do."

My patient started her own business. She applied for a government-run course that helped her create a plan for her home-based enterprise and gave her some financial assistance with start-up costs, as well. She could not have qualified for this help if she had not been unemployed.

I added to this list that she now had more free time and that she had become more compassionate and sensitive to other people and their ailments as a result of her own. She agreed, on both counts.

3. How we talk to ourselves affects how we feel. Negative thoughts drain, discourage and undermine us. Positive thoughts energize, encourage and support us.

I hate driving. Even as a teenager I waited a year before I bothered to get my learner's permit. In 1980 I bought a sporty car with a stick shift on the floor and felt like Mario Andretti for a few months, but after that driving felt like a drudge again.

My dislike of driving became a problem in recent years, because I do a lot of public speaking. More and more my presentations are out of town, and many require me to drive a couple of hours each way. My thoughts before these trips only added to my misery: "Well, here I go again, just what I love—two hours in the car. Boredom on the way, fatigue when I get there. What a drag." Just the spirited pep talk you'd want to give someone before a big game, right?

I finally admitted that my *attitude* was contributing to the problem. And since my work was going to continue taking me out of town, my situation wasn't going to change. I knew my conversations with myself would have to. Looking at the bright side, I came up with a new line of thinking. First, I enjoy my lecture and seminar work immensely, and driving is what gets me there. Second, it's an opportunity to visit scenic places and resorts. And third, the trips do have their pluses. On a recent drive home from a resort north of Toronto, I found myself tooling along on a gorgeous summer afternoon, windows and sunroof open, great sounds from the sixties on the tape deck, and I said to myself, "Hey, this is all right!" Last year I coined a phrase for these trips: "concerts on wheels." So now I load up with tapes and CDs and play music all the way there and all the way home. The time goes faster and it's much more enjoyable. Now I have a way of talking to myself about car travel that *supports* what I'm doing instead of *undermining* me. And it works.

Suppose your company has just gone through a merger and some downsizing. You have a new boss, added responsibilities and new procedures to learn. There's a lot of tension in the air and stress in your body. You could set out for work each day thinking thoughts like these: *Here goes another day in the meat grinder. There's too much to do, my boss is a jerk and they're playing favorites with their old employees. The whole thing sucks!*

Is that an uplift? Is that a springboard to a fun day? Feels like a lead ball in the stomach to me. Now try this: *Well, here goes another day of adventure. I guess these mergers take some time to settle in. My boss is an interesting guy, a bit too aggressive for my taste, but really bright and pretty funny at times. Bringing two cultures together is a real challenge. I'm glad to be one of the people they kept on when they downsized.*

Notice that this is a balanced, credible conversation. It's not pretending to be thrilled with the situation, but it is a reasonable attempt to be positive and put the best face on things. The result? A calmer mood and more open attitude.

The Glass Is Half-Empty and Also Half-Full

Most of the changes we face have positive and negative sides. But the gloomy side pulls us down, whereas the sunny side lifts us up. Why, then, would we want to dwell on the darker aspects of the situation? If the circumstances can't be changed, it makes good sense to concentrate on the things we *do* have an influence on: the way we approach the situation and the way we talk to ourselves about it. And amazingly that simple alteration can often make a huge difference.

Looking for Benefits When They Aren't Obvious to You

When benefits are obvious, acknowledge them. When they aren't apparent, look for them. This approach is known as **reframing**. It is based on the premise that there are many different ways of viewing things, all equally plausible and true to the facts. Let's go back to the examples at the beginning of this chapter. Water, stress and low interest rates each have their plus side and their minus side. Even a sunny summer day can be taken in different ways: bright, beautiful and inviting—or hot, sweaty and full of dangerous UV radiation. How we *feel* is a result of what we *think*. So why pick a point of view that makes you feel discouraged or unhappy? Why not choose to think about situations in a way that makes you feel good, that supports you? This is *most* important when you can't change the situation you're in. For example, if you have the flu, you can get upset about the activities you're missing, or you can snuggle into bed with a good book and enjoy the cozy relaxation. This is about being resilient and adaptable, making the best of any circumstance we find ourselves in. These skills are available to all of us.

Let's look at an example of reframing a situation involving change. In professional sports, being traded from one team to another is a common occurrence. With little or no warning, whether he likes it or not, the player finds himself in a new town with new teammates and coaches. Suddenly there is a change in job, city, housing—and a loss of friends, familiar surroundings and support system.

How do professional sportsmen deal with this? Their most important tool is their attitude, the way they choose to think about what happened. I did a seminar with the staff of a sporting-goods company, and I asked them to put themselves in the shoes of the departing player and reframe the situation: come up with positive ways to look at being traded. Here's the list of positive angles that the group came up with:

- The other team wanted me.
- It's a new challenge.
- Maybe it'll be a better fit for my skills.
- Maybe I'll get more playing time.
- It's a chance to start over, a fresh start.
- I'll meet new friends and teammates (or possibly reunite with former teammates).
- It's a chance to progress, to move ahead in a new organization.
- There will be an opportunity to negotiate a new contract.
- I'll finally get to wear sweater number 7.
- The climate is warmer (if traded to a southern team).
- It's a chance to play on a winning team (if traded to a playoff-bound club).
- It's a nice city to live in.
- Look who they gave up to get me!
- It's a chance to play with Cal Ripken or Michael Jordan (some star or childhood idol).
- Maybe I can really *help* this team, be a leader.

If change is going to happen anyway, whether we like it or not, it's helpful to see it in the most positive light possible. This is not a mind game or a gimmick. It's not pretending a hurricane is a sun shower. It is a constructive way of looking at the world in a light that is most beneficial to our mental health.

Reframing "Change"

Think about a change situation you're going through or struggling with right now. Take a moment to reflect on how you might reframe the situation so it feels less stressful.

Questions to ask yourself that help in doing this exercise include the following:

- How can I look at this to help me feel better about what's happened?
- How else can I think about this situation?

Or you might ask yourself:

- Why don't I think of it *this* way?
- What would I say to a friend dealing with a similar situation? (This question allows you to step outside yourself and be more objective)

Every time I do a change-management seminar, I ask the group, "What are the good things about change? What are the benefits?" This exercise invites people to expand their thinking, to widen their point of view, to take off their blinkers. Many are surprised at the number of positives they come up with, even in regard to things they usually find threatening. Here are some examples of advantages people suggested relating to change in the workplace:

- Opportunity to learn—to acquire new information and skills
- Challenge
- Chance to hone adaptation skills
- Possibility it will lead to a new job
- Chance to bring people forward in the organization (that is, to promote staff)
- Development of leadership skills for change process
- New teams, new people
- Fresh, new, exciting, adventure, refreshing, stimulating ("At least I won't be bored!")
- Learn about myself (limitations, abilities)
- Opportunity to be creative
- Opportunity to gain more control (that is, to influence the process and decision-making)

- Technology improvement
- More resources
- Learning experience (by going through the change)—builds confidence
- Opportunity to grow
- Promotes interaction—brings people together
- Makes me more marketable
- Improvement—makes us more efficient and competitive (as a company)
- New career opportunities
- Visionary, forward-looking, being proactive
- Gain knowledge about the company
- Cross-training will make me feel more useful and better about myself

Notice that some of these benefits are more meaningful or compelling than others. If even one gives you a sense of *Aha!* or *Gee, I never thought of that* or *I never looked at it that way before,* then the exercise was worthwhile.

Let me expand on some of the more commonly mentioned ideas.

"One thing about change: it's never dull!"

If you've ever had a job in which you were crashingly bored, you'll know there are few things worse. Change, even when difficult, is at least new, fresh and often exciting. There's a sense of adventure; it's dynamic. It keeps our lives from getting stale and routine.

We generally seek out variety in our lives. Do you re-read the same books over and over? Other than *The Rocky Horror Picture Show,* do you watch movies again and again? (Well, OK, my brother's watched *The Sound of Music* about ten times, but these are exceptions.) We buy new cars, get rid of old clothes and furniture, find new restaurants, visit new cities. If you had to choose between excitement and adventure versus stagnation and dullness, which would it be?

New learning, growth and portable skills

I finally broke down and bought a fax machine. Talk about techno-stress! I figured (wrongly) this would be a simple thing to install and use. And it would have been if I'd gone for a dedicated line. But my limited usage didn't justify such a large expense. So I opted for a split line, which took hours of my time to install properly (with assistance from the phone company and fax help line) and caused great anguish and frustration for all of us. However, once it was up and running, it was a pleasure. And of course I use it much more than I predicted. Setting up my E-mail system was a breeze in comparison.

> **"All true learning involves the awkwardness and discomfort of entering unknown territory. If you're afraid to be uncomfortable, you're not going to learn much."**
>
> SUSAN M. CAMPBELL

One of my patients told me: "I was resisting all the technology that was coming. [Then] I just decided to branch out." She enrolled in a computer course that included Internet skills. "I'm just so excited. It's so *neat!*"

Whether by choice or necessity, we're all learning new skills to keep up with our changing world. The bad news is that it's frustrating and confusing at times. The good news is that we end up with new tools and talents—portable skills that make us better at the work we do and more employable in the future. So if your company wants to train you in new areas, take advantage of the opportunity. It's really a win-win!

Opportunity for advancement

When a political leader steps down, it's usually open season among party members to become the successor. The changing of the guard presents opportunities that were not available when the leadership was set and the handpicked senior staff in place. The same thing happens when a baseball team changes managers. Either members of the coaching staff move up the chain of command or there's a general shakeup and a number of new positions to fill.

A chance to shine

In times of crisis a previously unknown person often emerges into the spotlight, demonstrating skill or courage they've never shown before. Military heroes like Audie Murphy (America's most decorated war hero and later a movie star), Alvin York and Canada's Billy Bishop come to mind. Or Sam Ervin and Sam Dash during the Watergate hearings. Companies in transition provide a less dramatic forum but opportunities nonetheless exist for displays of ability or leadership. When you're given more to do than you thought you could handle or are thrust into a realm of responsibility you don't feel ready for, seize the chance to show your employer what you can do. Now is the time to demonstrate your value to the organization.

Opportunity to meet new people and form new relationships

One negative side of change is the loss of relationships. But the plus side is the chance to find new folks to connect with. When I left medical school to do my internship, I was sad to leave so many good friends behind. But Edmonton was one of the friendliest places I've ever been, and I developed wonderful friendships there, a few of which have lasted to this day. I first met some of my closest friends in such faraway places as the Canadian Arctic and the Middle East. Talk about change! But in each case special people enriched the experience.

When people go through tough times together, they form bonds that can be deep and lasting. The people of Winnipeg drew together as a community when the outskirts of town were flooded (and the city center threatened) in the spring of 1997. A crisis in a company can do the same thing. Everyone pulling together and solving problems can produce great relationship rewards.

Change as opportunity

The word *crisis* doesn't usually produce happy thoughts. If someone tells you they're having a crisis, you don't say, "Oh, that's great! Can I come over? I'll bring deli and beer." You're more likely to wish them well and ask them to call you back when things settle down. But in Chinese the word *crisis* is written with two characters and pronounced "way gee." The ideogram looks like this:

Each character stands for a different concept: one for danger, the other for opportunity. Too often we focus on the danger part of change and fail to acknowledge the opportunity it presents. Dan Sullivan runs a very successful training program for entrepreneurs in Chicago and Toronto called The Strategic Coach. He says, "Some of our best opportunities in life come to us cleverly disguised as problems." Learning to solve problems leads to progress and growth. The problems become the stimulus for us to be creative and innovative, and make breakthroughs and discover abilities in ourselves we would otherwise never uncover.

Not only is change an opportunity, it's also a challenge. When a large manufacturer was taken over by another company in the eighties, fifty hours were required to build one unit of product on their assembly line. The new owners told the people at the factory that they'd have to get that figure down to twenty-seven hours if they wanted to stay in business—in other words, they had to cut their production time almost by half. That created a lot of consternation at the plant. But then they set to work on the problem. In the fall of 1992 I was asked to give a seminar for their management team. By that point they had cut their time to thirty hours per unit—an extraordinary achievement. They had almost reached the goal that had seemed literally impossible. They did it through hard work, creativity, innovation and teamwork—and by viewing the edict from their parent company as a challenge. When I met with them, there was a feeling of pride and accomplishment that was well deserved.

Change is a challenge
"What kind of man would live where there is no daring? I don't believe in taking foolish chances, but nothing can be accomplished without taking any chance at all.."
CHARLES LINDBERGH

We all need challenges in order to stretch ourselves, to develop and to grow. Let's return to the learning curve on page 20 to see what happens without change. Once we master a skill or situation, we lose our excitement and enthusiasm, our energy. Things become routine and we stagnate or become complacent. Only new challenges will stimulate us. Watch children when they play: once they've mastered something, they either lose interest or they change the rules. They add obstacles, try to do it faster or just start goofing around. It's not much fun to keep doing the same thing over and over, even if you do it well. We seek activities of "just manageable difficulty" (to quote psychologist Nicholas Hobbs). If it's too hard, we get frustrated or give up. If it's too easy, we lose interest. Most squash and tennis players usually look for opponents who are at their level or just a little better than they are. It's that challenge that brings their game up, keeps their attention and is much more satisfying than playing someone they can easily beat. Stretching ourselves not only helps us grow but is much more enjoyable.

Noted University of Chicago psychology professor Mihaly Csikszentmihaly made the point visually in this diagram from his superb 1990 book *Flow*.

The "flow state" is one in which we feel totally focused, completely absorbed in what we're doing. I've had this experience while playing sports, for example, a rally in doubles tennis where all four players are at the net volleying back and forth. You lose track of time; your concentration is total, you see the ball clearly and always seem to be in the right spot. Your movements are effortless, and you experience a feeling of being at one with your racquet and the ball. Nothing else exists for you in those delicious moments. It's like one of those movie scenes in which the actors are in focus, but the rest of the picture is blurred. I've also been in a flow state playing my trombone during a

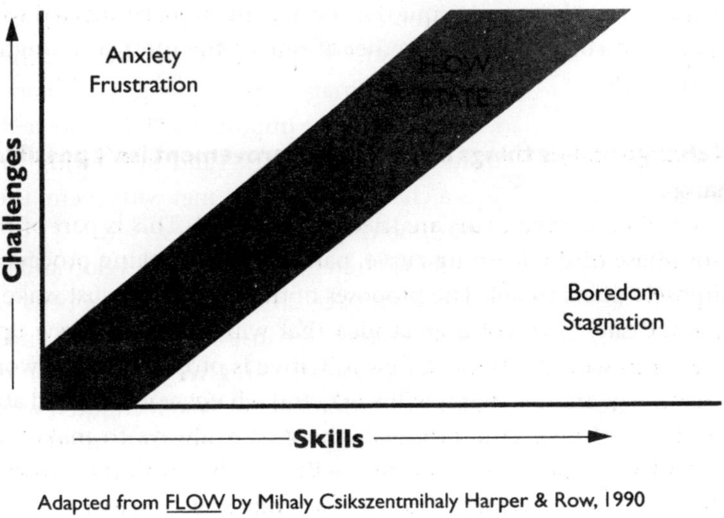

Adapted from FLOW by Mihaly Csikszentmihaly Harper & Row, 1990

difficult orchestra piece. I see the music with complete clarity, my eye moving along the notes with ease. Everything comes together and the playing becomes thrilling. It's an amazing feeling, and it's the result of an almost perfect match between the challenge at hand and my skill set or level of ability. The match isn't always perfect, of course, and that's the point. The amount of challenge has to be such that it stretches you and stimulates you to dig down a little deeper. If it's too much, anxiety and frustration will result. But without challenge, there is no personal progress, and the marvelous feeling of the flow state will be unavailable to you.

I remember when the idea of having fathers in the delivery room while their wives gave birth was first introduced. There was a lot of resistance in some quarters, including some members of the medical profession. "We don't allow family members as spectators during surgery! Why this?" The arguments ranged from risk of contamination to fathers fainting (which happened once to a patient of mine) to crowding the room. But the change evolved and has been standard practice for decades. The benefits have been numerous. Emotional support for the mother, men coaching their partners in the Lamaze breathing technique, fathers feeling more connected with their new babies and couples being together at one of the most meaningful occasions of their life.

Change brings progress
"The world hates change, yet it is the only thing that has brought progress."
CHARLES KETTERING

Not all change makes things better, but improvement isn't possible without change

Sometimes ill-conceived plans are tried and they fail. This is part of the trial-and-error phase of the learning curve, part of the risk-taking process. But no one purposely plans to fail. The proposer of the plan didn't just wake up one morning and say, "I've got a great idea that will definitely screw up everything. Let's run with it!" When a new initiative is proposed in the workplace, there's never a guarantee that it will work, and whatever can be said about the relative merits of a specific proposal, the *goal* is always to make improvements. And if it succeeds, everyone will say the initiator showed great foresight and courage. Which is how most progress gets made.

Change as a learning experience

Sometimes things happen about which you can't find anything good to say. Try looking at it as a learning experience. When I had infectious mononucleosis in 1969, it wiped out my entire summer. I lost twenty-two pounds, had zero energy and just lay around the house, barely able to read or watch TV. I slept most of the days away and as a result, for the first time in my life, developed insomnia. With my family asleep, I couldn't do anything that would make noise, there was nothing on TV (this was before VCRs), I couldn't phone anyone and I could only read for so long. One night I shaved off the beard I'd had for a year—just for something to do! But that illness taught me something. As a family practitioner, I encountered patients with these problems all the time. Now I had a perspective from which to understand their experience; it made me more empathetic and a better doctor. In fact, I coined a maxim after that for people seeking a new physician. My motto was: Don't just look for a doctor who's bright and experienced and personable; find one who's also been sick and knows what it feels like.

Another form of learning experience is the "wake-up call." Your company cleans house, going through a major reorganization. You get moved from your prestigious management job (and window office) to outside sales. It's called a demotion. You are not happy. The question to ask is: "What can I learn from this?" Maybe the writing was on the wall and you chose to ignore it. Perhaps your company wasn't as successful or as considerate of its employees as you thought. Or possibly you had gotten complacent. Instead of upgrading your skills and keeping ahead of market trends, you'd fallen into a comfort zone of just showing up for work and going through the motions. If so, you now know for next time what it takes to stay on top and will be better prepared when your chance comes again.

One of my patients lost his driver's license for a year for impaired driving. His lifestyle changed in a hurry. I asked him if he could see any positives in the situation and he quickly listed four:

- "I love riding my bike. Now I'm going to bicycle to work" (fortunately only ten minutes from his home).
- "I've been wanting to lose twenty pounds. Now I'll be getting more exercise, which will really help."

- "My life is pretty frantic right now. It'll help me slow down the pace if I can't drive anywhere."
- "One reason my life's been out of control is I can never say no to people. I'm always accommodating everyone else. Now, without a car, I'm going to *have* to say no—which I've been wanting to do for a long time."

These were all helpful ways to reframe a change in his life that he couldn't reverse. But I added a fifth benefit: "This is also a wake-up call to tell you that you have a drinking problem," to which he replied, "Oh, yeah, I guess that's true. Guess I better deal with that."

If You Can't Optimize, Neutralize

What if you can't see any benefits in a specific change? What if the very idea that this is a good thing is too much of a leap for you? There's another form of reframing that can be helpful. Instead of turning a negative into a positive ("optimizing" the problem), you can turn it into a neutral ("neutralizing" it). In a sense you take a "problem" and turn it into a "situation" (see diagram on the next page).

For example, you arrive at work and realize you have too much to do and not enough time to do it. This seems to be a way of life for most people these days. You can talk to yourself negatively—"This is impossible, I'll never finish, it's unfair, they're taking advantage of me"—which only adds to your difficulty. Or you can look for the positives—"This will be a challenge, I wonder how much of this I can get done, this will be a chance for me to practice my delegation skills." The third way of viewing this is to neutralize it, to take the negativity out of it without being upbeat. Say to yourself, "It is what it is," "I'll just do my best," or "I'll do what I can do and be satisfied with that."

With regard to change, if you can't see *any* positives (which is most unlikely), neutral thoughts like "This is the way it's going to be, so I might as well accept it" are better than negative thoughts. Even statements like "This is no big deal," "It's not the end of the world," "It's nothing I haven't seen before," or "It could have been worse" may be helpful.

If you want to learn about reframing, listen to sports people. Brendan Malone was the coach of the Toronto Raptors during their first season in the

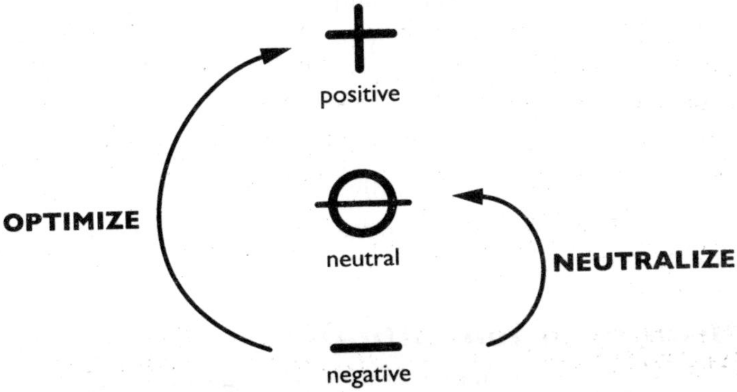

National Basketball Association. After lopsided losses in which the Raptors were blown out by their opponents, Coach Malone said, "Well, at least it doesn't happen very often," (that is, losing by such a huge margin), and "One good thing is that everyone on the team scored," (that is, at least one point). I remember a line by a baseball manager after his team got pummeled. He said, "Well, we got *that* out of our system."

It's OK to Make Mistakes

Another important form of neutralizing applies to situations where you have to learn new skills. Fear of failure or of feeling stupid and incompetent are among the reasons change is difficult for people. In his first book, *Unlimited Power*, Anthony Robbins said that there is no such thing as failure. There are only outcomes and results. And if you don't like the results, you ca work to improve them and bring about what you want. This is an excellent example of reframing a negative into a neutral. The first stage of the learning curve is trial and error. As British business writer Charles Handy says, "Getting it wrong is part of getting it right."

One way to increase your comfort with mistakes is to make lots of them. Stop playing it safe and take a few risks. I heard a great piece of philosophy from a forty-eight-year-old musician who told me she was starting to study the harp. I said, "Gee, I hear that's a tough instrument to take up as an adult," to which she replied, "I think you should always be a beginner at *something*—it keeps you humble." (It also keeps you comfortable with making mistakes and prevents you from taking yourself too seriously.) What a wonderful outlook for the times in which we live! Many people tell me, "If I can't do something well, I don't do it at all." That's not the attitude that leads to flexibility and resilience. And it is certainly not the mind-set to support you at times of rapid change. We should all be at the start of at least one learning curve at any given time.

Give Meaning to Your Situation or Experience

Another way to reframe a change is to make it meaningful for yourself on some level. The period between April 1984 and July 1985 was the most stressful of my life. In that fourteen months I got married, broke my foot, changed my career; my wife and I also had a house built for us and we had our first child. All but one of these events were positive, but all required a lot of adjustment. And there were two other, negative stressors that almost tipped me over. My father was diagnosed with cancer in May of 1984 and died the following May. And our baby had to have surgery when he was ten weeks old, which was very hard on us as new parents (and no breeze for the baby, either). The final sequence went like this: my son was born in January, his operation was in April, my father died in May and I gave up my family practice at the end of June. One of the ways I coped was to keep telling myself I was being tested—and educated. My new career was in the field of stress management, so I reframed my difficult experiences as real-life training for understanding what my patients go through and have to deal with. It made me more sensitive to the suffering of others.

When you're going through a difficult period of transition, ask yourself these questions: What has this been sent to teach me? What meaning or significance can I give to this experience that will somehow redeem it for me? How can I understand this in a way that is useful for me?

Two dramatic examples of giving meaning to adversity come from Holocaust literature. Nobel Prize winner Elie Wiesel wrote in his searing book, *Night,* that one of the things that kept him going through his internment at Auschwitz was his fierce determination to survive so he could tell the world what was happening to the Jews of Europe. He later dedicated himself to that mission, to bear witness to the world about the horrifying events of the Nazi era. Dr. Viktor Frankl, a psychiatrist and the author of the classic *Man's Search for Meaning,* felt he could be of help to others during his concentration camp experience at Auschwitz. For him the ordeal became meaningful as an opportunity to assist his fellow prisoners. Even in the most extreme human affliction, people who were able to give meaning to their experience found strength to endure.

In summary, change is happening faster and more extensively than ever before in human history. None of us can reverse this trend or avoid its effects. However, we can always change how we look at it. Learning to see the benefits of change helps us to deal with it. Remember, almost nothing is good or bad in itself. The ability to identify pluses when they're not readily apparent is a skill that confers an even higher level of resilience and flexibility.

This doesn't mean you should accept and applaud every change. Sometimes you should try to get changes modified, even reversed. But if the change is inevitable, standing off in the corner pouting is not helpful. Better to be as positive as you can in the circumstances. Ask yourself, What advantages or opportunities does this open up for me? How can I use what's happening to my benefit? Negative thoughts undermine you; positive thoughts support you. Take your pick. Change-averse people tend to see the glass as half-empty. Change-adept people see it as half-full. And *really* change-hardy folks are already trying to figure out how to fill the other half.

CHAPTER FOUR

We're All Change Agents

Belief in Your Ability to Deal with Change

A FEW YEARS AGO WE BOUGHT AN entertainment unit. It was seven feet high and had glass doors, a sliding swivel shelf for the TV set and other features. There was only one problem. It came in several boxes, unassembled. As we lugged the containers down to the basement I asked my wife, "Who do you think we should get to help us with this?"

She said, "No one. We're going to do it ourselves."

"Yeah, right!" I replied.

First of all, there were three hundred pieces, from seven-foot boards to tiny screws, and the instruction sheet consisted of five diagrams and no words. I didn't think we were up to this. (I'm not the handiest guy around the house.) My wife, however, was brimming with confidence and adventure. With a distinct lack of enthusiasm, I decided to give it a shot.

> ***"At times like these it's important to remember: there have always been times like these."***
> **UNKNOWN**

What happened was wonderful. Through a process of trial and error, we put the thing together. At times my wife saw how to do the next step, sometimes I did, and together we solved whatever problems came up. Not only did we end up with a fine piece of furniture, but we both had a feeling of satisfaction and accomplishment. I had so much fun meeting the challenge and working with my hands that I couldn't wait to get at the tables we'd also purchased. When I was up early the next day putting stuff together before breakfast, my wife wondered if she'd created a monster. Clearly I was on a roll.

Something else came out of this episode besides an entertainment unit. I changed my belief about myself being handy. For years I had carried beliefs about my ability to do certain things—beliefs that had limited my activities in those particular areas.

The Power of Belief

Self-limiting beliefs are common. Especially the *I can'ts*: I can't speak in public, remember names, be on time. We assume that these beliefs are the truth about us, so they *become* the truth. They are self-fulfilling prophecies. For example, I used to believe I couldn't carry a cup of coffee or tea without spilling, so my hand would shake. I became very careful with these drinks, walking slowly and focusing on the cup. Then one day it occurred to me that I'm never unsteady when I carry cold drinks like water or juice. What was the difference? Was the caffeine in the hot drinks piercing through the cup into my hand and causing it to shake? Not likely. This was about my thinking, my belief about what would happen before it happened. And then when it *did* happen, it simply reinforced my belief.

One reason people find change difficult is that they believe they can't handle it. They "know" that change is hard for them and they won't be able to cope. This belief limits their ability to manage change situations. If this applies to you, one way to increase your comfort with change is to challenge your negative beliefs about your ability to deal with it. Fortunately that's not hard to do, because we all have a pretty good history of being change agents.

A Lesson on the Track

I learned about the power of beliefs to determine behavior and outcomes when I was in high school. I took up track-and-field; the half-mile was my best event. But there was a guy in my school (I'll call him Joe) whom I could never beat. I always ran behind him. (I recognized him better from the back than from the front!) My coach even said to me once (in a piece of reverse psychology, I later realized) "Unless you've got more heart than I think you have, you'll never be a half-miler." One day we were running in a track meet and there I was again, about ten yards behind Joe after the first lap. Then for no apparent reason I started gaining on him. As we neared the curve I had an amazing thought. "Aw, c'mon, Joe," I said to myself, "you're holding me up here. If you don't speed up, I'll have to slow down to stay behind you."

Finally, out of sheer frustration and impatience—not determination, I assure you—I passed him, just so I wouldn't hit him or have to break stride. It was only after I was ahead of him that I realized I could *stay* ahead of him. It was like an adrenaline boost. I beat him that day and he never ran ahead of me again.

Had I suddenly acquired the ability to run faster? No, I had gained the *confidence* to run faster. I had changed my belief about myself. Instead of the certainty that I couldn't beat him, I now had the certainty that—with a little push—I *could*. And that's the reality I created ever after.

This story is about how our beliefs influence our behavior and the outcome of our actions. It's also about using a positive experience to challenge and revise inaccurate or outdated beliefs. This principle can be useful in dealing with the issue of change. If we have a record of overcoming obstacles and managing change in the past, we can use that personal history to amend our beliefs about our ability to handle change in the future.

Been There, Done That

We're all more practiced in making changes than we realize or give ourselves credit for. We all got through such experiences as starting school, leaving home, starting college, beginning a job, changing jobs, getting married, becoming parents and moving to a new city. At first, we always feel dislocated and awkward. But over time we adjust. Look back in your own personal memory bank and list the different situations you entered into and became accustomed to. Start with yourself as a child. You'll be surprised at how many adjustments you've made. (And we all got through puberty, didn't we?) I had a relatively stable childhood, but I still changed schools three times, went to four different summer camps and lived in seven differ nt cities by the time I was thirty.

Remember when you changed schools/moved to a new town/went to a summer camp/moved into your first apartment (take your pick)? You felt out of place, uncomfortable, maybe lonely at first. You wondered how things would work out. You missed your old familiar surroundings. These feelings are normal in a period of transition. With every new experience or phase in your life, your comfort and confidence decrease temporarily. But after a while you get into a routine, meet a few people, get more involved, and soon you're settling in and becoming more at ease. This adjustment takes different amounts of time for different people and often depends on the situation. But throughout your life you've been through this drill a number of times. It's important to remind yourself of this and to realize that you *are* flexible and adaptable, that you *are* able to adjust to change. You've dealt with change all your life. You've been an agent of change. And you can manage whatever change situation you're involved in now or will face in the future.

What Successes Have You Had?

In my change-management seminars I ask participants to think of changes they made in the past that they resisted at first or thought they couldn't handle, but then turned out OK or even very well. Most groups come up with an impressive list. Here's a sampling:

- Learning to use a computer or new software program
- Learning to drive (especially gearshift)
- Learning to fly a plane
- Skydiving
- Giving up smoking or drinking
- Overcoming the fear of public speaking
- Becoming a manager
- Starting my own company
- Learning to write with my nondominant hand
- Learning to live with a disability
- Moving to a different country/living in a new culture
- Learning a new language
- Becoming a stepparent

These are situations that people confronted with trepidation or even reluctance, but that turned out well after a period of adjustment. I'm not pretending that all were handled quickly or with ease. But they are testimony to the resilience and resourcefulness all of us have to varying degrees. We need to remind ourselves of that—in order to challenge the negative beliefs that often come up at times of change.

So what would be on your list? What situations did you meet with self-doubt and pessimism (or even grumbling and complaining), but that you then adjusted to? Let these be your touchstones at times of hesitation or skepticism.

We're Amazingly Adaptable

The VA Hospital in San Francisco has to be one of the most scenic settings for a health facility in the world. It sits on a high piece of land in the northwest corner of the city with a view of the Golden Gate Bridge to the north and the Pacific coastline to the south. When I went to work there in 1966, I thought I'd landed in heaven. We lived in the house-staff residence, just a few hundred feet from the hospital. There was only one problem. The foghorns on San Francisco Bay kept waking me up at night. On the fifth morning, walking to breakfast, I commented to my colleagues that I was grateful there had been no foghorns the previous night, and I had finally gotten some sleep. They looked at each other and laughed. Of course the noise hadn't stopped at all; I just hadn't noticed it. "Everyone gets used to it after a few days," one of them told me. This was an example of our built-in adjustment mechanism. Ever wonder how people can live near railroad tracks or airports? They get used to it.

When my high school guidance teacher urged me to apply to medical school, I told him I had no interest in being a doctor. Just thinking about blood and infections and giving needles to babies sent my stomach into spasms. Needless to say I got used to all of the above. But the turning point was in anatomy lab. Walking into a room filled with dead bodies wrapped in cellophane was a spooky experience. The strong smell of formaldehyde added to my uneasiness. But dissecting and exploring the body turned out to be fascinating, and we all adapted to the strangeness of the environment. An upperclassman told me that you've reached your first adjustment plateau in medicine when you can eat your lunch in the anatomy lab beside your cadaver—and the pinnacle is eating a tuna sandwich in that environment. I couldn't tell if he was having me on or if he was just being ghoulish. The next spring I passed this rite of passage and, although it would never be my preferred dining locale, I was able to eat there without it being a big deal. I never would have believed I could do something like that.

We've all had experiences of adjusting to situations of difficulty or deprivation, whether on a canoe trip, during a home renovation or after an injury to your dominant hand. People are amazingly resilient. The ultimate example is the way people are able to live in war zones. From Belfast to Sarajevo to Beirut, whole populations adjust to *real* deprivation punctuated by violence and smothered by ongoing fear. I'm not suggesting these conditions don't exact a terrible toll on people. It's just that it's a wonder to me that they can accommodate at all. Their ability to live and remain hopeful in such situations is inspiring testimony to the resilience of the human body, mind and spirit.

Don't Prejudge the Outcome—Keep an Open Mind

Question: What's pink and fuzzy?

Answer: Pink fuzz.

This was the first thing our twelve-year-old said to us when we picked him up at the end of two weeks at summer camp. He followed that with a riddle about two talking sausages. He and his buddy were sitting on his bunk swapping jokes with his counselor and a few cabinmates, his face all smiles. We gathered up his stuff, he said his goodbyes and we headed for home. In the car he regaled us with stories about his adventures. Clearly his first experience at overnight camp had been a success.

Contrast this scene to the conversation I had with him two weeks earlier when he lay in his room at bedtime and told me how much he dreaded going to camp the next day. "I made a mistake. I should never have signed up for two weeks. It was the wrong decision. What if I don't have fun? Can I come home early?" Even when he called home on the third day he said, "I can't wait for the two weeks to be over." But obviously things got a whole lot better after that.

Have you ever gone to a party with a sense of foreboding about how bad it was going to be? Maybe you said to your significant other, "Can't we get out of this? It's going to be deadly." Maybe you even hatched an escape plan—"What's the earliest we can leave without being rude? Let's meet at ten-thirty and get out of there." Then, at ten-thirty, one of you was having an awful time (as predicted), but the other one said, "I don't want to leave. I'm having a ball."

This illustrates the reasons not to prejudge the outcome of situations. When we predict what will happen, we sometimes bring about the result we feared—the classic self-fulfilling prophecy, or self-sabotage. This can be unconscious or arise from a lack of effort on our part ("Why try? It's no use. My heart's not really in this."). We can also waste a lot of time worrying about it ahead of time or a lot of energy fighting against it.

Here are some examples:

- In 1961 the province of Saskatchewan introduced the first government-funded health-care system in North America. The province's doctors were vigorously opposed to it; they even went on strike. Tommy Douglas, the premier, went ahead anyway. Once the plan was up and running the doctors never had it so good. They maintained their autonomy and freedom to practice as they liked (a major fear), had a much simplified billing system, were guaranteed payment for their services and had no bad debts or collection hassles. Their net incomes also rose as a result.

- A family in our neighborhood moved to Kingston, Ontario, a four-hour drive from here. The wife called me a few years later, having arrived back in the area, and we caught up on each other's news. She told me she had initially opposed the move to Kingston and dreaded moving there. She said, "George had to drag me kicking and screaming all the way down the highway. But after a while I loved it. When we decided to move back, I hated to leave. In fact, he had to drag me kicking and screaming all the way back."

- When President Harry Truman proposed pouring billions of dollars into Europe after the Second World War, including money for Germany, Americans were outraged. Who gives money to the enemy after such a

> horrific and costly war? But the Marshall Plan turned out to be a bold and brilliant idea that put Europe back on its feet and created trading partners for the U.S. It also stabilized the peace that had been signed. Truman had learned from the armistice terms after the First World War that if you crush your enemy after defeating him, you create resentment that only sows the seeds for future wars.

I'm not suggesting that every change will work out well. Nor am I saying that we should embrace every new situation indiscriminately. But we would save ourselves a lot of aggravation if we were more open-minded, especially in circumstances we can't change. Remember that the word prejudice comes from the word "pre-judge."

This leads us to one last belief: the usually unquestioned premise that change is difficult. Could it be that even this belief is inaccurate? In Rick Maurer's excellent book *Beyond the Wall of Resistance*, he quotes from an interview he did with Margaret Wheatley (she is the author of a bestseller called *Leadership and the New Science*). Here's an excerpt:

> A person in one organization said resistance to change is like a mantra we feed ourselves: "In every team meeting we get together and spend the first twenty minutes saying change is hard. People resist change." This is an unexamined belief about human nature. Our assumptions about stability and the promises of equilibrium were all false promises and that is not how life is. If people participate from the beginning of the change they are able to re-identify or change their identity so that it doesn't feel threatening....
>
> We do have a self-organizing capacity in us which means that we will change in order to maintain ourselves. Change is not foreign. In the natural world change is not a singular event you try to live through, it's just the way things are. I think the saying "People don't resist change, they resist being changed" sums it up.

In a sense Wheatley is questioning the very basis of this book. I began with the premise that change *is* difficult for most people, and I proposed to talk about some ways of making it easier and more comfortable. So what's the truth here? My take on it is that as an *observer* of human activity, I have noticed that change is hard for a lot of people. But perhaps it's not an inherent truth about us. People certainly vary greatly in their capacity to accept and deal with change, and generally speaking, we become increasingly resistant to change as we grow older. So it's not an immutable fact that change is and always will be hard for us. In fact, what I'm doing in this book is suggesting ways in which change can be made easier. If change were irreversibly difficult, I'd probably be writing about something else.

When I make suggestions to patients (for example, that they give up caffeine or get up earlier so they're not so rushed in the morning), they sometimes reply, "That's going to be hard." When I hear that, I ask, "How do you know?" or "Why do you say that?" I tell them it might be difficult, which is far more likely if they begin with that premise. But it also might be a lot easier than they think. Why not take a positive approach—or at least keep an open mind?

In summary, beliefs have a profound effect on the way we think and behave. As Henry Ford said, "Whether you believe you can do a thing or believe you can't, you are right." In a time of rapid, extensive and ongoing change, it serves us badly to hold negative beliefs about change or our ability to deal with it. We would do well to challenge those beliefs and revise them. We need to acknowledge that we're all change agents and accept that we will continue to be in the years ahead. Whether it is difficult or easy is largely up to us. This is an area *we* control. We need to seize that control and use it constructively.

CHAPTER FIVE

What's So Funny about Change?

Keeping, and Using, Your Sense of Humor

EVERYTHING IN LIFE IS EASIER IF YOU can laugh about it. With all the layoffs and downsizing in recent years, the air around most workplaces has been thick with tension for a long time. But someone at the Hospital for Sick Children in Toronto decided to blow some humor through the fog of worry by putting up the following sign in the outpatient department in 1996: Due to cutbacks, the light at the end of the tunnel will be turned off until further notice.

> ***"Life is too serious to be taken seriously."***
> OSCAR WILDE

Did this affect the rate of restructuring? No. Did it create any new jobs? Hardly. Did it lighten the mood and lessen the stress even a little? You bet. Humor isn't about changing what happens. It's about changing our *reaction* to what happens. And those who use humor as a coping strategy are generally more resilient and adaptable when faced with change.

Humor Reduces Stress

Laughter relieves tension. You cannot laugh and feel tense at the same time. Physiologically it's not possible. Because the minute you laugh you relieve the tension. I watched this happen one day in my office. A woman was telling me about her experience the night before when she tried on her bathing suit. It was April and they were preparing for a Caribbean cruise. She'd gained some weight over the winter and her suit didn't fit. This brought up a lot of weight issues for her and triggered some painful memories and emotions. I was just listening as she talked about those feelings when suddenly she stopped. Her face changed, she smiled and then said, "You know what? I've just solved my problem. This year I'm going to swim in the dark!" With that we both burst out laughing and the tension disappeared. It was as if she'd decided in that moment to stop feeling sad and frustrated and down on herself. Seeing the funny side of her situation enabled her to pull herself together and raise herself up, to find the words and wit to break the mood. Was this woman a standup comic or humor writer? No. She was simply a person who was willing to be playful and, like millions of others, had the ability to find amusement in everyday situations. We can all tap into our sense of humor, and benefit from it.

Humor doesn't have to produce a thigh-slapping joke to be helpful. Think of a meeting you were at where things were getting pretty tense. Then perhaps someone said something funny and everybody roared with laughter. That night you told the story to your spouse, but the joke fell flat. You finally said, "Well, I guess you had to be there." That's probably true. Because if you weren't there to feel the tension, you couldn't experience the relief of the remark that broke it. In the right circumstances it doesn't take much to generate a laugh. And the humor is a gift to everyone in the room, because they all benefit from the laughter.

Laughter in the Workplace

Nowhere is humor more needed these days than at the office. When times are tough, people tend to get serious and intense, and one of the first casualties of this somber mood is laughter. Yet humor can be the perfect antidote to those uptight feelings. Dr. Joel Goodman, a humor advocate and academic from New York, uses the phrase "From grim and bear it to grin and share it." Create a playful, fun environment in your office and people will beat a path to your door to work with you.

> Question: Is the glass half-empty or half-full?
> Answer: The reengineering department says it's just that there's too much glass!

I was doing a seminar for a company that had downsized, resulting in everyone being asked to do more than they had before. We were talking about reframing, and one of the participants said he worked at a counter in which he not only served the onsite customers but those who phoned in. Then he was given the added responsibility of being the troubleshooter for staff problems. There were times when he was besieged from all sides and felt overwhelmed. "At times like that," he said, "I reframe the situation in a way that really helps. I say to myself, I *love* it when they fight over me!"

What's Funny about Change?

There's nothing inherently funny about change. But if you look, you can find or create a wealth of humor in change situations—or any other situation, for that matter.

For example, here's a good line to use when you're snowed under by the sheer volume of work to be done: "I feel like a mosquito at a nudist colony. I know what I'm supposed to do. I just don't know where to start."

When I interned in Edmonton, we earned the princely sum of $4300 for the year. For this we worked an average of a hundred hours a week (including on-call coverage every other night and every other weekend). Sometimes we grumbled about being "paid slaves," and one of us said, "Do you realize we're earning less than a dollar an hour?" to which someone else replied, "You're wrong. We're earning about $50 an hour—but they're *paying* us less than a buck an hour!" But the best line of the year came from a surgical resident (he didn't make much more than we did): "I am wealthy, not in the magnitude of my possessions but in the modesty of my requirements!" Given that we had barely enough time to sleep, much less enjoy leisure pursuits, there really wasn't much opportunity to spend the meager salary anyway.

Merger mania has been part of the business landscape for several years and will likely continue. Sometimes the possible new names for merged entities are very funny. For example, if El Al airlines of Israel decided to merge with Alitalia, the Italian national carrier, they could call the new company "Val, I'll Tal Ya." And here's one that was passed to me after a seminar I did on humor in the workplace: "Did you hear about the merger between Xerox and Wurlitzer? They wanted to manufacture a reproductive organ!"

Stretch your humor muscles by thinking up your own merger scenarios and create funny names for them. For example, if Chock Full o' Nuts joined with Beef Jerky they could form a company called "Chock Full o' Jerks."

Good-news, bad-news jokes are a great way of injecting a bit of humor into tense situations. Again they don't have to be hysterically funny to be welcome. For example: "The good news is that we're finally going to have some free time around here. The bad news is we just lost our major client." Or: "The good news is that, with this new cell phone, my staff can reach me anywhere. The bad news is that, with this new cell phone, my staff can reach me anywhere!"

We're often faced with difficult decisions at work where none of the options are appealing. Woody Allen had a line about the no-win dilemma: "More than anytime in history mankind faces a crossroad. One path leads to despair and utter hopelessness, the other to total extinction. Let us pray that we have the wisdom to choose correctly."

You might have a no-win situation at work, such as when you feel you can't please your boss or you can't do anything right. It reminds me of the man whose aunt comes to visit and brings him two neckties as a gift. This guy doesn't even wear ties, but to please his aunt he puts one of them on for dinner that night. He's waiting for her to notice and be pleased with his gesture. After a few minutes she looks up from her soup and says, "So what's the matter? You didn't like the other tie?"

Humor about Health

Illness creates unwelcome and often painful changes in our lives. Humor can at least give us a welcome respite. When my father was very ill, he was hospitalized several times. It's ironic that, despite our upset and worry on those occasions, there were also moments for laughter. My dad never lost his warm sense of humor, even in his final few days, and we rarely passed up an opportunity to kibitz with him or find something funny about what was going on. The lightness and laughter were blessings to all of us.

One of my patients developed breast cancer and was devastated with fear. Before her surgery she met the surgeon in his office and he explained what he intended to do. He'd remove the lump and as little other breast tissue as possible (called a "lumpectomy"). If there was evidence of spread to the lymph nodes, he'd have to do a mastectomy. In summing up, he said, "You'll either have a small dimple in your breast—or you'll look like *me!*" She loved the joke, and she appreciated his trying to help ease her tension. This surgeon, by the way, is a skilled, kind and empathetic man whom his patients adore. His remark was made in the context of a caring, concerned consultation. It was neither flip nor disrespectful. He knew this patient, understood how she herself used humor and took his lead from her.

Unfortunately she did require a mastectomy. On her first visit back to see me, she related, with a hearty laugh, what her best friend said when she first saw her after the operation: "So which side did they do?" Again the context was important. This was a loving friend who shared her dry sense of humor. The comment was therefore welcome and appreciated.

Norman Cousins wrote a landmark book called *The Anatomy of an Illness* in which he related the benefits of laughter for him when he was battling a painful, degenerative disease called ankylosing spondylitis. He decided that conventional medicine was not offering him sufficient improvement. So he prescribed laugh therapy for himself. He asked people to bring him old Marx Brothers movies, which generated real belly laughs for him. Deep laughter actually stirs up the body in a positive way—humor specialists call this an "internal massage." It improves the circulation, increases oxygen intake and stimulates the release of endorphins, the feel-good brain hormone.

Humor can also be useful in dealing with illness of close relatives. Multiple sclerosis is a difficult and at times disabling disease, often affecting relatively young people. When I was in training, I cared for a man who developed M.S. and was confined to a wheelchair. Not long after, research on a promising treatment was reported in the popular press. Early tests on monkeys showed hopeful signs. The next day his wife came in with the newspaper and jokingly said, "I'm going to start him on a diet of bananas. After all, if it works for monkeys . . ."

A baby was born at our hospital with a prominent birthmark on his face. His parents were extremely upset at first, despite the fact that the baby was otherwise healthy and was quite physically attractive. We assured the couple that there were treatments to make the mark less noticeable, and as they went through a period of adjustment to the situation, they began to ease their feelings with jokes. I overheard the father say, "At least we know they won't send us home with the wrong baby!" and, "All those other kids have such boring features."

When I heard those comments, I knew this man was mobilizing one of his best coping mechanisms—humor—and to me it was a sign that he was dealing constructively with his pain. And as the years went by, the child grew into a handsome young man with a barely observable skin discoloration.

Humor to Ward Off Fear

One of our greatest weapons against fear is humor. We make jokes about things we're most afraid of, like death. Again, Woody Allen: "I don't believe in a life after death, but I'm taking a change of underwear anyway." And this line was attributed to Harry Truman: "It reminds me of the man who woke up to find himself lying in a coffin. He said, 'If I'm not dead, what am I doing here? And if I *am* dead, how come I have to go to the bathroom?'"

Fear of Alzheimer's disease has led to a multitude of jokes. Humor is one of the few weapons we have as yet against this unfortunate condition. Here's an example: "Two good things about Alzheimer's—you keep meeting new people and you can hide your own Easter eggs."

We also tell jokes about areas in which we feel uncomfortable or insecure. That's why there are so many gags about sex. For example: Two sophisticated eight-year-olds are talking. One says, "Hey, I found a condom on the veranda last night." The other asks, "What's a veranda?" (You didn't really expect me to tell a racy story *here*, did you?)

A line I heard from a guy on his fiftieth birthday went like this: "I'm not as good as I once was. But I'm as good *once* as I ever was!"

Humor about Transitions

One change we all experience is the passage through different stages of life, from infancy and childhood to adolescence, to young adulthood and on through middle age to retirement and old age. Some of these transitions are difficult, even painful. The loss of faculties as we age is of particular concern to seniors, and a lot of people fear the fading of eyesight, hearing, memory and sex drive. This creates very fertile ground for humor. Laughter is one of the best weapons we have to deal with situations over which we have no control.

An elderly but avid golfer had to stop playing because his vision was deteriorating and he could no longer follow the flight of the ball. His friend said to him, "That's no problem. My eyes are fine. I'll come along and watch the ball for you." The golfer was grateful and delighted. They set out to play. On the first tee, the golfer took his drive and got away a very nice shot. His friend did as he promised and kept his eye on the ball's flight. He said, "I see it. I see it." As they strolled off the tee toward the ball, the golfer asked, "Which way did it go?" His buddy replied, "I forget!"

At a recent class reunion one of our classmates gave a presentation on "Memory and the Aging Brain." It spawned two memorable lines. One guy quipped, "The older we get, the clearer our memory becomes for things that never happened." To which someone retorted, "Yeah, the older you get, the better it *was*."

My uncle is eighty-two and slowing down physically, but he's lost none of his great sense of humor. We were talking to him about plans to do something next year and he said, "I don't know. We'll see. These days I don't plan that far ahead. I don't even buy green bananas anymore."

Retirement holds great appeal for some people, while others view it with trepidation. Wives are notorious for fearing the time when their husbands will be home all day, every day. This gives rise to lines like "I vowed to take him for better or worse—but not for lunch," and "Since he retired I have twice as much husband and half as much money."

Couples growing old together provide fodder for stories like this one. A couple in their eighties are sitting in the living room when the husband decides to go to the store. He asks his wife if she wants anything and she says some ice cream would be nice.

"What flavor?" he asks.

"Vanilla."

"OK."

"Why don't you write it down so you don't forget?"

"I won't forget. Do you want any sauce on it?"

"Sure. Chocolate. But why don't you write it down?"

"Vanilla ice cream, chocolate sauce. I'll remember. Do you want nuts on top?"

"Yes, thank you. Walnuts. I wish you'd write all this down."

"I'll be fine. See you in an hour."

One hour later he returns. He shuffles across the living room to where his wife is sitting and hands her a brown bag. She opens it and takes out a bagel with lox. She looks at him with an expression of frustration and exasperation. "You forgot the cream cheese!"

How Do I Look?

Another area of transition we all go through has to do with physical appearance. As we age our bodies change shape, wrinkles develop and hair turns gray or drops out. As a follicly-challenged individual, I've noticed a lot of jokes about baldness over the years. I liked the T-shirt that said, "All males have a certain amount of testosterone. If some men want to waste theirs growing hair, that's up to them!"

Or how about: "Men who go bald from the front are thinkers. Men who go bald from the back are sexy. And men who go bald from the front *and* the back just *think* they're sexy!"

Sometimes friends can use humor to help us adjust to new stages. Timing, kindness and sensitivity are paramount. Here's a sample from my twenty-second birthday. I was already starting to lose my hair and was feeling a bit touchy about the subject. It was the end of my third summer on staff at the National Music Camp in Michigan. A surprise party was thrown in my honor at which the following song was sung (to the tune of "On Top of Old Smoky"):

On top of Old Posen
All covered with hair,
That is until lately
Now the hair isn't there.

It went on for several verses. I didn't know how to react; I laughed and felt like hiding at the same time. One of my pals put it in context for me: "This room is filled with your best friends. We know you're sensitive about your hair and we thought it was time you lightened up about it. In this whole room you're the only one who notices or cares. The rest of us love you just the way you are."

Their use of humor was one of the watershed moments in my eventual acceptance of an inherited family trait.

It's OK to Be Playful—at Any Age

Humor is more than jokes and laughter. It's also about playfulness. As we get older we often lose our youthful exuberance and willingness to goof around. What a shame! The word *silly* is usually a putdown word, as in "Stop being so silly. Act your age." But actually it's a wonderful word that comes from the Middle English word *selig*, which means "prosperous, happy, healthy and blessed."

Playfulness is as much an attitude as it is an activity. It's about seeing things in a light and offbeat way. Being playful is like looking through a fun filter, viewing the world through a light-giving lens. (My son is wonderful at this. When he was three, he fell through a slightly ajar front door and tumbled onto the floor. Within two seconds he said, "Look who just dropped in!" Last year we went horseback riding, and while the horses were being saddled, he walked up to one of them and said, "Hi, Molly. Why the long face?" Humor and play are an innate part of who he is—but for others it's a skill that can be acquired through practice.) Playfulness is about being joyful and free and clowning around. It's about taking yourself less seriously and giving yourself permission to have fun. Playfulness can include loud ties, funny T-shirts or funky hats. When safe sex became a societal concern, a friend of ours showed up at a party wearing a pair of very colorful earrings—fashioned from small condoms. Talk about a conversation piece.

When I opened my practice in stress-management counseling, I received several coffee mugs with funny sayings on them. One was a Garfield cartoon with this line: "You are entitled to my opinion." A friend gave me a small pillow embroidered with: "My Decision Is Final. The Answer Is Maybe." Last year I learned how to juggle. I keep three small colored beanbags on my desk at work and every so often I take a short juggling break. It gets me out of my chair, gives me a short exercise break and reminds me to stay loose and playful. It's hard to take yourself seriously while you're juggling beanbags. As someone said, "Having fun is more important than being funny."

Humor and Creativity: the Perfect Match

In dealing with change, humor isn't helpful only as a stress reliever. Its other benefits include waking up our bodies (laughter is a great energizer), bringing people together (for team building and group cooperation) and enhancing creativity. This latter function reflects the fact that the part of the brain (located on the right side) that controls humor also controls creativity. It relates to our ability to think conceptually, in ideas and pictures rather than words and logic. You *get* a joke, you don't *understand* it. If someone has to explain it to you (which you process in your analytical *left* brain), it's not funny anymore.

The more people learn to see humor in situations, the more they develop the ability to see things in different ways, which is the essence of creativity. When I was in high school, the clock had stopped in the room where we studied French. A student put a sign up beside the clock that read, "This clock doesn't work. Why should *I?*" Everyone thought that was terribly clever. But our French teacher went one better. He put up a sign next to the first sign that read, "Time passes. Will *you?*"

Using humor in this way leads to other skills such as flexibility, problem-solving and being innovative. It's a way of stretching your "creativity muscles." Creativity is one of the elements of resilience—and resilience is a key survival skill in our rapidly changing world. So laugh, stay loose and think laterally!

In summary, is there anything funny about change? Sure there is. Just as there is amusement to be found in any sphere of life. But the humor isn't in the situation itself—we have to find it or create it ourselves. And doing so brings a host of benefits. It relieves tension and stress, brings people closer together, relieves boredom, helps keep things in perspective, enhances creativity, energizes and motivates, promotes flexibility and helps us feel better about ourselves. We can use humor to deal with work pressure, difficult people, illness, life transitions, disappointments and loss. The Four Horsemen of Humor are **laughter**, **playfulness**, **fun** and **lightheartedness**. Laugh your way to change-hardiness. Give yourself permission to start today, especially in the workplace. And remember to share it with others.

CHAPTER SIX

Where Am I?

Stages in the Change and Change-Adjustment Process

MY WIFE GAVE ME A CARD YEARS AGO that went something like this: On the front someone was walking toward a car carrying a suitcase. A very upset person was walking behind, beseeching the departing traveler, "Can't you stay a few more minutes?" When you opened the card, the speaker had prostrated himself on the ground with his arms wrapped around the ankles of the person leaving. He was saying, "I can't stand short goodbyes."

"Life is made up of meetings and partings."
CHARLES DICKENS

The card was a playful dig at my propensity to drag out partings and leavetakings, whether from a party, a holiday visit with friends or a place I'd become attached to. When we moved into our newly built house in 1984, moving day was hard for me. Much as I looked forward to living in my first house, I felt really sad to be leaving my small and somewhat cramped apartment. I went back twice after the movers left to collect some things and lock up. Before locking up for the last time I lingered for several minutes, wandering in and out of the now empty rooms, trying in some ritualistic way to say goodbye to a place that had been my home for several years. Many warm memories flooded back and I wanted time to just experience them. I was having trouble letting go. Moving forward isn't so hard for me. But letting go is difficult, evoking feelings of sadness and loss. No wonder my father used to observe that I didn't take kindly to change.

"Letting go is difficult. Hanging on is harder."
UNKNOWN

I never fully understood this phenomenon until I read William Bridges' remarkable book *Transitions* (first published in 1980 and still in print). In it he talks about the stages in the process of change. We each find certain aspects of change tougher than others, and we usually develop our own characteristic ways of coping. The subtitle of Bridges' book is *Making Sense of Life's Changes*, with a further subtitle "Strategies for coping with the difficult, painful, and confusing times in your life." It's a book I highly recommend to everyone. I won't attempt to paraphrase it here. However, the three stages of change that Bridges describes are important for us to know.

It's important to realize that change is an ongoing **process** that takes place over time; it is not a single **event**. That's why the word "transition" is so helpful here. We sometimes think of change as something that happens quickly—you quit one job and start another the next day, or you move directly from one home to another. Then we're confused when we have trouble adjusting, or when the settling-in period takes longer than we expect. Bridges helps us recognize that change takes time *internally* even when it may take place quickly *externally*. A mistake we commonly make is to hurry the change process and not give ourselves time to deal with the emotional issues involved.

The Three Stages in the Change Process

According to Bridges' model, every change starts with an **ending**, proceeds through an in-between stage he calls the **neutral zone** and finally comes to a **beginning**. I always thought of change as the start of something new. I never gave much thought to the ending or to the neutral zone. And thus I missed a lot of the reasons I (and others) struggled with change. Let's look at these stages as they apply to common events in our lives.

Take marriage, for example. You're in love, you have a wedding, you go on a honeymoon and then you set up house and start a life together. The focus is on getting married and moving forward. But there is an ending involved, as well. You leave the home you lived in before and all the people you lived with. You leave behind a certain freedom and spontaneity. Single people generally do whatever they like whenever it suits them. Marriage, wonderful institution that it is, entails thinking about someone else. Decisions are made jointly. Successful couples do a lot of compromising. He likes the window open at night, she gets cold; she's chatty and chirpy in the morning, he likes quiet; he plays hockey twice a week, she likes to go dancing; she wants to visit her parents on Sundays, he wants to watch the football game. Life gets more complicated. It's not without its rewards, of course. But in the first blush of love and enthusiasm, we sometimes forget that an ending has taken place, a phase of our lives has come to a close. Sometimes the endings are significant. If the newlyweds lived in different cities, one of them will have to move. Certain activities and even friendships may end if they're inappropriate to the marital situation. We need to acknowledge these things and the feelings they evoke.

Then there's the transition period. You come back from the honeymoon, move in together and start the adjustment period. It's not just the myriad little things like who gets which side of the bed, who does the dishes and what time supper will be. It's getting used to checking with your spouse before accepting invitations, telling him or her you'll be out on Tuesday evening or late for dinner on Thursday. Decisions about spending money and religious activities have to be discussed. You may start living together on a given day, but the settling-in process can take months, even a year or more. So even though the start of a marriage is about a beginning, the other stages are there as well.

High school graduation is an interesting time, often involving mixed emotions. Is it an ending (of a phase of your education), a completion of a certain body of learning? Or is it a beginning? Graduation ceremonies are often called Commencement Exercises, clearly focusing on the aspect of starting the next step in life, be it a job or going to college. So graduation is both an end and a beginning, with the emphasis varying for each individual. Some people can't wait to get out of high school and don't even show up to receive their diploma. Others feel great sadness at leaving one of the happiest phases of their lives. For many it's a time of limbo. Previously their life had a rhythm and structure. Now they may be undecided about what to do next, drifting from one temporary job to another trying to find themselves. Some can't wait to move on to the next stage and barely take notice of the leavetaking. But there are definitely three stages to this transition.

I loved high school and found it hard to leave. So I went back to visit many times over the next year or two, maintaining contact with the building, several teachers and many friends in the grades behind me. But I know people who have no fond memories of high school. For them graduation was a great relief. I struggled in my first year of university. I felt lost and lonely, trying to find my niche in the activities, social structures and new routines of campus life. Others made that adjustment more quickly and comfortably. I felt out of sync with my classmates in pre-med, many of whom formed into groups and cliques around sports, their old high school friendships and so on. I felt like an outsider most of the year. I even wondered if I'd ever fit in and feel the comfort and security I'd enjoyed in high school. Then something truly astonishing happened. I was elected class president for the following year. I couldn't believe it. Suddenly things started to fall into place and the next five years were wonderful and memorable. But I've never forgotten how discouraged and alone I felt that first year. In later years and situations, it was a touchstone for me. I've learned that I acclimatize slowly to new situations, but that things usually work out extremely well. Understanding that pattern has helped me to be patient and optimistic.

Stages in Our Reaction to Change (Specifically Endings)

William Bridges identified three stages in the change process. It's helpful to know what stage you're in at any given time, partly to keep you oriented and partly to guide you in finding helpful coping strategies.

"At this stage it is important to take note of what you are letting go of and grieve for what you will no longer have. It's a good idea to name these things specifically and create a ritual in which you say goodbye to them."

SUSAN M. CAMPBELL

But it's also helpful to know where you are in the stages of your *reaction* to change. For this information we should turn to the groundbreaking work of Dr. Elisabeth Kübler-Ross and her classic bestseller, *On Death and Dying*. In it she described the five stages that people go through in dealing with their own impending death or the death of a loved one. These stages translate very well to other forms of change, especially when the element of loss is prominent, such as loss of a job, separation, divorce, children leaving home, retirement, illness or disability.

Dr. Kübler-Ross identified the following five steps in the grieving process.

Denial → Anger → Bargaining → Depression → Acceptance

To illustrate these stages, let's imagine someone who's just found out he has advanced cancer. The **denial** phase is marked by incomprehension and disbelief. He may say things like "This can't be true, I feel just fine," or "There must be a mistake. They must have someone else's specimen." Then **anger** may set in. "This isn't fair." "I'm too young." "It's all those smokers at work—*they* caused this!" Or the anger may be at himself, a form of self-blame: "I got what was coming to me." "How could I have been so careless?" "I deserve this for all the stuff I've done." The **bargaining** stage might feature statements such as "I'm going to make a fresh start: good diet, lots of sleep, exercise." "I'm going to beat this thing." In other words, "If I just do this or that, the problem will go away." **Depression** usually sets in when the person realizes that he or she does indeed have cancer and the treatments have not cured it. There is a feeling of profound sadness and foreboding. Finally the stage of **acceptance** arrives when he says, "Well, there's nothing more that can be done," or "This is the way it is."

Over the years experts have noted that these five stages are not as separate and sequential as first envisioned. As Dr. Kübler-Ross herself notes, not everyone goes through all these stages, or necessarily in that order. Some stages are skipped, and others may be gone through more than once. It's now considered more accurate to think of the grieving process as a mix of emotions or what a colleague of mine calls the "chaos of feelings." Rather than depicting them in a line with arrows, we can more accurately represent them in a random way (see below), or in a circle with arrows going in many different directions (see diagram on the following page).

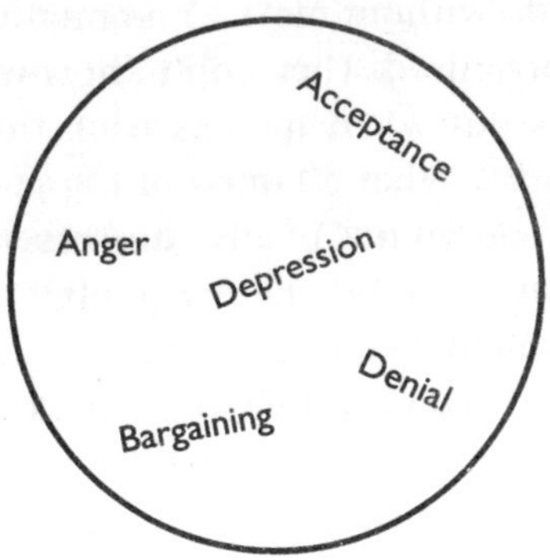

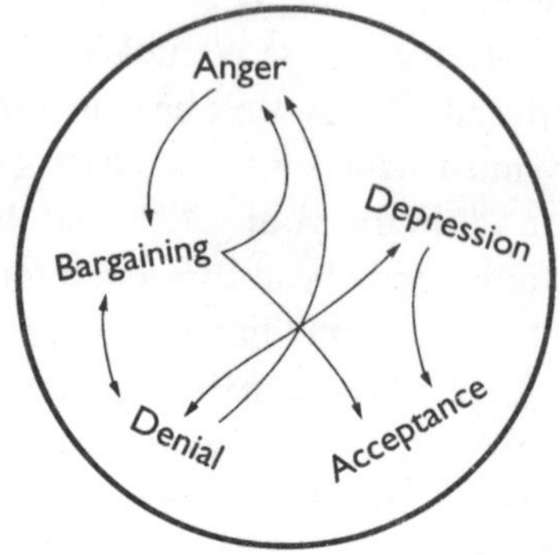

Another profound change is the breakup of a marriage, an event that provokes highly individual reactions, which may include **anger** ("After all I did for him, sacrificing to put him through school," or "How dare she do this to me! I treated her like a queen"), **depression** ("This is awful. I don't think I can make it alone," "What a loser I am," "Life feels so empty"), **bargaining** ("I'll promise to spend more time at home if she comes back," "I'll agree to go for counseling/do more around the house/control my temper"), **denial** ("Oh, he'll be back," "She just needs some time to cool off," "This is only temporary") and **acceptance** ("I guess it just wasn't a good fit. It's nobody's fault. We just weren't happy together. It's time to move on").

Let's look at a person who's just lost her job in a downsizing. Her first reaction might be **bargaining** ("I'll present a proposal to come back on a contract basis. I know these accounts better than anyone. And I'll beef up my skills so they can't do without me"). Then might come **denial** and disbelief ("They're so disorganized. They don't know what they're doing. The VP will straighten this out when he gets back from his trip"). Perhaps **anger** will be there too: ("What a bunch of ingrates! I work my buns off for them and then they dump me"). Enter **depression** ("I'm exhausted by all this. I don't care anymore. What's the point?"). Back to **bargaining** ("I'm going to ask Martha to go to bat for me. She's a personal friend of the general manager. And if I can't get my old job back, I'll apply for the opening in marketing"). Then **acceptance** ("OK, enough of this moping around and spinning my wheels. What's done is done. I got a decent severance. I'll just have to learn to play by the new rules"). Then a final flareup of **anger** ("I'm furious at them for putting me in this mess. They had to hire two people to replace me. Why didn't they just leave things as they were?"). And so on.

It helps to know that these reactions to loss are normal and predictable. So if you experience these feelings, in any order, don't be discouraged or think you're not handling things well. You're going through a process that takes time. Try to get yourself oriented and understand which emotions you're encountering so you can deal with them most effectively. And realize that depression, and even acceptance, can come and go. One of the best ways to cope is to talk about your feelings to someone else. It can be a relative, a friend, a mentor or a professional counselor. Writing in a journal can also be helpful. Guillermo Vilas, a prominent tennis star from Argentina in the 1970s, once told an interviewer about his journal-writing, "When my life is going well, I live it. When it's not going well, I *write* it."

The Neutral Zone

In a car with a standard transmission, you can't shift gears without first going through "neutral." The change process works the same way.

Endings are hard for me and many others, but the neutral zone can also be difficult.

This story was related to me by an amateur athlete. His unorthodox tennis serve had always been a problem. It became apparent that, with it, he'd gone as far as he could in the game, and that he needed to go back to the beginning, unlearn his bad habits and develop a correct serve. However, that took time. And in the interim his game fell apart. He'd given up his old motion and hadn't yet mastered the new. He was lost in between, frustrated and embarrassed. His sense of competence was gone, and he felt like an inept person. One day he thought, "Nuts to this. I'm going back to my old way. At least I kept the ball in play." But he couldn't find that serve anymore either. He was truly in the neutral zone: the old way was gone and the new way hadn't kicked in yet. He had no choice except to persevere—or give up the game. He went through a transition period of awkwardness, dislocation and frustration. But eventually he mastered the new serve.

Years later he went through a similar experience with his forehand shot. Only this time the neutral zone became so quickly uncomfortable and dispiriting that he let himself go back to the old way (inefficient as it was) rather than struggle with a shot that felt too awkward. He later found a teacher who was able to *modify* what he was doing rather than change it radically. It was less dislocating, felt more comfortable and allowed him to continue playing while he was perfecting the new stroke. So here were two different experiences with the neutral zone. In one case, my friend soldiered on through the difficulty. In the other, he abandoned the project and found an easier way to achieve the same result.

Some people try to avoid the neutral zone because it's unpleasant. In some cases avoidance is impossible—the period of being in limbo goes with the territory. In other cases, it may not be the smartest thing to do. A patient came to me with a dilemma. She was unhappy in her marriage but didn't want to be alone. She'd always been popular but had trouble with intimacy, so she went through a succession of relationships over the years (including two marriages). But these liaisons followed a pattern. She never left a relationship until she had the next prospect lined up. There was never a time when she was on her own or "playing the field." She'd avoided periods of casual dating (seeing several men, none seriously) and especially had shunned the notion of not dating at all for any period of time. The result was that she'd never learned to be alone, self-sufficient and able to enjoy her own company. The mere prospect of it frightened her.

This created a perplexing problem. Because she was unwilling to experience the neutral zone—and to learn from it—she made a lot of very bad choices.

As unpleasant as the neutral zone can be, it is often a necessary middle stage of change. It's a time for contemplation, clarification, getting to know yourself. And it doesn't have to be difficult: you can make it a comfortable, even enjoyable period. With my unhappily married patient, I reflected back to her that she was putting up with unhappy relationships just to avoid being alone. I suggested that maybe it was time to face that fear and, perhaps, to discover that being alone isn't so bad (easy for me to say—a guy who was happily single till age forty-one!). I thought she'd be more likely to make good choices in the future if she could develop the strength and self-acceptance to be able to say, "I don't have to put up with jerks just to have company. It's OK to be alone—and better than having *bad* company." A friend of mine made a profound statement after she and her fiancé mutually decided to break off their engagement. "It's not pleasant, but I know I need to go through this. And even though it's lonely, it has great integrity to it." She realized there are times in life when you can't (or shouldn't) shortchange a painful transition, and that by experiencing it and learning from it, you grow and become stronger and wiser. The neutral zone is a necessary part of change—and of life.

Another tale of the neutral zone involves an accountant who was unhappy in his work and kept talking about quitting his job and doing something entirely different. He had a restless and curious mind and mentioned several ventures that sounded fascinating to me and were clearly exciting to him. But when it got to the point of following up on them, he became uncomfortable. Even though he was financially secure, it seemed too big a step. Even more unacceptable was the idea of taking some time off from his secure job just to explore other career avenues. He was reluctant to be in the neutral zone, possibly because he'd gotten used to a certain standard of living, and possibly because he had a high need to be in control: living an unstructured existence, even temporarily, seemed threatening to him. The result is that he never took stock or redirected his life. He simply changed jobs in the same field, a kind of timid response to his occupational rut.

The neutral zone is one in which people often feel confused, disoriented, lost, rudderless, in limbo. However, the neutral zone can be viewed as a time of freedom and possibility, of new adventures and experimentation. It's also a time for reflection and self-discovery—an unappealing prospect to people who don't care for introspection and just want to keep busy so they won't have to think about things too much. Maybe we can learn something from the large number of high school graduates who take a year off before starting college or a career. They travel, earn some money, teach skiing or work at a resort, partly to take a break from years of study but often just to clear some time to think about what they want to do with the rest of their lives.

As Susan M. Campbell states in her excellent book *From Chaos to Confidence*, "You may notice a tendency in yourself to escape the discomfort of not knowing by engaging in compulsive activity or busy-ness. Do not rush to fill in the blanks with answers."

Beginnings

I'm a slow starter. I've learned that about myself. In new experiences I tend to feel like an outsider, wondering if I'll ever fit in or catch on to a new activity. My father and older brother taught me how to drive. One day I was getting frustrated with parallel parking and said to my brother, "I'm never going to get the hang of this." He immediately said, "Of course you will. You're a good athlete. Fai less coordinated people learn to drive." I beamed (praise from an older sibling will do that to a teenager) and felt reassured. And later I passed my test and got my license.

Two years later another driving experience had me again thinking I'd never catch on. I was working at a summer camp when the owner purchased a new boat. My friend Paul and I were sent to pick it up in Toronto, three hundred miles to the south. So off we went in a half-ton pickup truck, which we would use to pull the boat and trailer on the return trip. Paul drove the truck because I didn't know how to drive a gearshift. No problem. However, when we got to the waterfront in Toronto, we learned that the boat was at a marina on Centre Island and could only be reached by ferry. Paul had to take the ferry because he knew how to drive the new boat. I had to drive the truck to a loading ramp several miles away.

The moment of truth had arrived. I not only had to learn to use a stick shift, but I had about two minutes in which to do it. Paul gave me a few instructions and off he went. I then proceeded to make dozens of new friends by tying up traffic on Lakeshore Boulevard while I tried to master the complexities of the gearshift and clutch. I can't count the number of times I lurched forward, almost hitting other cars, and then stalled the truck by taking my foot off the clutch. It was a hot summer day and my fellow drivers (already cranky with the heat) didn't see this as a propitious time or place to be conducting a self-guided practice session. Their yelling and honking only added to my nervousness and ineptitude. It amazes me that I ever got the truck to our planned meeting spot. (By the way, I eventually mastered the skill and drove cars with standard transmissions for fifteen years.)

Beginnings of any kind are stressful. For example, starting a new job. You have to figure out where everything is, learn the new procedures, meet new people and sort out your own role and place. When you move to a new city, you need to find out where to go to buy bagels, get your shoes repaired and have your hair cut. New routines, new relationships—it all takes time, and can feel overwhelming at first. But slowly you catch on, and eventually you fit in and start to feel comfortable. Finally you get used to the place and its rhythms and feel at home.

Knowing I start slowly means I don't get concerned anymore. I used to wonder, Will this ever work out? Will I ever get used to this? Now I trust that eventually I will. It helps to look back at events I found difficult at the time and to realize I recovered from all of them. These events *were* tough, but I handled them. It's helpful to understand the stages of change and to realize there is a pattern to the process. Then you can determine where you are in the sequence and what will likely follow. It keeps you from getting discouraged when you can't yet see the way ahead.

Don't Rush the Process

A patient of mine was fired after years of loyal service to an organization in which he'd done a superior job and felt valued and secure. He received a generous severance package and an excellent letter of reference but still felt bewildered and badly treated. He had never been fired before, had lost much of his self-esteem and was very worried about his future.

When I asked if he was angry, he made an interesting reply: "Being angry isn't going to do me any good. I have to find a way to turn this around, turn it into a positive. I want to get back on my feet quickly." It had only been a few days since his dismissal, and it seemed to me that it was too soon for him to leap back in. He was still experiencing an "ending," and I knew he would have to spend an undetermined amount of time in the neutral zone. He needed to experience his feelings and deal with them before moving on. I explained the chaos of emotions concerning loss and grieving and asked where he thought he was. He pointed to depression. But he also acknowledged that at times he felt resentful. I drew a different diagram on my presentation board outlining yet another way of looking at the stages involved in our reaction to change:

Event → Emotional Reactions → Coping Strategies
(Acknowledging and Expressing Feelings)

I suggested that when an upsetting event occurs in our lives, we need to acknowledge and work through the feelings that result before we try to employ coping strategies to deal with the aftermath. Psychologists tell us that denial of feelings or burying of emotions is unhealthy. Rather than ignore feelings, gloss over them or dart around them, we do better by recognizing them and allowing ourselves time to work through them. In that way they're less likely to resurface at a later time, often triggered by a similar or related event (like someone responding with profound and prolonged sadness to the death of a pet, partly because it may have echoed the earlier death of a relative, where the feelings of grief and loss had been suppressed).

There are two steps in dealing with emotions: one is to experience them, the other is to express them. Betty Rollin wrote an important book about her involvement with breast cancer, which was later turned into a movie for television. The title is instructive. She called it *First, You Cry.* That's the normal response of women with this disease. It's important to allow that emotion to happen and allow time for it to be expressed. The intent is not to *dwell* on sorrowful feelings and remain stuck at that stage, but to allow natural reactions to occur and to work through them with patience and understanding, taking as much time as you require. Being "brave" and stoic may impress others, but usually it's a form of denial.

One of my patients struggled with emotional pain when her husband left her. She said, "I have times of screaming anger, but I get tearful when I get *here* [my office]." I suggested she not try to suppress her crying, to which she replied, "Crying doesn't *solve* the problem!" I agreed. But that's not its purpose. Its function is to release feelings of hurt and pain and tension. After acknowledging and expressing our emotions we can then get on with repairing, problem-solving and developing coping strategies.

How quickly people move through the stage of experiencing and expressing emotions is an individual matter. There are no "right" answers, although there are general ranges that serve as guidelines. When my father died, I booked off work for two weeks. I simply wasn't ready to interact with patients and concentrate on their needs any sooner. It took me several months to be able to function more or less normally. To recover from the death of a spouse can take a year or more. Allow yourself a period of time in which to react emotionally. During that process certain healing activities are necessary and helpful; especially important are the venting of feelings and getting support from people to whom you feel close.

Dealing with anger is a somewhat different story. First, realize that anger is a normal reaction to many situations. Don't judge yourself harshly for feeling that way. Sometimes the anger seems inappropriate; for example, the anger that is sometimes felt toward a spouse who has died may seem irrational. After all, he didn't want to die. But anger isn't always rational. You may think that he didn't take proper care of himself, or that he abandoned you, however unintentionally. You may feel angry because you were both about to retire and start relaxing, traveling and having the fun you kept putting off during your working years. Anger is a feeling. It isn't right or wrong. It's no more to be judged than if you feel hungry, sad, thirsty, tired or worried. The healthy thing to do is to acknowledge the feeling and experience it.

Now we come to the second part: expressing the anger. There are some helpful guidelines for this. First, don't hold the feelings in. It's healthy and constructive to express them. Second, avoid doing so in a way that is hurtful to others. If you're angry because you were fired from a job, writing nasty letters to your boss or defaming him publicly may feel cathartic at the time, but will land you in hot water and damage your reputation and career aspirations. And if it's public, your words may come back to haunt you. What you need to do is ventilate your feelings in a way that is safer and less direct. It's only important that you say it, not that your boss hear it. Another method that many people find beneficial is to write a letter to the person you're angry at, saying anything and everything you want to express, in whatever colorful language you choose. (As Mark Twain once said, "There are few enough words in the English language that express our true meaning—and we must learn to use *all* of them!") Once the letter is written, destroy it (shred it, throw it in the fire, flush it down the toilet, whatever). Don't send it (too inflammatory) and don't leave it around where it can be found by others (too risky). Don't even file it. Get rid of it. Another piece of advice: Don't reread it. The purpose of the exercise is to express the anger and get it out of your system. This is healthy and therapeutic, and unburdens you of the anger. But if you reread the letter, you end up experiencing the anger and internalizing it all over again. Not a good idea.

Carol Tavris wrote an excellent book simply called *Anger,* in which she questions the benefit of venting anger, especially if it is prolonged or done repeatedly. I agree with her that if it goes on too long, expressing anger may not be constructive. But in the early stages of anger, I think it's important to get it out. And then let it go. Another way of venting anger is through physical activity. It can be using a pillow as a punching bag, chopping wood or smashing a squash ball. One woman told me she went to a driving range and rented a bucket of golf balls. On each ball she wrote the name of her boss with a pencil. Then she teed them up, one at a time, "and whacked the living shit out of them." Then she calmly got back into her car and drove away, leaving her fierce hostility safely behind her.

The next step, employing coping strategies, is the stage where you start mobilizing yourself to move forward. It can include reframing the event (to think of it in some acceptable way), planning a strategy, resuming regular activities and so on. In the case of the woman who lost her job, it included outplacement services, a job search, psychological testing for a possible career change and seeking financial advice on how to conserve her severance package.

In summary, there are several stages in the process of change and several different models or ways of looking at them. Knowing where you are in the process can help you get your bearings and feel less confused. Understanding the stages helps make the natural course of change—and our reactions to it—more predictable. As William Bridges pointed out, all change starts with an ending, moves through a transition period (the neutral zone) and finally leads to a new beginning. Even when the change is rapid, the three stages are experienced internally. Dr. Elisabeth Kübler-Ross identified five stages in the grieving process and dealing with endings and loss. They include denial (disbelief), anger, bargaining, depression and acceptance. I have added my own conceptualization, in which the event is followed by a variety of emotional responses (essentially the ones described by Kübler-Ross), and my premise is that we need to take time to acknowledge and experience the emotional reactions before moving on to coping strategies. The intent is not to dwell on the emotional responses or become stuck in them, but neither is it to ignore or speed through them. In this area time is a helpful healer. Although, as one colleague notes, time alone heals nothing. It is the work that is *done* in that time, even subconsciously, that leads to healing.

PART TWO

Taking Action

CHAPTER SEVEN

When the Going Gets Tough, the Tough Get Strategic

Starting to Deal with Change

ONE DAY SHE WAS A SINGLE MOTHER in a good, well-paying job. The next day she was unemployed. It was the story of the times (mid-nineties). She'd been caught in a downsizing once before and had no means of support except some savings. She was shocked and for a few days she fell apart. Then she wondered if somehow she could get her job back. She became angry at what happened. She felt sorry for herself. The future looked scary. Then she sank into depression like a torpedoed boat. Several stages of the grieving process had flooded over her and overlapped.

> ***"Pick battles big enough to matter, small enough to win."***
> JONATHAN KOZOL

But she was a resilient and capable individual. She'd faced adversity before and had overcome great obstacles. Now she started to mobilize herself for action. She called me immediately because she recognized her need for support and a place to sort out her feelings. She called a lawyer about a possible case for wrongful dismissal, but decided not to pursue that avenue. However, the lawyer helped her secure a good severance package. One of the provisions was outplacement services, in which she enrolled quickly. The services included career counseling, a valuable process for her. The counselor was a sympathetic, insightful individual who became another source of emotional support. She drew up a financial plan to conserve her limited funds. She updated her résumé and touched base with her many friends, drawing on the support system she'd developed over the years. In addition, she joined a support group of unemployed executives in her community. After numerous job interviews she decided that her best security lay not in working for someone else, but in developing her own enterprise and becoming self-employed. After some investigation of an area that had interested her for years, she found a career opportunity that was a great fit. She enrolled in a government-sponsored program for starting a new business. Armed with a business plan she'd drawn up, she created some promotional literature and a snappy brochure, and within months she was busy with new clients. This whole process evolved over more than a year. There were inevitable small setbacks, but the general direction was upward.

This story illustrates an important aspect of resilience. People who bounce back are people who take *action,* who take the initiative. They don't sit back and wait for the world to come to them. Dealing with change is like dealing with winter. There are ways we can *think* about it that help create a positive mind-set and attitude. And there are things we can *do,* actions we can take, to make it easier, more comfortable and even more enjoyable.

"After the anger, rage, sorrow and complaining, what do I do *next?*" Once people stop lamenting and venting their feelings (understandable and normal behavior, of course, in the immediate aftermath of sudden change), it's amazing how creative they can be. They start to realize they *can* be resourceful, *can* be courageous, *can* be risk-takers and *can* be problem-solvers. This chapter is about what to do—after the dust has settled—to deal with change constructively and strategically. It's about "doing solutions" and taking action. It involves being active instead of passive, and also knowing what you can change and what you can't—taking action on the former and letting go of, or accepting, the latter. The result is constructive behavior and an increased sense of control.

Get Organized

I hated studying for exams. Who doesn't? The self-discipline, the volume of work, the intense concentration, the sitting indoors on beautiful days—what a drag! I break into a cold sweat just thinking about it. Over the years I evolved a system. The first thing I did was clean off my desk and straighten out my work area. Then I sat down and listed all the work I had to cover in each subject, by chapter number or topic. Next I made a schedule of when I would cover each item. Then I went to bed. That was it. (Probably just looking at all the stuff there was to do made me tired.) That planning session got me focused, helped me see the big picture, organized the material and gave me a sense of momentum. I'd made a start without actually doing any work. I used to wonder if it was just a clever way of procrastinating, but over time I realized it truly was a necessary step. It eased me into the task, but it also got everything in place for maximum efficiency.

Let's look at a major change for most people: starting a new job. What happens on day one? First, orientation: you get shown around, introduced to the physical surroundings and the people you'll be working with. You're told about procedures, given your job description and so on. Then you set up your own work area. Ding! There's the bell. End of the first day. Did you turn out any work? No. Was it productive? You bet.

Whatever the new situation you're dealing with, get organized first. Find your bearings. One of the best pieces of advice I ever got was from the nurse I hired to help me open my first solo medical practice. She said, "Start as you mean to continue." In other words, develop good work habits from the beginning—and then stick with them. It establishes a pattern for you and lets others know what to expect. There's a Zen saying: How you do anything is how you do everything.

Work Smart

In today's rapidly changing workplace, with all the downsizing, there's often too much to do for people who've kept their jobs. This is the "survivor syndrome," where you're asked to do more with less and pick up the tasks your departed co-workers used to do. There isn't enough time and the pressure is unrelenting. The tendency in these situations is to work longer and harder. But that becomes counterproductive because it leads to exhaustion and inefficiency. The key is to *work smarter*. Here's how:

Prioritize tasks. Decide what's most important and do that first. Then go on to the second-most-important item and so on. More time is wasted on low-priority, low-value, discretionary activities than you can imagine. And remember, as consultant and author Stephen Covey has noted, the most urgent task may not be the most important. We could spend our lives dealing with crises and responding to deadlines, only to realize that what really needed doing never got done.

Avoid clutter. Especially in your work area, but at home, as well. It's easy to become distracted by items strewn around your desk, reducing your concentration. You lose inordinate amounts of time looking for things. You feel overwhelmed or pressured with this constant visual reminder of work that's waiting for your attention. And clutter can lead to confusion and inefficiency. Kurt Vonnegut tells a story in his book *Slapstick* about his brother in upstate New York. The man was a research scientist whose lab was a scene of utter chaos. When asked how he got any work done, he pointed to his head and replied, "If you think this laboratory is bad, you should see what it looks like in *here!*"

Work on one thing at a time. Studies show that every time you leave a task and come back to it, there's a readjustment time on your return. It takes a few seconds or minutes to remember where you were and get back into the same mental frame. Don't jump from one item to another. If I write my notes immediately after seeing a patient, I can do it quickly because my thoughts are already in gear and the session is fresh in my mind. But if I write up my notes at the end of the day, it takes much longer, and they're not as useful later on.

Set aside blocks of time. If you're working on high-concentration tasks, such as writing a speech, preparing a report or doing month-end accounts, carve sufficiently long blocks of time out of your schedule so that you can get a lot done at one sitting. Depending on your ability to sit and concentrate, these periods might be thirty to ninety minutes long. Don't fragment tasks into too-short chunks of time, because you'll lose time trying to refocus and remember where you were. This is about building momentum. And when you're in a good groove ("in the zone," so to speak), stay at it as long as you're productive.

Limit interruptions. Close your door when you want to be left alone. Have the answering machine or service take your phone calls when you do high-concentration tasks. Work somewhere other than your office (a quiet room down the hall, a conference room or library). Do focused mental work at quiet times (for example, before nine or after five if you work in a busy office).

Delegate. If you have people to assign work to, don't do anything yourself that can be done well by someone else. As Dan Sullivan, president of The Strategic Coach program puts it, "Delegate everything but genius." Do the things that you are uniquely good at—and enjoy—and delegate everything else if you can. That's the ideal. But remember, delegating is not passing the buck. It's assigning tasks to the person most appropriate and qualified to do it, not just dumping your In basket into theirs and then going for coffee.

Work fresh. This is especially important for maximizing your peak energy times. If you're a morning person, do your most demanding work in the morning when your efficiency and stamina are highest. Do lower-concentration tasks and items of lesser priority in the afternoon. Reverse this if you're sluggish in the morning but come fully alive after lunch.

Take time-outs. No one can go full tilt all the time. We all need a time-out every couple of hours, even if it's only a short break of five minutes. This is discussed more fully in Chapter 9.

Avoid perfectionism. Common sense tells us that nothing is perfect, but our less logical selves keep striving for this unattainable standard. Of course this doesn't apply to everyone, but if you're someone who has extremely high expectations (of yourself and others), here's a quick tip: *Give it up*. It's a huge waste of time and energy—and most things don't have to be done to such a high standard anyway.

Avoid unrealistic promises and deadlines. Most people want to be agreeable and accommodating in an era of high customer expectation, tough competition and job insecurity. But this often leads to overly optimistic promises or agreements to unrealistic time frames for completion of work. Pressure and strain are put on you at a time when the stress of life is already high enough. And if you can't meet your obligations, things get even worse as you disappoint or anger others and are left feeling guilty, embarrassed, incompetent or all three. Give yourself an out if you're not sure you can fulfill a promise. Or say you'll do your best but don't make a firm commitment. As for deadlines, negotiate them carefully so you have some buffer time built in for unavoidable delays and interruptions.

Learn to say no. At times of rapid change, we often feel out of control and under pressure. Taking on chores open-endedly only adds to these feelings and leads to that overworked and overwhelmed feeling. At some point you have to slow down the onslaught and take control of your life. "No" is a good word to use for this purpose. It conveys respect for your own time and energy and honesty to the other person. In the present service-oriented, team-approach atmosphere of most workplaces, "no" may feel like a message of uncooperation or unwillingness to pitch in and be a team player. But if delivered properly, "no" will engender people's understanding, a respect for your situation and an appreciation of your candor. Here are some guidelines regarding this simple, though often uncomfortable, skill.

Learning to Say No

Benefits of Saying No

1. Takes pressure off you, less stress
2. People know where you stand
3. Increases your own self-respect
4. You feel more in control (of your self and your life), less like a victim
5. Reduces anger and resentment, increases general happiness
6. Frees up more time for yourself
7. Increases your energy
8. People are more appreciative when you do things for them (don't take you for granted)

When Is It Appropriate to Say No?

1. When you're exhausted or stressed out
2. When you're already overloaded and have no time
3. When you have higher, more important or more pressing priorities

4. When the requester's expectations are unrealistic
5. When it's not your job (area of responsibility)
6. When it's not your area of expertise and someone else can do it better or faster
7. When there's no benefit to you
8. When you feel the request is a slough off or buck-passing

How to Say No Acceptably

1. Express your wish and willingness to help (even when you have to decline)
2. Give an explanation
3. Make a counteroffer (to do it later or to give partial assistance)
4. Suggest alternatives (other ideas or people to help)
5. Ask what it's for (to help them clarify their situation)
6. Ask them to help you trade priorities (i.e., "What would you like me to set aside in order to help you?")
7. Ask for time to think about it

Use technology and other resources. There are a lot of great tools around. Use them. Don't write a letter if a phone call will do. Use fax and E-mail if they can save you time. Hold a telephone conference-call meeting instead of trying to assemble people from different places in one location. Use call-forwarding if you want to work from home. Use a dictaphone to dictate letters, even if you have to type them up yourself. It may sound like a make-work project, but it actually saves time. Use a word-processor instead of a typewriter. You don't have to be a "techie" to avail yourself of these labor-saving devices.

Conclusion: working hard doesn't work anymore. The key to success in the future is to **work smart**.

Acquire New Skills

As the world changes, new skills are required. In almost every field, from teaching to nursing to factory work, we've all had to learn how to use computers. Accountants have had to become financial advisers. X-ray technicians have needed new skills to use ultrasound, CT and MRI machines. If there's one overall message about adjusting to change, it's this: Don't rest on your laurels. You have to stay current and keep up. You have to make lifelong learning a part of your life.

"What you're learning is more important than what you know."

UNKNOWN

There are two kinds of learning. **Knowledge** is about acquiring information relevant to your field. **Skills** are hands-on abilities (using equipment) or organizational techniques (such as time management). The more you learn the better you'll be able to do your job. And the more employable you'll be if you *lose* your job. Business writers like William Bridges and Charles Handy tell us we'll all have several different jobs/careers in a lifetime. The more portable the skills you learn, the more mobile and versatile you will be.

Seek out and enroll in training courses. If at all possible, get your company to pay, and preferably take the courses during the day—on company time. After all, the capabilities you develop will benefit the organization as well. But if your company won't fund your learning, pay for it on your own. Think of it as an investment in yourself. When I was in grade eleven, I decided I wanted to learn how to type. My high school didn't offer such a course to general students, so I found a class that ran two evenings a week and signed up with a classmate of mine. We were the only people under age thirty in the group. Going to night school was a wonderful experience. Everyone was very nice to us (we were like the class mascots), and we met people from every walk of life, including a lot of new immigrants. The one thing we all had in common was our desire to learn a new skill. And learning to type was one of the smartest things I ever did. It's repaid my time and effort a thousandfold.

What do you need to learn? Just about anything and everything will be beneficial. Organizational skills, prioritizing, delegating, assertiveness, time management, money management, computer expertise, keyboard abilities, selling yourself, marketing, entrepreneurial skills, relaxation techniques, stress management, public speaking, leadership skills—even learning how to learn. They'll all add to your overall competence and confidence. Emotional aptitudes are also important. Interpersonal skills such as negotiation techniques and conflict management are a must in many jobs. My only warning is don't overload yourself. Take one course at a time. Pick things you're most interested in first. And make it fun.

As for knowledge and information, lifelong learning is essential because new facts are being discovered and ideas created at a dizzying rate. In many fields information becomes obsolete quickly and you have to keep up. Fortunately there are many ways to do this. My preferred method is reading: books, magazines, newspapers, newsletters—there's a vast array of options. But don't overwhelm yourself with stacks of journals and periodicals. Be selective. And don't forget to read for pleasure, as well. Other information sources are TV documentaries and public affairs programs, CD-ROMs, the Internet and public lectures (there's a constant flow of free or inexpensive presentations in most communities on a wide assortment of topics, including parenting, health, financial management and the environment). Just keep learning and you'll keep growing—at any age.

Be Creative

A local radio station asked for suggestions to beat the February blahs. The most imaginative idea I heard was from a man who videotapes baseball games all summer and throws them in a drawer, unlabeled. When winter comes, he settles into his favorite chair, randomly selects a tape, shoves it in the VCR and enjoys an evening of baseball, complete with pictures of hot sunny weather. He puts his mind into a summer mood, completely forgetting about the cold and snow just outside his window. That's an example of the creative mind-set in action.

New situations at work are great laboratories for new ideas, because everything's in flux and companies are more open to experimentation and innovation than they are when routines are already in place. Telecommuting is an example of creatively giving people the option to work from home with the use of new technology. Flex-time was an innovative way of allowing employees to adapt work, home responsibilities and time concerns (the time wasted in rush-hour traffic) more comfortably into their lives. Job-sharing was someone's resourceful idea to allow people to balance their desire for paid work with their wish to spend more time at home raising their kids. We take these concepts for granted now, but they all emerged in one generation as more women entered the workforce and people searched for ways to make the world of work more flexible and compatible with new lifestyle patterns.

Here's a funny story about a variation of job-sharing that I encountered during my internship. On my obstetrics rotation I was slowly getting to meet all the staff obstetricians. One evening I noticed that the attending faculty man on call was Dr. Nelson. I'd been curious to meet him because of his first name—Frewbarr. When I saw him on the list, I said, "Oh good, I'm finally going to meet Frewbarr Nelson tonight. What nationality is he?" The doctors and nurses on the ward cracked up. Then someone explained, "He's from England and his name is Tom. His partners are Dr. Frew and Dr. Barr. We call them Frew-Barr-Nelson because their patients aren't assigned to any one doctor. They're simply patients of the clinic. They see them all at different times during their pregnancy and get delivered by whoever's on duty when they go into labor." Job-sharing had become so well established that it had evolved into name-sharing (at least on lists and schedules!).

The following anecdote demonstrates a schoolteacher's creative approach to a discipline problem. I read about a teacher who was struggling with a high-energy, fun-loving student who consistently disrupted her class with his wisecracks, jokes and funny faces. She tried all kinds of conventional methods of discipline, but the kid was irrepressible. Finally she hit on the solution. She made him a deal. If he would refrain from cutting up in class, she would give him the last fifteen minutes of each day to entertain his fellow students. "Done!" he reportedly said, and the bargain was struck. This turned out to be a classic win-win. Actually it was a win-win-win. She got his cooperation in class, he got center stage on a daily basis and the other pupils were treated to a funny send-off at the end of each day. This teacher not only used creativity to deal with a problem, but she must have had a decent eye for talent, too. The class comedian went on to become a movie star. His name is Jim Carrey.

This story was about *lateral thinking*. Sometimes you have to harness the energy that is working against you. There is a paradox in kite-flying. To launch a kite you have to run *against* the wind, not *with* it. Sometimes things are not as they seem. And often there's more there than we can see. Learn to use your mind in unique and unaccustomed ways. Dare to think "out of the box" and do things differently.

Anticipate the Future

Entrepreneurism is an area where creativity and innovation are vital. Secure full-time jobs are vanishing, and more and more of us are becoming self-employed, contracting our work out to a succession of "clients" or "customers" and forging strategic alliances with others for joint ventures and projects. It's new and different but also extremely exciting. In the Information Age, consulting, training and many other kinds of services are in demand. The possibilities are endless, bounded only by our imagination and ingenuity.

If you are thinking of joining the entrepreneurial economy, there are three ways of deciding where to branch out. One is to follow your passion, as Marsha Sinetar put it in her bestselling book, *Do What You Love, the Money Will Follow.* That's how I got involved with stress management. I became so fascinated with it that I decided I wanted to do it all the time. The second is to go with your skills and strengths. If you're good at teaching, consider becoming a trainer and present seminars. If you're a computer hotshot, start a consulting service to help people solve software problems. If you're an ex-policeman, develop a niche investigating white-collar crime or insurance fraud. If you're good with your hands, do freelance work in construction and home renovation.

> **"Throughout the centuries, there were men who took first steps down new roads armed with nothing but their own vision."**
> AYN RAND

The third way of employing yourself is to figure out future trends and jump into the vanguard. Think about where things are headed and position yourself to take advantage of opportunities in those areas. As hockey superstar Wayne Gretzky put it, "Don't skate where the puck is. Skate to where it will be." By anticipating the future and planning for it, you can make yourself a part of it.

What will the world of tomorrow look like? Take an example from the field of medicine. The trend is away from hospital stays and toward community services and ambulatory care. To that end, hospitals have closed down large numbers of beds, day surgery has been introduced, rapid discharge after childbirth has become the norm and so on. New trends are emerging from this radical shift. Members of the nursing profession who are out of work because of the changes should be paying attention to the new job opportunities those very same changes are opening up. One is that more nurses will be needed in the community to provide home care to patients no longer being admitted to hospital or those being discharged earlier (and sicker) than in previous days. The other is that nurses still on duty in hospitals are stretched to the limit by having more patients to deal with than when staff-patient ratios were more balanced. The net result, I believe, will be an increasing need—and demand—for private-duty nurses, not only in patients' homes but also in hospitals Alzheimer's patients, for example, need a more constant level of supervision than ward nurses can provide. Nurses anticipating this need could start to offer their services for one-to-one bedside nursing on a shift-work basis. They could join an agency that contracts out nursing professionals, or they might start their own agency, recruiting well-trained colleagues, marketing their services, arranging schedules and managing the financial end.

Other trends in medicine for unemployed nurses to pursue include the move to more midwife-assisted births (many nurses have already become trained midwives), nurse practitioners and forms of alternative medicine (wellness counseling, massage, reflexology, therapeutic touch and so on).

One cash-strapped hospital came up with a brilliant idea to generate revenue. (After all, there are only so many times you can raise prices for parking or cafeteria food!) They started to rent space to local business enterprises, who then provided their services and products to members of the hospital staff, ambulatory patients and visitors. Everything was considered, from a doughnut kiosk to a photo-finishing center. There are a lot of people who move through hospital corridors on any given day. This novel idea provided convenience for them, a new source of business to the vendors and an inflow of much-needed income for the medical facility. Another win-win-win situation.

People will work less and have more free time in the future. Charles Handy predicts that the wage-earner of tomorrow will work 50,000 hours over his/her lifetime, as opposed to 100,000 hours in the last generation. The result will be folks with less money and more time on their hands. They're going to need a few things that enterprising individuals can start figuring out how to provide. First they'll need advice on time and money management. Inexpensive leisure activities will be an area to explore. As baby boomers live longer, a whole industry will emerge to provide services to seniors, including retirement planning and counseling. It's already happening. Volunteerism is increasing as the number of healthy seniors increases, and jobs that didn't exist a generation ago have begun to appear in the area of coordinating and directing the work of volunteers.

Be a Team Player

Change in the workplace can have the same effect as a stink bomb in the middle of a party. The group disintegrates as everyone heads for cover and only looks out for Number One. That's an unfortunate outcome, because there is strength in numbers—safety, too. This is not just about togetherness. It's about cooperation. It involves doing what you can to make the change work. You don't have to become a cheerleader for a new policy that you think is a disaster. But unless your objections are very significant, you'd be better served by making an honest attempt to be a willing partner and support the new ideas. When change is a done deal or fait accompli, further opposition is not helpful—to you or to the new enterprise. It doesn't mean you can't continue to give input and suggestions. Just make them constructive rather than destructive. Don't complain.

There are times when we have to decide whether to fight or fit. One man I counseled didn't get along with his new boss, who had started a restructuring program in the company. He was resisting his boss's initiatives and resenting his ideas. The outcome was friction and conflict—and a lot of tension and stress. One day he bounced into my office and announced, "I'm doing great." He explained, "I decided there's going to be a new me at work, so I've been going in with a new attitude. And I'm feeling much better. If you can't beat 'em, join 'em! Now I'm doing things they wanted me to do that I'd been resisting. I'm doing what *they* think is a good job, not what *I* think is a good job. I'm all caught up in my work and I don't have the weight of the world on me." He had given up his stance of resistance, confrontation and trying to work around his boss. This was not capitulation or caving in. It was a strategic decision about when it's useful to resist and when it's futile. It's about knowing when to give up the opposition role and start working for the greater good.

A last word about being a team player. Avoid negative people, who complain, sabotage and drain you. Be positive, constructive and conscientious. And be a support to others, giving encouragement, advice and a helping hand.

Ask for Help

You don't have to reinvent the wheel. Being creative doesn't mean you can't listen and learn. Seek out mentors and coaches. Read what others have written about similar situations. In specific things like writing a résumé or designing a brochure, find out who can help you. In general areas such as surviving a divorce or learning to live with a disability, get all the advice and direction you can. And respond in kind when others seek out *your* expertise and guidance.

Manage Your Health

Sudden change can be overwhelming. If a family member gets sick or dies unexpectedly, or you lose your job without notice, the emotional reaction can leave you feeling helpless. Gradual change is certainly challenging, but rapid change is even harder because there's no preparation time. Just getting over the shock drains a lot of adaptation energy. The tendency for many is to get so caught up with immediate details and coping emotionally that they forget to attend to their own needs.

One of my patients went through a terrible ordeal when her brother, to whom she was very close, was diagnosed with cancer. He started chemotherapy, but the prognosis was not good and he eventually died. My patient was a very caring, giving person, and it was natural for her to shift her focus almost totally to her brother's needs. But in so doing she neglected herself. She skipped meals, didn't sleep or exercise enough, withdrew from her friends and activities and devoted herself entirely to her ailing sibling. In the short run she was able to sustain this routine, but as the months wore on, the strain became obvious. I urged her to start pacing herself, not only to get through this difficult time herself, but also to be able to continue to give support to her brother. She needed to eat regular meals and a balanced diet, not just junk food on the fly. She had to go to bed at a reasonable time and get a full night's sleep. I suggested she get back to her regimen of regular exercise. She started using alcohol as a coping tool until I asked her to stop. I encouraged her to make some time for friends and relaxation. After all, she needed to receive support, as well as give it.

People in crisis often ignore their own most basic needs. The concepts of self-care are not complicated. In fact, they're pretty simple and mundane, but the benefits are profound, and they're most important at times of strain and difficulty. If your business is failing and you're spending every waking moment trying to rescue it from the brink, you'll actually have more energy for the task—and make better decisions—if you take care of yourself and your essential needs. Self-neglect is not a formula for adaptability. But resilience and self-care go hand in hand.

Put Your Financial House in Order

Of all the changes in the past ten years, the one that's probably hit the hardest is economic. The majority of families need two wage-earners just to keep their heads above water. Debt is a widespread blanket that's covering, if not smothering, everyone. Workers who have lost jobs have begun depleting their savings. Full-time work has been replaced by part-time employment, usually meaning less income and loss of benefits. Governments are cutting back on unemployment and welfare payments. There's no evidence that this trend will be reversed anytime soon. Simply put, most of us are going to have to learn to live on less money.

Mention money today and you touch a nerve. People are more comfortable talking about their sex lives than their monetary situations. Several patients have told me they started sleeping with someone after their first or second date but wouldn't even consider inquiring about their partner's finances, even months after sharing the same bed. "Ask him about money or his income? Are you kidding? Don't you think that's a bit too personal at this stage?"

However, talk about money we must. It's the only way to get a handle on the situation. When my patients list money problems as a source of stress, I lead them through the preparation of a financial statement. It's a sobering exercise for many, but a crucial one. And no matter how bad things may be, all of them get a sense of relief to finally put the cards on the table. They feel that at last they're getting organized and facing realities they know are important. Another positive aspect of this activity is that some people are pleasantly surprised to find that things are not as bad as they'd feared.

What should you write down? There are two parts to this drill. One is to list all your assets (bank balances, savings, investments, equity in home, car and so on) and liabilities (outstanding loans, debts, mortgage and so on). Then subtract one from the other to get your "net worth."

Assets		**Liabilities**	
Bank Balance(s)	$ ________	Loans Owing	$ ________
Savings	$ ________	Mortgage	$ ________
Investments	$ ________	Credit Card Balances	$ ________
Equity in House	$ ________	Back Taxes Owed	$ ________
Equity in Car	$ ________	Other Loans Owing	$ ________
Other	$ ________		
Subtotal (A)	**$ ________**	**Subtotal (L)**	**$ ________**
NET WORTH (A-L)	**$ ____________**		

If it's a positive number, you want to keep it that way and improve on it. If it's negative ("in the red"), you have to take immediate measures to reverse the situation, including selling off some assets if necessary. I prepare a "net worth" statement at the end of every month, plotting the final number on a piece of graph paper and then joining it to the dot from the previous month. There are inevitable ups and downs, but if the overall trend isn't upward, I take action to rectify it.

The second part is to set out a monthly cash-flow statement (see diagram on page 120). Here you list income from all sources (wages, investment income if any or loans you've received) and all expenses. The latter includes

Monthly Income

Salary	$ ________
Investment Interest	$ ________
Other	$ ________
Subtotal	**$ ________**

Monthly Expenses

Fixed

Rent/Mortgage	$ ________
Phone	$ ________
Insurance	$ ________
Loan Payments	$ ________
Cable TV	$ ________
Hydro	$ ________
Other	$ ________
Subtotal	**$ ________**

Variable

Food	$ ________
Gas & Car Repair	$ ________
Clothes	$ ________
Entertainment	$ ________
Gifts	$ ________
Travel	$ ________
Miscellaneous	$ ________
Subtotal	**$ ________**

Net Monthly Cash Flow

Income	$ ________
Total Expenses (Fixed & Variable)	$ ________

NET TOTAL **$ ________**

fixed expenses (such as rent or mortgage, phone, insurance, car payments, cable TV) and variable expenses (such as food, entertainment, gifts, travel). Then look at the two numbers.

If there's more coming in than going out, you're on the right track. But if the outflow exceeds the inflow, if there's "too much month at the end of your money," you have to act quickly to turn it around.

"Wants" vs. "Needs"

Insecurity is one of the toughest aspects of change to deal with. And *economic* insecurity is especially stressful. My father always warned me about debt. "Interest will kill you," he said. But we're a consumer society. We buy stuff—often stuff we don't need and can't afford. If ever there was a time to address this issue, it's now. We've been on a collective spending spree for decades, fueled by government largesse and the wonder of credit cards. We can buy on a whim, live beyond our means and not pay till later—*much* later. Governments are finally wrestling with their financial overextension by slashing spending, and the results aren't pretty. As Al Jolson used to say, "You ain't seen nothin' yet!" That's because our politicians woke up so late in the game and have so far only been attacking the deficit (the annual overspending). They haven't even begun to tackle the accumulated debt from years of such deficits. In Canada the total debt at all levels of government is nearing one trillion dollars, a number most of us can't even comprehend. In the United States the number is much higher.

If governments (who love wooing us with our own money) have realized the jig's up and the binging has to stop, we as individuals also need a personal wake-up call about our own finances. The best book I've ever read on this subject is *Your Money or Your Life*, by Joe Dominguez and Vicki Robin, which looks at our relationship with money. As a friend of mine once told me, "When people talk about money, it's never about money." Think about it. What does money mean to *you?* Security? Freedom? Power? Status? Success? Money is only a vehicle for obtaining things. When you look at a five-dollar bill, what does it represent to you? It's worthless in itself—just a piece of paper. It only has value in terms of what it can buy for you. We exchange these pieces of paper for **survival needs** (food, shelter, clothing), **comforts** (nice furniture, carpets, cars, air-conditioning) and **luxuries** (jewelry, travel, theater tickets, fancy restaurants). One way to get control of our finances is to understand the difference among these three categories. Especially important is defining the difference between a *need* and a *want*. The next step is to discipline ourselves to curtail spending on wants. I'm not suggesting that we should *never* buy anything we don't need. But these discretionary purchases should be made more selectively and mindfully, depending on our overall financial picture.

Dominguez and Robin use a brilliant visual tool in their book to distinguish between needs and wants. They call it the "Fulfillment Curve" (diagrammed in modified form on the next page), plotting satisfaction versus money spent. They point out that, past a certain point, the satisfaction and fulfillment you get from spending money diminishes. At some point you start spending without thinking and consuming without appreciating. If you go out to a restaurant on occasion, it's a treat. If you go out several times a week, it loses its specialness. You become blasé or take it for granted. When theater tickets started to become very expensive, we canceled our subscription and started to go only to selected productions, maybe two or three times a year. We make a real occasion out of it. It's become more enjoyable because it's less frequent. The authors call the top of their curve, the point where satisfaction starts to decrease, "Enough." The question each of us has to ask is "How much is enough?" What do we really *need* for a satisfying life? Some of my patients have restrained their spending for several months to get their finances into better balance. One called this his "austerity program." He limited his outflow of money and questioned every purchase. He and his wife ate at home, he took his lunch to work and stopped paying for entertainment. Instead they watched TV, went cycling, got together with friends, rented movies or played board games. No movie theaters, no new clothes, no restaurants or traveling—nothing but necessities. It was amazing how quickly his finances turned around once he slowed down his spending. And the quality of his life during this period was fine. When his finances were OK again, he loosened the purse strings and got out a bit more. This exercise was not about deprivation. It was about being frugal and mindful of how he spent money.

Your financial situation can also be improved, of course, if you earn more money. But this is not where I recommend you start. Working longer hours or at more than one job will only wear you out. And the extra money you earn will just flow out like water through a sieve, and you'll be no further ahead. People tend to live up to their income. The key is to curtail your spending.

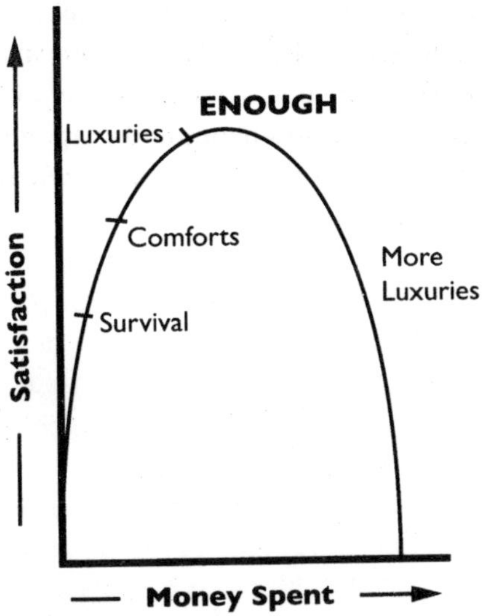

Something else to consider: When you earn a dollar, you only get to keep about seventy cents (or less) because of taxes. But when you *save* a dollar, you save one hundred cents. My advice is to spend less before you try to earn more.

To better handle change, finance is an area where all of us should take action. When your money picture is in disarray, your alternatives are limited. People who have money in reserve are more flexible and resilient: they can quit a job they hate, go away on vacation when they're exhausted and ride through business slumps in which their income falls. Change-hardiness depends on physical health and emotional well-being, but our financial condition also has an impact. This isn't about wealth. It's about matching what you have and what you earn with what you spend and save. If they're not in good balance, you need to take action. And you'll be thrilled with the benefits when you do.

In summary, when dealing with change, we need to adjust on two levels: making the mental shift and taking concrete action. Get organized, work smart, learn new skills, be creative, anticipate the future and plan for it, be a cooperative, positive force in the change process, take care of your health and, finally, manage your money and be mindful in your spending. This is no time to be timid or sit on the sidelines! Look at this era of change as a time of opportunity—and get involved. Resilience and adaptability are not only states of mind, they are reflected in specific actions. So when the water gets rough and the going gets tough, *get strategic!*

CHAPTER EIGHT

Don't Just Jump In

Planning, Practicing and Preparing for Change

IT'S MOVING DAY. IS EVERYTHING PACKED? The movers will be arriving at 7:30 sharp. Are you ready for them to start taking boxes to the van? Or are you planning to do some last-minute packing while they're loading the furniture? Do you find it's taking longer than you predicted to fill those cartons? Are you getting irritated because the moving guys are a lot faster and more efficient than you'd imagined? Are you running way behind by the time the truck's ready to roll? Do you start figuring how much you can put in your own car because now you're holding them up? (And you're paying for their time!) Are you sweating and feeling panicky? Are you already promising yourself you'll be better organized next time?

"To reach any significant goal, you must leave your comfort zone."
HYRUM W. SMITH

Welcome to the world of poor preparation for change. It's obvious that planning and preparing for events makes life a whole lot easier, but not too many of us are so well organized that we've never experienced that last-minute panic and disarray. If there's going to be change in our lives, then being proactive and learning to anticipate and plan in advance are essential skills. We need to develop a more forward-thinking focus. These habits are part of the resilience repertoire.

Be Prepared!

Every Boy Scout knows that this motto is an important piece of life wisdom. We need to be prepared not only for specific situations, but for change in general, for whatever might come along. A lot of the anxiety of a new situation can be reduced if we plan ahead. In 1969 a friend of mine decided to move to Spain.

Months before his departure, he did a number of things to get himself ready for the transition to a new country, climate and culture. He talked to many people who'd lived there about jobs, weather, housing, the local currency—everything. He started reading about the country and its history. He enrolled in Spanish classes in Toronto. He got names of people to look up in Madrid. Notwithstanding some normal trepidation about moving five time zones away, he felt a sense of ease and comfort by the time he departed. His planning and preparation had given him a head start even before he got on the plane. He made a comfortable adjustment, got a job and stayed for more than a year.

When you know about a particular change in advance, anything you can do to prepare for it will make the adjustment easier. Learn what you can about the new job, becoming a parent, living in that city. You don't have to become obsessive about it, but some familiarity will definitely help you settle in and adapt more quickly. Whom do you need to talk to? What would you like to know? What resources will assist you?

A friend of mine is a master at this kind of research. Years ago he planned a trip to Club Med on Paradise Island. It happened that I was going there two weeks earlier. When he heard that, he asked me to do some reconnaissance for him. This guy is a classic Type A individual. He wanted to do as much as possible in his seven days at this "summer camp for adults," so he wanted to know how best to manage the system. For example, he had me find out how he could book a tennis court within an hour of his arrival. I found the whole thing rather amusing and compulsive, but by scoping out the situation ahead of time he was able to jump in and start participating as soon as he'd unpacked. This is a literal example of hitting the ground running.

Psychological preparation is as important as physical/logistical planning. A woman once told me about the stress of her job. She said that everyone she dealt with was rude, hostile and sometimes verbally abusive. I asked her where she worked. "In my company's complaints department" she told me. She had a problem all right, but it wasn't just the environment in which she worked. She apparently hadn't come to grips with the fact that unhappy, complaining customers *were* her job. She could have chosen to quit if it wasn't a good fit for her temperament, but eventually, by matching her expectations to the reality, she was able to cope better.

Imagine this scenario: You've just been promoted at work. You're now going to manage people who were recently your co-workers and peers. What can you expect in your new role? Well, for one thing, there'll be an adjustment period, during which you'll feel disorganized and maybe a little out of your depth. There'll be new things to learn (information, procedures, reporting protocols) and you'll feel inept for a while. Good to know that in advance. You might also anticipate a shift in your relationship with the staff who are now reporting to you. This isn't inevitable, but it's a probability. You might notice they're less relaxed around you. The chatter and gossip at lunchtime may hush when you approach. It could be an awkward time. But if you expect that nothing will change and it'll be business as usual, you're setting yourself up for an unpleasant surprise. Mental/psychological/emotional preparation is extremely important when you enter a new situation.

Look what's happened over the past twenty-five years in the field of obstetrics. Women used to have babies with a minimum of preparation. They went into labor without much advance information about what to expect, and in the hospital things would be done to them (shave prep, enema), sometimes without explanation. Doctors, nurses and/or midwives would monitor the labor and "deliver" the baby with or without some form of anesthetic. If there were problems, events might move swiftly for safety reasons, but again the mother might not be told much. "We don't want to scare her" was the rationale—as if it wasn't frightening to see people scurrying around with worried looks on their faces, talking in hushed tones. Nowadays expectant mothers (and their husbands) are given a lot of opportunity to prepare for this natural and exciting event in their lives. Prenatal classes explain all the phases of pregnancy and the different stages of labor and delivery. There are diagrams, a movie of an actual birth, answers given to questions, misconceptions clarified and fears allayed. There's a tour of the maternity wing of the hospital, including labor rooms, delivery suites and nursery, and couples are walked through the exact procedure that will be followed from the moment they arrive at the hospital door. In addition, relaxation and breathing techniques are taught and practiced for the different stages of labor. The net effect of all this is that expectant parents today are *prepared*: they're much better informed, more comfortable and confident when the first labor pains begin.

Preparing for the Unknown

How do you plan for change when you don't know what form the change will take? It's fine to say you want to be a good change agent, to be resilient and adaptable, but what steps can you take to achieve that? There *are* specific skills you can develop to prepare yourself for the unknown effects of change in your life. Let's look at them.

Become a Lifelong Learner

This phrase has become a cliché in recent times, but it's an absolute essential for the change-hardy individual. Whatever your field of work, things are changing, often rapidly. In the insurance industry new products are being offered, and woe betide the agent who doesn't know about them. Lawyers need to keep abreast of all the changes in law and precedents—the legal system is constantly evolving. If you're an accountant, tax rules and regulations are in continual flux, and you have to be on top of the latest wrinkles. The field of medicine is changing so much and so fast that most of the drugs and procedures used today weren't even available when I graduated. Teachers should know about new theories and innovations in the field of education. New sales and marketing ideas are springing up regularly. The face of management has changed dramatically. Industrial skills and procedures are anything but static. And on and on it goes.

You need more than just facts and information. You have to keep upgrading and adding to your skills, especially in the technical area. Computer literacy and expertise are becoming necessary in every field of endeavor. Fax machines, E-mail, voice mail, cell phones—technology is booming and it's best to join the parade and learn to keep up.

I should also mention literacy in general. The information age is upon us, and the ability to read and write clearly and well are paramount requirements for functioning in the world of tomorrow.

In addition to information and skills, keep abreast of general trends. Read widely. What's on the horizon in the field of technology? Demographics? World events? This kind of general awareness affects all kinds of current decisions and long-range plans. Do you lock into a long-term mortgage? Where should you invest your money? What new businesses show the most promise for entrepreneurs? Keep your eyes and ears open. A good sailor is always watching the water and weather for signs of change. A sudden wind shift can create a danger to your boat, especially if it's not anticipated. But it can also provide an opportunity to pick up speed if you see it coming and prepare your craft to take advantage of it. Keep a close eye on what's happening around you. And every so often, check the horizon to see what's coming.

Stay Flexible and Light-Footed

In addition to keeping up with events and developments, you also have to be able to move fast when situations change. Think of white-water rafting. This is an exhilarating activity that my family and I recently tried. It can turn dangerous in an instant, so there was a lot of preparation. We were suited up with helmets, wet suits, boots and life jackets. After a short orientation session, we practiced (in calm waters) different paddling strokes for different situations and were given instruction about what to do if various mishaps occurred. There was a big component of psychological preparation as well, so that by the time we hit the white water we felt comfortable and confident.

However, on this kind of thrill ride, confidence isn't enough. We had to be alert, attentive and ready to react instantly to the instructions of our guides, who were superb. They had to read the water, know the currents, anticipate quickly, know what orders to give and then do so calmly and at the right time. Events can occur so fast that seconds make a difference. The heightened vigilance is needed to do the sport safely—but it also adds to the excitement of the experience.

Highway driving requires the same light-footedness and ability to react quickly. You have to watch immediately ahead, beside and behind you—and also keep an eye on the road further ahead. You need to be aware of other drivers and anticipate their behavior. Good defensive driving requires you to keep scanning the scene and planning what you'd do if this or that problem arose. In addition, you make constant adjustments in speed, distance from the next car and the lane you're in. The margin of safety is smaller than we appreciate. I was driving in Michigan years ago with a friend whose father was a highway patrolman. He said something to us I never forgot. "Just remember, at sixty miles an hour every one of those telephone poles you pass is only a tenth of a second away from your car." That's a piece of news to wake you up and keep you vigilant!

How do you stay light-footed in day-to-day life? Do you keep a packed suitcase under your bed, wear sneakers all the time and keep a full tank of gas in your car? In a word, no. It would be exhausting to live every day as if you were white-water rafting or riding a galloping horse. But there are some basic measures that are practical and important. Have some food in the fridge in case you can't go out. Have some money in the bank to deal with emergencies. It's a good idea in today's working world to have your résumé up to date and in a drawer nearby. And if you don't have a résumé, write one (and get help with it—there's a skill to doing this). Keep your ear to the ground about job opportunities in your field in case you're suddenly laid off. You don't have to run scared to be prepared. In fact, having general plans for different contingencies is more likely to *relieve* anxiety than to cause it. You just need to anticipate possible problems and be ready for them. Then you can relax.

Hope for the Best but Prepare for the Worst

In terms of general preparedness think of situations that could arise and how you would deal with them. This is how to develop a proactive mind-set. I'm not talking bomb shelters and doomsday scenarios here. Just things like "What would you do if you lost your job?" Circulate your résumé? Start networking, find out what's available in your field, take courses to develop your skills? Why not do some of that now? And be poised and ready to implement the other plans if needed. "What would I live on if I lost my job?" Deal with that question now. Would you start spending less to conserve funds? Why wait? Most of us buy things we don't need. Be more mindful in your purchasing. For example, many people have put off buying big-ticket items like appliances and furniture because of insecurity about their jobs. That's a sensible thing to do in uncertain times.

Take care of your health. *You* are the most important resource you have. Unexpected events and changes are challenging enough when you're at your best. They're much tougher, even unmanageable, if you're sick.

Make sure you have a will and keep it in a place where your relatives can find it easily. Be certain you have life insurance, enough to cover more than your funeral if you have dependents. Get disability insurance if you don't already have it. Have a list of people you can call on for help (especially child care) if you get sick or have to go into hospital.

People in relationships often fall into stereotyped roles, leaving gaps in their skill sets—perhaps in areas where their partners are strong or have taken over. It's helpful to close those gaps before you *have* to. For example, men should learn how to manage a household (cooking, laundry, grocery shopping) so they can step into that role if required. Similarly, women should develop facility in money management (paying bills, investments, dealing with banks). Of course these roles aren't always gender specific, but in most marriages there is a division of labor.

In general, the message is: Hope for the best but **prepare** for the worst. Then get on with living your life.

Practicing Change

Another way to prepare for change is to practice it ahead of time. But how do you practice something as abstract as change? By inviting it into your life. Any kind of change. All kinds of change. Just as long as it keeps you loose and flexible and nimble. This is the best way to develop resilience and adaptability so you'll be able to deal with new situations when they come along. Notice this isn't an "if" anymore. Change has become a certainty.

If you want to keep in shape for skiing, you don't have to ski. You can run, cycle, climb stairs or work out with weights. Anything that keeps your muscles strong yet limber will pay off. Similarly you can practice change by stretching and strengthening your change-hardiness. Anything that takes you out of your comfort zone is a form of rehearsal for other, as yet unidentified, new situations or unexpected circumstances. And the less wedded you are to the status quo and the less you need predictability in your life, the more adaptable you will be.

For example, are you disturbed when your route to work is blocked by road construction? Start exploring other ways of getting to work. What other streets could you take? Are you close enough to walk or cycle? How about public transportation? Now that you've identified alternatives, why not take another route to work on occasion just for variety? Mix things up a bit. You might even discover a way that's more scenic or less congested with traffic. I take the train into Toronto whenever I can because it's relaxing. My uncle used to drive the back roads between his work in Rochester, New York, and his home in Canandaigua. I asked him why he took such a long route, especially at the end of a tiring day (he was a psychiatrist). He said it was more enjoyable driving out in the country, much prettier and less hectic—a time to decompress and wind down. But he could always switch to the highway if he wanted to save time or in case of bad weather.

I've changed my work schedule about ten times over the years. Different starting times, finishing earlier or later, seeing patients only in the morning or all on one day in order to free up a whole day just for writing. I do it for expediency or efficiency at times, and at others just for comfort. But I also do it for variety—so my days don't all look exactly alike—and to keep myself limber. Then if change is required, I'm ready to deal with it.

But varying patterns isn't the whole story. Leaving your comfort zone involves putting yourself in positions you're not entirely comfortable with—on purpose. Taking on challenges—for example, playing a different position on your baseball team, agreeing to give a presentation at work even though public speaking isn't your favorite thing, accepting an invitation to a party where you don't know anyone. If you intentionally put yourself in such situations, you still maintain some level of control—yet you're stretching your flexibility muscles and broadening the horizons of what you can tolerate or feel comfortable with. And the more you do this, the easier it gets. Many people who fear public speaking (and there are millions of them) join Toastmasters, where they purposely agree to do the very thing they fear: public speaking. But they're introduced to it on a gradual and incremental basis. First just stating their name and where they're from, then a one-minute speech about something, then two minutes, then five and so on. Eventually many go on to give full-length presentations with a measure of comfort and ease they would not have thought possible at the outset.

Practice specific changes that might be useful at some time in the future. For example, try living on less money for a while—it's amazing what you can learn to live without, and the experiment helps you realize that, if push comes to shove, you can live at a lower level of spending and life will go on satisfactorily.

Travel also affords a great opportunity to leave your comfort zone. Especially when you go to places very different from your home. Another country or climate, a big city if you're a rural dweller, or a place with unfamiliar customs or a different language. These are all ways to expand yourself. Going on canoe or camping trips is a great adaptability builder because it involves living close to nature, in good weather or bad, with a minimum of creature comforts. Sleeping in a tent, cooking out of doors, washing in a lake, performing natural bodily functions without porcelain toilets—all of these departures from everyday living build resilience and resourcefulness.

I went through a period where I tried all kinds of different things. It was the most adventurous time of my life. I lived in the Canadian Arctic, got my pilot's license and flew bush planes. Then I went to live in Israel, in a small flat in Jerusalem. We had no heat, no phone and only one appliance, a refrigerator. We cooked on two gas-fed hot plates and washed our clothes in the bathtub. For a city boy from Toronto it was an interesting adjustment. As my friends got wind of my eagerness for adventure, they found new challenges for me. I worked on an archaeological dig and was later invited to the summer excavation for a month as the dig doctor. I also got to be the team doctor on a one-week trip through the Sinai Desert in an open-sided truck with an eclectic mix of thirty-five fascinating people. The daytime heat was oppressive, the nights were cold, bathroom breaks were taken without even the luxury of a tree to duck behind—the truck would stop in the middle of the desert, and men went off on one side, women on the other. We got to see and do some incredible things—including a six-hour climb of Jebl Musa, the biblical Mount Sinai. Was I out of my comfort zone? Absolutely. Did I have the trip of a lifetime? You bet. Did it increase my comfort in dealing with unusual situations? I'll say.

NBA star Michael Jordan purposely took himself out of his comfort zone during his two-year experiment with baseball. Here was this phenomenally successful basketball player giving up his illustrious career with the Chicago Bulls to try his hand at a sport he'd have to enter in the minor leagues. He intentionally put himself in the position of apprentice, a newcomer learning the game from the ground up. Granted, he'd played some baseball and was a superbly conditioned and gifted athlete. But here he was in

Birmingham, Alabama, playing Class AA ball, driving around the countryside by bus and appearing in small ballparks around the Southern League. This wasn't Deion Sanders playing two sports at the major league level. This was the best-known athlete on the planet deliberately taking on the role of student and novice—in full view of the American public and media. What kind of courage and humility did that take? And think of what he learned from the experience!

Movie actors sometimes stretch themselves in similar ways. Dustin Hoffman and Richard Dreyfuss go back periodically and do stage acting, a very different discipline (although one they've been trained in). Other stars leave their familiar turf or source of their success to try their hand at different roles. Meg Ryan was America's darling for a while after her delightful comedic roles in *When Harry Met Sally* and *Sleepless in Seattle*. So what did she do next? She played an alcoholic in *When a Man Loves a Woman*. Tom Hanks took a big chance playing a lawyer dying of AIDS in *Philadelphia*. What did he get for his trouble? An Academy Award. Woody Allen left his patented and highly successful comedy persona to direct the very somber *Interiors* and play a serious acting role in *The Front* (about the McCarthy-era blacklist nightmare). Some stars try their hand at directing, taking a chance on the other side of the camera. Why do highly successful people leave their areas of comfort to try something new, and in such a public way? One reason, undoubtedly, is the need for change and challenge, or a wish not to be typecast. But what they gain from it is equally valuable: flexibility, adaptability and personal and professional growth. And every time they do it, it makes the next time that much more comfortable.

In summary, dealing with change becomes much easier if you plan and prepare for it. This applies to specific changes but also to new situations in general. There are measures you can take now to prepare yourself for a shift in circumstances, or even adversity. Developing contingency plans, financial security, a support system and good health are measures that will enhance your resilience. Practicing change on a regular basis helps to improve your adaptation skills and increase your feelings of confidence and self-reliance. Just as fire drills teach us how to respond in case of fire and desensitize our fears, practicing change takes the mystique out of new situations and lets us develop game plans for handling them. All this preparation and practice builds up your "change immunity" so that new circumstances and rough water don't seem so foreign or intimidating. And remember, the more you leave your comfort zone *voluntarily*, the easier it will be when you have to leave your comfort zone *involuntarily*. And stretching yourself will eventually actually cause your comfort zone to *expand!*

CHAPTER NINE

Change Is So Exhausting!

Generating and Maintaining Energy for Change

HERE'S A TYPICAL NEWS STORY OF THE NINETIES: Company restructures. Many layoffs. Major reorganization. Roles reassigned. Employee dislocation. Long hours. Much pressure. High stress. New learning.

Are we having fun yet? Here are two responses. Guess who's coping better.

Worker #1: "I'm bagged. This sucks. How long do they think I can go on like this? I get home exhausted. The first thing I need is a drink—well, OK, *two* drinks. I can't be bothered to cook, so I grab a burger and some fries on the way home. All I'm up for is crashing out in front of the tube for the evening. And some comfort food—where would I be without nachos and Coke? And my fave, chocolate ice cream with fudge sauce. I drag myself up to bed after the late news. Gotta keep up with world events. Set the alarm for six and hope I can bag a few Z's before morning. Oh, God, when will this end?"

"Progress might have been all right once, but it has gone on too long."

OGDEN NASH

Worker #2: "This is tough sledding. My mind aches at the end of the day. Can't wait to get home and change clothes and get out on my bicycle. I need to move my body and get some fresh air. Think I'll have lasagna tonight with veggies and salad. Better pick up some fruit on the way home. Maybe I'll just read tonight and have a quiet evening. Gotta be in bed by ten. Tomorrow I think I'll invite Wendy to an early flick for Friday night. This work schedule's a grind, but it won't last forever."

As corny as it sounds, a healthy lifestyle is imperative if we're going to manage transitions well. Change management includes energy management, and that means generating vitality and maintaining it at a good level. Energy depends on basic lifestyle habits. It's all pretty straightforward and not that hard to do. And the payoffs are considerable.

What does change have to do with energy? Dealing with change is demanding: it requires **adaptation energy**, both physical and mental. Without it we'd have difficulty adjusting to new situations or concentrating on new tasks. I remember how tiring it was for my children when they started grade one and had to stay in school for a full day, and when the workload picked up in grade five, they came home more fatigued at first. We forget that mental challenge and effort can be as taxing as physical work. If you want to be resilient and adaptable, you need energy. If you wish to be flexible and resourceful, you should show up rested, fit and fresh. If your work requires creativity and innovative thinking, you have to be sharp. It's that simple. And the recipe for keeping up your energy is equally simple. It consists of the following:

1. Good nutrition
2. Adequate sleep
3. Regular exercise
4. Minimal caffeine
5. Time-outs and leisure

There's nothing mysterious or flaky here—just the nuts and bolts of a healthy lifestyle and good common sense. And while it's not flashy, it works. When I follow this recipe, I feel like a world-beater. When I don't, I feel like a slug.

Let's explore each of these items in a bit more detail.

1. Good Nutrition

Think of food as fuel. You'd never take a motor trip without making sure there's gas in the tank. Our bodies run on the same principle. The only source of energy we have is in the food we eat. Skipping meals or eating empty calories (for example, doughnuts) makes no sense.

The Guidelines Are Simple:

- Eat regular meals (preferably breakfast, lunch and supper)
- Make sure your meals are well balanced (eating from all the food groups). Here is an outline from *Canada's Food Guide*:

Milk products (2–4 servings/day): milk, cheese, yogurt, ice cream

Meat & alternatives (2–3 servings/day): poultry, fish, meat, eggs, beans, tofu

Vegetables & fruit (5–10 servings/day): fresh veggies (including potatoes), fruit, salads

Grain products (5–12 servings/day): whole-grain cereals, whole-wheat bread, bran muffins, bagels, buns, rice, pasta

Choose a variety from each group to get the best mix of vitamins and minerals.

- Avoid junk foods, sugar, fried foods and fats.
- Drink 6–8 glasses of water a day. Hydration is important.
- Eat slowly and chew your food well. It not only aids digestion but makes mealtime more relaxing instead of a stress-filled race against time.

Most of us know this stuff but only pay lip service to it. Nutritionists tell us we should eat five to ten portions of vegetables and fruit a day. American research shows that ninety percent of U.S. citizens eat less than the minimum of five. Eating smarter is an essential part of an energy-management program.

2. Adequate Sleep

One of the best-kept secrets of success is sleep. Yes, I know that Thomas Edison thought sleep was a waste of time, and Buckminster Fuller was said to go for weeks sleeping only three hours at a time. And I concede that neither of these gentlemen was an underachiever. But for the vast majority of us mortals lack of sleep makes us tired, grumpy and inefficient. Juliet B. Schor, in her excellent book *The Overworked American,* states that "According to sleep researchers, studies point to a 'sleep deficit' among Americans, a majority of whom are currently [1991] getting between sixty and ninety minutes less a night than they should for optimum health and performance." My wife teaches time-management courses. She cited a study to me showing that forty-four percent of people who feel time-crunched (and who doesn't these days?) steal time away from sleep. We're simply not getting enough.

How much sleep do we need? Each of us has our own set of internal clocks and individual requirements, but most of us need seven to eight hours a night. Dr. Stanley Coren, a psychologist at UBC in Vancouver, wrote a wonderful book called *Sleep Thieves,* in which he states that our need is closer to nine hours a night, which is what Americans were averaging until 1913. What happened that year to change the pattern? Edison brought out his tungsten filament lightbulb, and life hasn't been the same since. This artificial light not only allowed folks to read and sew after dark but made it possible for them to work at night, as well. Shift workers take note: Edison's your man if you want to complain about those graveyard shifts.

I often ask patients a number of questions about their sleeping habits:

- How much sleep do you *think* you need to function at your best? Most people know from experience. This isn't about how much you can get by on. It's about how much you need to feel great and perform optimally. I can live on six hours a night for weeks at a time, but I need eight to feel my best.
- Do you wake up rested or tired? You should feel refreshed when you awaken.
- How is your energy through the day? We all have fluctuations, which I'll discuss later ("ultradian cycles"), but if you're dragging around much of the time, you're sleep-deprived.

- Do you require an alarm clock to wake you in the morning? If so, you're probably sleeping too little. You should awaken naturally and spontaneously when your body has gotten the amount of rest it needs.

According to Stanley Coren, the best measure of whether you're getting adequate sleep is something called the "sleep latency period." This is the amount of time it takes to fall asleep. If you're out like a light the minute your head hits the pillow, as many people proudly state, guess what? It means you're not getting enough sleep. Normally it takes about ten to fifteen minutes to fall asleep and more than twenty if you're fully rested. If you conk out in less than five minutes, it means you're very sleep-deprived and your body is craving sleep.

How does sleep deprivation affect our adaptability to change? It reduces it. We become less efficient, make more mistakes and learn less well. Dr. Coren introduces the term "sleep debt" to describe the shortfall between the sleep we get and the amount we need. For example, if you need eight hours a night and you only log seven, you have a sleep debt of one hour for that night. If this goes on for a week, you have an accumulated sleep debt of seven hours. You start to show the kind of effect that people exhibit when they lose all seven hours in the same night, albeit not to the same degree. Your concentration is reduced, your mental reflexes are slowed and your mood is affected; you may show some irritability or feel a bit depressed. This will not stand you in good stead when you're trying to get used to new procedures, learn new tasks and get along well with new team members at work.

Dr. Coren gives us some good news though. We can "repay" our "sleep debt" when we get behind. A few full nights of uninterrupted sleep can get you caught up. Then, of course, if you don't start getting your full allotment on a regular basis, you'll just fall behind again.

There's another way in which sleep relates to adaptability—it influences learning. New situations often require us to master new information and skills. That process is affected by the amount of sleep we get, because new learning involves laying down new circuits in the brain, and that takes place partly when we sleep. That's when we process and consolidate new information so we can recall or use it more easily the next time around. Research studies show that if you learn a new skill or manual task and then get a good night's sleep, you will be more adept at reproducing that skill the next day than a person who *doesn't* get adequate sleep. Different parts of the sleep cycle seem to play specific roles in the acquiring of memory. Losing slow wave (or deep) sleep has an overall effect on concentration, attention span and short-term memory development the following day. Losing REM sleep (rapid eye movement sleep, which is when we dream) affects memory consolidation from the day just past. The guess is that deep sleep builds up whatever resources and capacity we need for short-term memory the next day, allowing us to take in information or new learning and to store it. REM sleep is most important for laying down memories from the previous day. Since deep sleep takes place in the first few hours of sleep and most of our dream sleep occurs in the second half of the night, getting a *full* night's sleep is essential for optimal memory development. So in changing work situations, getting enough sleep is critical.

Guidelines for Sleep:

- Determine how much you need and get it on a regular basis.
- Go to bed and get up at the same time as often as possible. Our bodies love routine.
- If you want to get extra sleep, going to bed earlier is better than sleeping in. Sleeping later is better than nothing, but it throws off your body's sleep-wake cycle for the next day.
- Sleep in a room that is dark, quiet and cool. Light, noise and too much heat interfere with both the quantity and quality of your sleep.
- Sleep on a firm (but not *too* firm) mattress.
- Avoid stimulation such as vigorous exercise, arguments, exciting movies or books before bedtime. Similarly, disturbing thoughts and images will interfere with sleep. That's why I strongly oppose watching television news before bed. I also urge people not to watch TV in the bedroom at all. The content of most programs (sports, comedy, drama) produces some

form of arousal or stimulation. Sleep experts tell us the bedroom should be used only for sleep and sex (especially important if you have trouble falling asleep).

- Avoid large meals or rich food in the mid to late evening.
- Avoid caffeine in the evening and late afternoon (see discussion of caffeine below).
- Limit alcohol to two drinks in an evening (it has a stimulant effect as it wears off).

3. Regular Exercise

Most people think of physical exercise as a *drainer* of energy. But, paradoxically, it's also an energy *producer*. It may tire you out at the time, but it energizes you afterward. I used to play hockey with a group of guys on Wednesday nights from ten to eleven-thirty. We called ourselves the WNHL (Wednesday Nighters' Hockey League) and we all had snails on the front of our jerseys (true story!). I'd get off the ice exhausted and practically crawl home, whereupon I'd be up till two in the morning, feeling totally energized and infuriatingly awake. There are two reasons for this. When we exercise, our bodies become highly stimulated. A lot of wake-up and feel-good hormones start circulating (such as adrenaline and endorphins), and their effects last for several hours after the exertion.

The other explanation is that when we exercise, we improve our level of fitness. This includes not only strength but stamina and endurance. Exercise improves the function of the heart and lungs and makes them more efficient. We breathe faster and deeper when we exercise, so we take in more oxygen. The body gets better at absorbing that oxygen into the bloodstream. The heart beats more quickly during exercise, so the blood circulates faster, carrying the oxygen to all parts of the body, especially to the muscles that need it most during strenuous activity. The tissues get more efficient at taking up the oxygen and using it at the cellular level. So exercise improves the delivery and uptake of oxygen. The best measure of fitness is not strength or even endurance. It's something called "oxygen uptake and utilization" and has to be measured in a lab. The fittest people are those who have the best capacity for absorbing oxygen and getting it to the individual cells of the body. Exercise is absolutely the best way to improve the body's efficient use of oxygen.

A word about oxygen. Remember learning about combustion in school? Where you lit a candle, covered it with a drinking glass and within seconds the candle went out? The teacher explained that, as the candle burned, it consumed all the oxygen under the glass. Conclusion? Oxygen is essential to combustion. The same principle applies to the human body. We also burn fuel, which we get from our food, and that's why we need good nutrition. But we can't burn that fuel without oxygen except for very short periods. And the more oxygen we have, the more fuel we can burn—and the more energy we produce. The science behind this is dramatically convincing. If you burn one molecule of glucose in the presence of oxygen, the output of energy is ten to twelve times greater than burning a molecule of glucose without oxygen.

Which brings us back to the subject of exercise. The more we exercise, the better our bodies get at taking in oxygen and using it efficiently. The result is substantially increased energy. And that improved fitness doesn't just help us the next time we exercise or play sports. It serves us all day long. Our bodies are stronger, our minds sharper, our health better. If you want to generate and maintain energy to help you deal with change, exercise is a crucial part of the program.

Guidelines:

- Exercise a minimum of three times a week, preferably four or five.
- Exercise a minimum of thirty minutes each time. Longer than an hour is fine, but the benefits aren't much greater unless you're an athlete in training. If you don't have half an hour, twenty minutes is better than none.
- Pick aerobic forms of exercise (walking, jogging, swimming, bicycling, skating, racquet sports like tennis and squash, basketball, hockey, touch football, exercise classes, Stairmaster). The word "aerobic," coined by Dr. Kenneth H. Cooper, refers to activities that improve oxygen uptake and utilization, which is exactly what we're trying to achieve here.

- Pick activities you enjoy. Otherwise you'll get turned off and it will feel like a chore. Variety is a good way to keep it interesting. Do different kinds of exercise. Perhaps jog twice a week and vary the routine with walking, tennis and/or cycling on other days.
- Physical activity other than exercise is also valuable. Mowing the lawn, housecleaning, gardening, taking stairs instead of elevators—these all contribute energy-producing benefits for the body.

4. Minimal Caffeine

Caffeine is such a socially accepted substance that we forget it's a drug. It's a stimulant. Actually it's a *strong* stimulant. It jazzes up our bodies and increases our metabolism rate. The result is that it increases the rate at which we burn fuel. "Hold it," you may say. "Caffeine increases energy. I can't start the day without it. I need that kickstart to get going." What we have here is another paradox. Caffeine is a stimulant in the short term (increasing energy), but over time it *depletes* us of energy by cranking us up so we utilize more energy than we need to.

A colleague of mine is a microsurgeon (this does not mean he is a tiny person!). He does surgery under a microscope (repairing blood vessels and nerves). He told me he used to drink a couple of cups of coffee in the morning and thought nothing of it. But when he started operating under the microscope he noticed a slight shaking of his hands. With his naked eye he saw nothing. His hand looked perfectly steady. But under the mike there was a slight tremor. That's when he realized the impact caffeine was having on him. He found he was OK with one cup of coffee, so he limited himself to that.

That's how subtle the effect can be. On a larger level can you imagine what would happen to your energy if your arms and legs were trembling continuously all day long? You'd be exhausted by noon! When your car idles too fast, you take it in for a tune-up. Why do you do that? Well, it's partly because it's noisy and because your car leaps forward when you let up on the brake. But you also know it's burning more gas than necessary. The same thing happens in your body. When your "motor" is revving faster, it's using up more fuel—which is inefficient and costly.

Caffeine Does Not Supply Energy

Only foods that can be broken down into glucose supply fuel. All caffeine does is stimulate the body to produce more energy (from the fuel that's already there) and get it into the bloodstream. It's like squeezing water out of a sponge. If the liquid is there, squeezing will make it available. But it doesn't put any moisture *into* the sponge. Caffeine is like a big fist squeezing short-term energy out of our bodies and not putting anything back. So it eventually depletes the energy that was there by making it more readily available and using it up more quickly. The result is that, over time, caffeine actually drains us.

And it gets worse. Caffeine interferes with sleep. You may be thinking, "Not me! I can drink a cup of coffee at bedtime and fall asleep in minutes." True enough. Not everyone gets insomnia from caffeine. But there is a subtle effect that became apparent only when researchers started studying subjects in sleep labs. Here's what they found. When we fall asleep, we go into a very deep level of sleep for more than an hour. This is called "level 3-4" sleep or "slow-wave" or "delta-wave" sleep. Then we enter a lighter phase called rapid eye movement, or REM sleep, and that's when we dream. Then we go back into deep sleep again (I call it "the sleep of the dead"—if something wakes you, you don't know where you are for a few seconds.) This is again followed by a REM phase. We alternate deep and dream sleep like that all night long in roughly ninety-minute cycles.

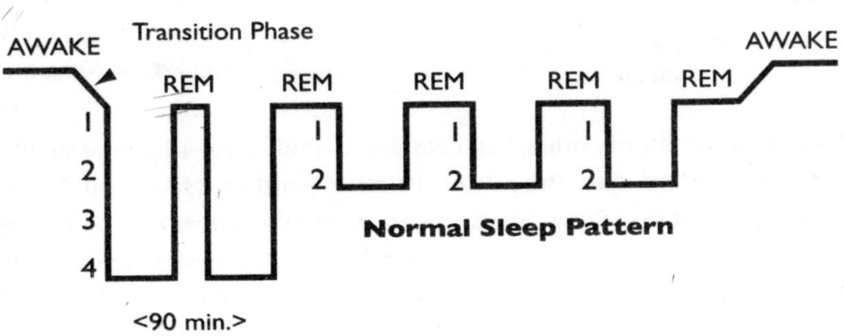

REM=Dream Sleep

From Jon Shearer, Ottawa

But not all cycles look the same, as illustrated in the diagram on the previous page. Notice that the first two cycles are deeper than all the other cycles throughout the night. What researchers discovered is that those first two cycles of deep sleep (corresponding to the first three hours of sleep) are the ones that replenish us physically. This is where we get the physical restoration that raises our level of daytime energy. It's why Buckie Fuller could function with only three hours of sleep at a time. He was getting the most important and restorative part of the night's rest.

Now let's look at what happens when you have caffeine in your system. Even if you fall asleep and stay asleep all night long, you never reach the level of delta sleep that restores your physical energy. Caffeine fragments your sleep cycle, it interferes with the architecture of your sleep. You end up with the same *amount* of sleep (quantity) but not the same *benefit* (quality).

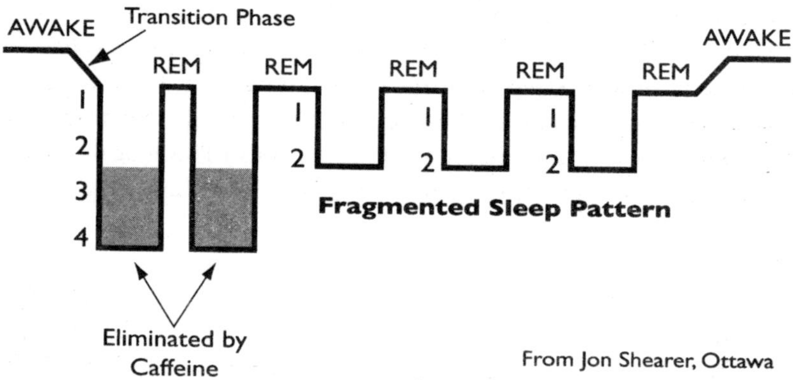

Caffeine is found in coffee, tea, cola drinks (and some other forms of pop like Mountain Dew) and chocolate. It's also found in certain medications, including painkillers. Read labels or ask. Caffeine enters the bloodstream within minutes, peaks at about an hour, *but stays in the system six to ten hours* (and longer as we get older). If you drink several cups a day, the effect is cumulative and magnified. So if you're going to drink caffeine, do so in the early part of the day (preferably before noon) and limit yourself to one or two cups, depending on your tolerance.

I urge all my patients to go off caffeine for a few weeks as an experiment to see what effect it has on them. The best way to find out what it's doing to you is get it out of your system completely. Three weeks is ample time to test it. A warning: **Don't stop caffeine abruptly or you'll get bad, migraine-like, withdrawal headaches.** Wean yourself gradually (for example, cut back by one drink each day until you're off completely). Then stay off for three weeks.

Most of my patients feel better without it, many dramatically so. They feel calmer, more relaxed and less stressed. But they also report sleeping better and having more energy. That's the paradox: removing a stimulant produces more energy. The explanation is that (1) you stop revving up your body, and (2) you get a better quality of sleep. In effect, you get off the "caffeine roller coaster" of stimulation and withdrawal, stimulation and withdrawal (which is exhausting). Try the experiment for yourself. The odds are about four to one that you'll feel better without it.

5. Time-Outs and Leisure

In every sport except the marathon, time-outs are built into the game. Hockey players rest between shifts and again between periods. There's half-time in soccer and football, pitstops in car racing, a minute between rounds in boxing and so on. No one would even consider doing otherwise. Not even athletes can maintain the pace. Without breaks they would run out of juice (a.k.a. energy) and risk injury. Their performance would also be adversely affected. Leave a hockey player out there for fifteen minutes at a time and see how effective he is.

In the work domain, the same principle applies. You wouldn't expect a ditchdigger to work nonstop for hours at a time. If you've ever shoveled snow, you know you have to stop periodically and give your muscles a rest. The same premise goes for animals. If you have a horse pulling a plow in your field, you're not going to work him for several hours without a time-out. Not if you want the best from him.

Then why is it that people in white-collar jobs think they can start work at eight in the morning and go till six or seven at night without a break (not even for lunch) and assume that somehow makes sense? How do they think

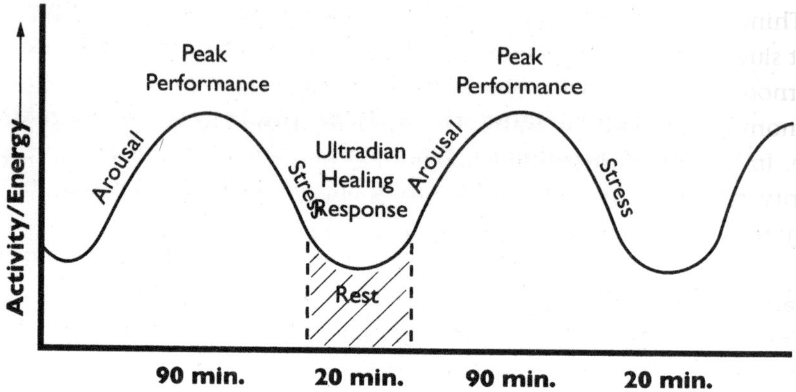

they can work efficiently and productively for all those consecutive hours? The fact is, they can't. And those who think otherwise are fooling themselves. Mental work is just as taxing as physical work but in a different way. It would help if we all started thinking of the brain as a muscle. It can get fatigued, it can get overloaded, it can stop working well.

Aside from the pleasure of taking time-outs, periodic breaks in the workday are indispensable to energy management and high performance. Science backs this up. Dr. Ernest L. Rossi explains this in his fascinating book *The 20 Minute Break*. Just as we have cycles of deep sleep and dream sleep through the night, we also have rest-activity cycles throughout the day called "ultradian rhythms"—*ultradian* means "many times a day," as opposed to our twenty-four-hour "circadian rhythm" of sleep and wakefulness. Actually these latter cycles each run twenty-five hours (*circa*—approximately; *diem*—day), but that's another story! Each ultradian cycle (I prefer to call them "energy cycles") lasts 90 to 120 minutes (see the diagram above) and consists of more than an hour in which our physical energy and mental function are enhanced, reach a peak and start to diminish. This is followed by a lull or low period in which our bodies go into a state of rest, in a sense preparing for the next wave of increased energy and activity. This is determined physiologically, and we've all experienced it, although we may not have known it has a name and happens to everyone.

Think of what happens to you around midmorning, when you start to feel a bit sluggish. Or that trough we all get into after lunch and/or in mid to late afternoon. Another dip occurs sometime in the evening. These fluctuations are normal, and we'd do well to start noticing them and heeding their message. In the trough, we're not functioning optimally. Why not give up the twenty minutes that aren't productive anyway and prepare to make maximum use of the next energy upswing when it appears?

When to Take a Break

You're feeling good, on a roll, working efficiently, you're on the upswing or near the top of the cycle. Enjoy it and make the most of it. But then you notice signals from your body that it's winding down temporarily. You may start yawning and sighing; you feel tired (sometimes I experience a wave of fatigue that rolls over me within minutes), lose your focus and concentration, start to daydream or find you're making mistakes or errors in judgment. Or you may have a feeling of restlessness, where you want to get up and stretch and move around. Some people start to feel hungry or have an inclination to go to the bathroom. These internal messages signal a shift into the rest phase of the cycle. Unfortunately most of us aren't sufficiently tuned in to our bodies to notice. Some feel it's a sign of weakness and don't want to admit they slow down at times. Others ignore the cues when they arise (especially when they're busy and a lapse would be inconvenient). So we usually just override them by continuing to work. Worst of all, many people try to mask or overcome the signals with stimulants like caffeine ("I'm starting to fade here. Better grab some more java.").

How to Take a Break

If we decide to heed our body's message, what should we do? Well, since the message is "I need a break now, to rest and recover for the next cycle," we should be good to ourselves and take a time-out. Dr. Rossi calls this an "ultradian healing break" (which produces the ultradian healing response). It's not only kind to our bodies, but it produces maximum efficiency in our performance.

What is the best way of taking a twenty-minute break? Ideally, through some form of rest, Dr. Rossi suggests. Find a quiet place and get comfortable (sitting or lying down). Close your eyes and let your breathing get naturally deeper and slower. Observe your body and notice where you feel the most comfort. Focus on that area and feeling and let it spread throughout your body. Let your thoughts go wherever they may. Your mind-body knows how to do the rest. You've created a state of deep relaxation in which your mind-body restores itself biologically and biochemically. As Dr. Rossi puts it, "The essential feature of this stage . . . is *not doing*: allowing the inner mind-body to do its own work in its own way." You create the optimal conditions and then let yourself float, observing whatever thoughts and insights arise, without trying to program or direct what's happening. Just experience the pleasurable healing that's occurring deep within you. Anyone who's learned meditation or other relaxation skills will immediately recognize the similarity between those modalities and Dr. Rossi's technique. His "ultradian healing response" is very similar to what Dr. Herbert Benson describes as the "relaxation response." Both are natural processes that the mind-body does automatically once we create the setting. And both are remarkably beneficial and reviving.

What if you can't, or choose not to, take a break in this manner? There are many other ways of taking short time-outs in the course of a day. A friend of mine calls these "mini time-outs" or "snapshot vacations." You can take the traditional coffee break (which I prefer to call a "refreshment break," since coffee is not on my list of recommended beverages), go for a short walk, take a bathroom break (the only room where you can lock the door and no one accuses you of being antisocial!), listen to music, stare out the window, daydream, take a social break (on the phone or by the water cooler), browse through a magazine, have a humor break (a comedy tape or book of cartoons), do a crossword puzzle or wander outdoors. Stopping for lunch and supper also provide ultradian breaks and you get a double benefit: nutrition plus a chance for your mind-body to refresh itself. The options are limited only by your imagination. The only caution is that the time-outs be easy and restful, not too strenuous or stimulating.

A Word about Napping

Taking a short nap ("cat nap" or "power nap") is a wonderful way of taking an ultradian break for those who can fall asleep in the middle of the day. I was taking naps for thirty years before I learned they had a name. Actually most of my naps were inadvertent. I'd just doze off and come to a few minutes later, feeling a bit embarrassed, depending on the circumstances ("Er, ah, sorry. Was I gone long?"). But I noticed I'd be amazingly refreshed. Finally I gave myself permission to take a proper nap and label it as such. I'd ask someone to wake me or set a timer for twenty minutes. But usually I'd wake up spontaneously before the beeper went off. The reason these mini-sleeps (optimally only five to twenty minutes in length) are so beneficial is that you immediately fall into a deep sleep ("delta sleep"), which is very restorative. Oversleeping (beyond an hour) usually leaves people feeling sluggish.

The idea of napping during a workday, especially at the office, is unthinkable to most people. It sounds like the height of sloth, a suggestion that would go over with a resounding thud if they mentioned it to their boss. I've been on a crusade for years to gain acceptance for the idea of napping in the workplace. First I've learned, from personal experience, the profound benefits of power naps. They work. My efficiency used to flag noticeably from about three o'clock on. A midafternoon nap increased my performance remarkably for the rest of the day. At first I wondered, "How can I take twenty minutes out of a day that's already too full?" But when I looked at the payoff, I realized that twenty minutes of napping can give me hours of productivity. Anyway, why should napping have a stigma attached to it? If someone says, "I'm going for my coffee break now," no one even looks up. If they say, "I'm going for a walk, I'll be back in twenty minutes," everyone says, "See you later." What's the difference if they go for a nap? In all three cases they're gone for twenty minutes and come back refreshed. Why should it matter what they do to reenergize themselves? I'm awaiting the day when, on noticing an employee napping, people won't say, "Look at that guy Wilson, dogging it again." Instead they'll say, "Isn't that great! There's Wilson recharging his batteries!" There are many countries where an after-lunch siesta is not only acceptable but considered natural and beneficial, and Dr. Rossi states in his book that "Americans take an average of one or two naps per week, and one-third of the population naps four or more times each week." Anything that's so common can't be all wrong.

Articles in the *Wall Street Journal*, *Atlantic Monthly*, *Toronto Star* and other publications indicate that the trend is starting to change. Napping is being acknowledged as probably normal, more widespread than anyone knew—or admitted—and obviously helpful to many. In fact, a company in New England is building a new plant that will include a napping room for its 250 employees. Napping works, is not illegal and harms no one. It's a good idea whose time has come. So let's all snooze our way to more energy and productivity.

Further Thoughts about Time-Outs

- If you can't always take a break when you need it, take it when you can. It'd be a little awkward in the middle of an important meeting to say, "Whoops, my body just told me it's time for a break. See you later." So just take the next convenient opportunity.
- Plan ahead. If you usually hit low ebb at about three in the afternoon, arrange your schedule as best as you can to take a break around then.
- If you can't take twenty minutes, take ten—or even five. A short break is better than none at all. Or just switch to low-concentration tasks for twenty minutes. Make a phone call, do some filing, riffle through your mail. Sometimes a change is as good as a rest.
- If you're on a roll, feeling energized and working effectively, don't stop just because of the clock. Listen to your body. The rhythm is not as precise as the diagram suggests. We're all different, and our rhythms can vary from day to day.
- If you take a break at midmorning, stop again for lunch, take a midafternoon time-out and break again for supper, you will have divided your day into ultradian cycles. So it's not that unnatural or complicated. Most paid workers get two coffee breaks and time off for lunch. Dr. Rossi's ultradian healing breaks mesh perfectly with that work pattern.
- Take different *kinds* of breaks throughout the day (relaxation, refreshment, exercise or social). Variety is a good idea here.

A Look at Leisure

Twenty-minute breaks aren't the only kind of time-outs we need. Longer periods of leisure time are also necessary for optimum energy and functioning.

Many people say they don't have time, and they blame this on externals (work pressure, family demands and so on). But I think there's another issue here, and it's contained in the meaning of the word "leisure." I used to think it meant rest and relaxation. But it literally means "permission" (from the Latin *licere*, "to be lawful," the same root as the word "license"). If we are reluctant to take time for ourselves, it's not because of a shortage of time, but because we feel that it's not allowed: we feel selfish and guilty when we do things we enjoy. But not giving ourselves permission to relax is shortsighted. Hobbies, golf, reading, playing the piano, going to a movie, visiting friends, playing cribbage or chess—these are all activities that are diverting, satisfying and nourishing. When we balance our lives to include these pastimes, we give our bodies extended periods of pleasure and rejuvenation. It's a smart and healthy thing to do. And unless you take it to extremes, there's absolutely nothing to feel selfish or guilty about!

I advocate doing something for yourself every day. Make the time—an hour is ideal, but at least thirty minutes a day. And make it a priority, not just something you do at the end of the evening if you have the time and energy. Sol Gordon and Harold Brecher wrote a book with a great title that captures this philosophy beautifully: *Life Is Uncertain. Eat Dessert First!* Think of some things you used to enjoy but are no longer doing. Put them back in your life. Not all of them every day, but one here and another there. And put them in first. I'm a runner. I've been running for eighteen years and I do it on my lunch hour. It's a priority and there aren't many things that I allow to get in the way. When a patient of mine took up transcendental meditation, he told me he meditates for twenty minutes twice a day. I asked him how he finds the time to do that. He said, "I make the time. When something works as well as this does, you make the time." He made a commitment to himself, put that in his schedule first and then worked around it, adjusting his other activities (including work) accordingly.

Here's an exercise you can do to discover where your time goes now and to explore ways of accommodating some leisure in your life. Draw a large circle and turn it into a twenty-four hour clock. Then divide it into sections to reflect your typical day at the present time. Don't forget to include commuting time in the portion called "work." See the example given on the next page from my own schedule.

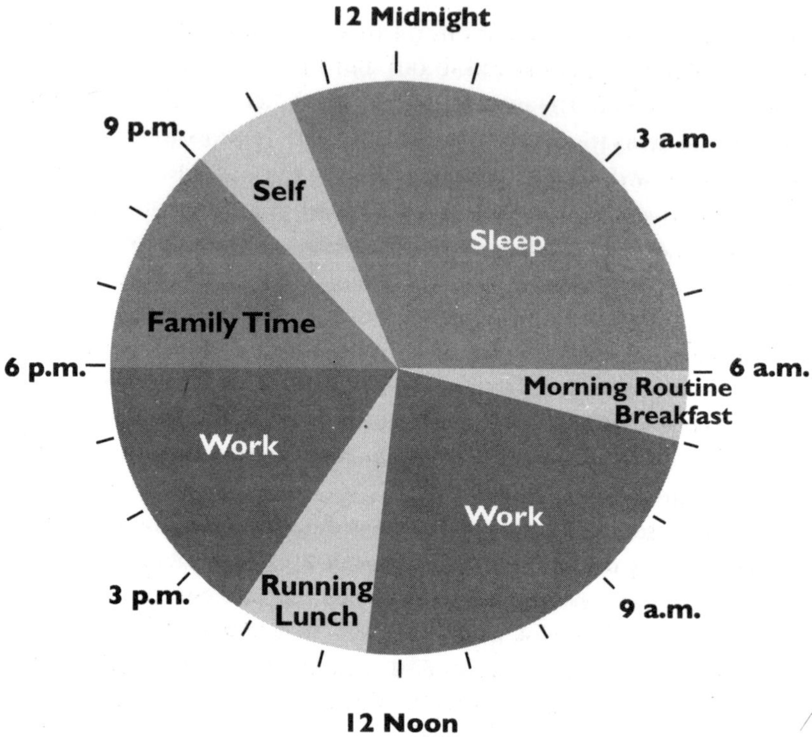

When you're done, look at it for a minute and reflect. What do you notice? How do you feel? When I do this in seminars, people often make comments such as, "I've got no time for myself," "I'm not getting enough sleep," "This is depressing—my whole life is work" and "I can't find myself in here anywhere."

Now do a second clock, the way you'd like it to be. Start with the time you'd like to be going to sleep and waking up. Put in your work and commuting hours next, but only if they are fixed hours you can't change. If you have any flexibility in designing your work timetable, consider changing it on the diagram. Next, think about the things you'd like to be doing but aren't including at the moment. It might be a walk or bike ride after supper, a relaxing bubble bath at bedtime, playing your guitar or reading in the evening—whatever you would enjoy. Put one or two of these in next. Then add the other ingredients of your life to fill in the remaining time (playing with the kids, meals, household chores and so on). Note that this exercise isn't about putting yourself ahead of your family. It's about making sure you're in there *somewhere* by scheduling yourself first. This exercise allows you to see what's possible if you take the time to envision it and then plan it out. Now, try the revised schedule. The benefits will quickly be apparent. You'll have more energy, be more productive and generally feel happier. And if that happens, everyone wins: your family, your employer and you.

In summary, dealing with change requires extra energy for adjusting to new circumstances and for facilitating new learning (skills, roles and information). It's important to start each day feeling fresh, fit and in a good frame of mind. Managing our lifestyle choices to support the need for energy is very important. Energy depleters include stress, overload, overwork, poor diet, insufficient sleep, alcohol and too much caffeine. Factors that enhance energy are good nutrition, adequate sleep, regular exercise, minimal caffeine and routine time-outs and leisure.

There is another payoff. In addition to enhanced energy and productivity, we profit emotionally and psychologically. As discussed in Chapter 2, the reasons change is difficult include feeling a loss of control and a decrease in self-esteem. When we take good care of ourselves, we feel more in control of our lives, feel better about ourselves, enjoy improved health and enhance the overall quality of our lives.

CHAPTER TEN

I Can't Go That Fast!

Pacing the Rate of Change–and Pacing Yourself

In 1980 Canada went metric. We started buying gas in liters instead of gallons. (It felt so British, we should have been calling it "petrol.") Going from zero to sixty in under ten seconds was no longer high praise for a new car because we'd switched from miles to kilometers—and sixty kph was less than forty mph. Room temperature went from seventy degrees to twenty-one (fahrenheit to celsius). Weighing a hundred kilograms didn't sound like much until you did the conversion—and ended up with 220 pounds! And I'm still baffled when I hear someone is 185 centimeters (whatever happened to "six foot one"?).

"The trouble with the future is that it usually arrives before we're ready for it."
ARNOLD H. GLASOW

This was a huge societal switch that changed our frame of reference for almost everything we did. Everyone was doing calculations in their head or carrying little conversion tables around with them. But the government understood how long it would take for people to change the way they think, so they phased in the program gradually. Speeds, temperatures, weights and measures were given in both systems for several years to allow people time to adjust (many weather reports still give both readings). This example shows the importance of pacing the *speed* with which change takes place.

My wife is a superb mother. She is affectionate, patient, playful and funny. She is also sensitive and intuitive. One of the things she learned (and taught me) over the years is that our kids adapt much better to situations if they're told in advance what is going to happen. This gives them time to prepare psychologically and helps them feel more secure. It's a way of making changes appear gradual rather than sudden. This is another way of pacing the rate of change.

The speed with which things happen affects their impact on us. Generally speaking, gradual change is comfortable. Abrupt change is jarring and dislocating. A local company decided to switch software programs on their computer system. But they made the change in a single day. And without much notice or preparation. BAM! The conversion was hard on everyone. And the fear of other sudden changes lingered for some time.

Of course, it's not always possible to ease changes in over time. If Britain ever decides to switch to right-side-of-the-road driving, I *don't* think they're going to invite people to implement it at their own rate of comfort. That kind of change has to be made all at once by everyone at the same time. But when it's possible, unhurried transitions allow people to adjust more easily.

We usually don't have much say in how *imposed* change takes place. We can only hope that our employers and leaders are smart and sensible about implementing new procedures, rules, laws and ideas. And, of course, some changes *can't* be programmed in advance (like the sudden death of a CEO or a highly-secret-until-announced merger). But whenever possible, people should be given (or take) the time to get used to new physical realities and to adjust psychologically. When I changed careers at age forty-two, I arranged to stay in the same office for almost eighteen months. When I got married, we didn't move into our new house until six months later (and even then it wasn't ready!). It was very helpful to be able to make the transitions gradually. Contrast this to a colleague of mine who moved to the United States to practice: his last day in Oakville was a Friday and he was on the new job first thing Monday morning. The change involved a different house, neighborhood, city and country, as well as a new office, hospital, colleagues and patients. And he only had one weekend to adjust! I would have found that quite a jolt. I know it was more stressful than he expected. I think people should take at least a week's break between jobs just to clear their heads before they shift gears.

Whenever you can, arrange for change to be phased in. If it's a change you control, pace yourself for a comfortable transition. For example, if you're going away to school, go there ahead of time to get acclimatized. Scope out the campus, the dorm situation, the town. See if you can get your schedule set up early or obtain a reading list—anything that will ease your arrival and settling in. Some people who take jobs in another city spend some time commuting until they adjust to the work situation. *Then* they move their family and deal with the next phase of change, involving a new house, neighbors and so on. This is an example of the Swiss-cheese method of breaking tasks into smaller parts so they don't seem so overwhelming—taking a bite here and a nibble there until everything is done or all the pieces are in place. When couples decide to separate, the timing can usually be worked out so the emotional pain and dislocation is more gradual. Even when change comes from the death of someone you love, it's less of a shock if there's some warning than if the death is sudden and unexpected.

One of my patients had her husband leave her somewhat suddenly. Within months she decided to move to her old hometown to start life anew. I wondered out loud if this wasn't too soon and simply adding other changes to cope with. She was just adjusting to her new marital status, which was very stressful. It seemed unwise to add the stress of a major move, including new house, new job and new city—even though it was a place she'd once lived. However, she went ahead with her plans and seemed quite upbeat about the whole thing.

This story brings up an important fact about change: we all have different styles, preferences and tolerance levels. Some people prefer to get on with it, while others want a more measured pace. Some want a clean break; other people like overlap. Some individuals do fine with rapid change; others are thrown for a loop if too much happens at once. So the observations and suggestions I'm making here are not one-size-fits-all. You should also take into consideration the state you're in at the moment. If your stress level is already high or your health compromised, you'd be well advised to go slowly. If you're fit and keen and rarin' to go, you'll be able to handle more and faster.

It's known, for example, that major life events (whether positive or negative) have a stressful impact on us, and the effect can last as long as a year, even two years in some cases. Also, the effects are cumulative, so the more you have the greater the overall effect. Most people have seen the Holmes-Rahe scale published in the *Journal of Psychosomatic Research* in 1967. This is a list of major events that can occur in a person's life (everything from having a baby to losing your job to going to jail), and many of the items are listed as "change in . . ." (for example, work responsibilities, schools, residence). Each item is given a numerical value corresponding to the stressful effect it has on a person (for example, death of a spouse is the highest at 100, getting married is 50 and trouble with your boss is 23). Events don't have to be negative to be stressful. Buying a new house, being promoted at work and winning a lottery are all positive events, but they're also stressful: they require adaptation and adjustment, which in turn drains us of energy.

After you've completed the Holmes-Rahe test (on the next page), which has forty-three items on it, you are asked to add up the points of all the items you've experienced in the previous twelve months. Their research implied that your chance of getting sick in the near future corresponds statistically to your total score (for example, if you score 300 or more, the odds are eighty percent, 150–299 gives you a fifty percent chance and so on). I have simplified this list, divided it into positive and negative events and left out the numerical scoring system (see page 161).

But the message is still the same: the more changes you encounter, the more your system is called upon to adapt and the more physiological stress you experience. If you're a resilient and stress-hardy person, you will be able to tolerate more than someone who is less adaptable. But we're all affected to some degree and everyone has a limit. We need to monitor our stress level and the amount of change that's occurring—and then pace ourselves accordingly, slowing down the rate of change wherever possible and necessary.

How Much Change Is Enough? And How Much Is Too Much?

This is a very individual judgment, differing from person to person and even fluctuating in any one person from time to time. We each need to find a point of comfort between too little change (which produces staleness and stagnation) and too much (which leads to chaos and distress). Three faculty members from the University of Western Ontario (Howard, Cunningham and Rechnitzer) wrote a book in 1978 called *Rusting Out, Burning Out, Bowing Out,* referring to the effects of understimulation and overload on the job. As the Learning Curve (page 6) and Flow diagram (page 52) show, we function best when there is a balance between feeling bored and feeling overwhelmed. Some stability produces comfort and security, but too much sameness leads to

Life Event	Numerical Value
1. Death of a spouse	100
2. Divorce	73
3. Marital separation	65
4. Jail term	63
5. Death of a close family member	63
6. Personal injury or illness	53
7. Marriage	50
8. Fired at work	47
9. Marital reconciliation	45
10. Retirement	45
11. Change in health of family member	44
12. Pregnancy	40
13. Sexual difficulties	39
14. Gain of a new family member	39
15. Business readjustment	39
16. Change in financial state	38
17. Death of a close friend	37
18. Change to different line of work	36
19. Change in number of arguments with spouse	35
20. Mortgage over $10,000 (≃ $175,000 in 1998 dollars)	31
21. Foreclosure of mortgage loan	30
22. Change in responsibilities at work	29
23. Son or daughter leaving home	29
24. Trouble with in-laws	29
25. Outstanding personal achievement	28
26. Wife begins or stops work	26
27. Begin or end school	26
28. Change in living conditions	25
29. Revision of personal habits	24
30. Trouble with boss	23
31. Change in work hours or conditions	20
32. Change in residence	20
33. Change in schools	20
34. Change in recreation	19
35. Change in church activities	19
36. Change in social activities	18
37. Mortgage or loan less than $10,000 (≃ $175,000 in 1998 dollars)	17
38. Change in sleeping habits	16
39. Change in number of family get-togethers	15
40. Change in eating habits	13
41. Vacation	13
42. Christmas	12
43. Minor violations of the law	11
TOTAL POINTS	—

Positive Events	Negative Events
1. Getting married	1. Death of a spouse
2. New child	2. Divorce or separation
3. New job or occupation	3. Death of close family member
4. New house	4. Serious injury or illness
5. Move to a new city or neighborhood	5. Loss of job
6. Promotion	6. Demotion at work
7. Acquiring large sum of money	7. Losing large sum of money
8. Marital reconciliation	8. Death of a close friend
9. Outstanding personal achievement	9. Child leaving home
10. Business success	10. Being victim of crime
11. Vacation	11. Serious illness in family
12. Christmas	12. Close friend moving away

Retirement is another significant life event but I list it separately because it is positive for some, but negative and detrimental to others.

apathy and loss of enthusiasm. We've lived in our house for fourteen years and feel no urge to leave, although we redecorate rooms from time to time. But we have friends who have moved every couple of years for the past quarter-century. They probably think we're in a rut. We think they live in a whirlwind. The important thing is to determine what works for you and what your comfort and tolerance levels are—then be guided by them. The two factors to consider are the *amount* of change and the *rate* of change. And err on the side of caution. It's usually easier to speed up a notch than to slow things down when they're in full flight and you're gasping for breath.

Don't Change Your Job, House and Spouse in the Same Month!

Another aspect of pacing is to maintain stability in as many parts of your life as possible during periods of rapid change. So if you're going through a major reorganization at work, that's not the time to take on the chairmanship of your college alumni or to volunteer to organize the charity golf tournament. Similarly, if you're in the midst of a marriage upheaval, you'd do well to put off changing jobs until the dust settles. Having your attention and emotional energy pulled in several different directions is extremely stressful. The old adage "If you want something done, give it to a busy man" may not be so great for the busy man himself—especially if he gets overextended. The next thing you know he calls you at the eleventh hour to tell you he won't be able to finish the task because he got overloaded and didn't realize it at the time.

William Bridges uses a great metaphor for this principle in his excellent book *Jobshift*. He notes that a rock climber can only move a hand or a foot if the other three limbs are stable and stationary. In a recent moment of youthful exuberance I decided to try a variation of rock climbing in Whistler, BC. Fresh from the exhilaration of whitewater rafting, I joined my kids in climbing a twenty-four-foot wall, using hand- and footholds randomly placed all the way up. My sons made it look easy, but it was a struggle for me. And it really reinforced Bridges' message.

The Value of Routines and Rituals

One way to maintain stability in your life during periods of rapid change is through continued use of customs and rituals from your previous routine. Let's imagine you've moved to a new town. Your job, house, surroundings and activities are totally different. But there are ways of preserving elements of familiarity from your previous situation. These help to ease the transition, establishing touchpoints of comfort and stability. You've probably taken your old furniture with you. Chances are you'll set up the rooms much as they were in your old house. You'll arrange the personal effects that make a house a home, everything from pictures to mementos. Your morning routine will be maintained, with the same wake-up time and order of activities. You'll have your noontime walk or after-work squash game as you used to do.

Family traditions are especially helpful to continue: eating meals together, the Saturday-night movie, Friday-night dinner in the dining room, Sunday brunch at a restaurant. Bedtime routines of reading and singing to young children, evenings of playing board games or cards, weekend bike rides or reading the New York Times. These are all rituals and patterns that needn't change no matter where you live. It's not about getting into a rut. It's about preserving links with the past. My family and I have developed a tradition for New Year's Eve. Wherever we are, we go to a late-afternoon movie with our children, then out for dinner and home for the rest of the evening. The first year we did this we were amazed at the number of young couples in the restaurant, dressed as casually as we were and spending the evening with their kids. Building personal and family traditions is an excellent way of buffering the winds of change. And it doesn't preclude your adding other customs over time that fit your new surroundings or situation. Eventually you might even replace some old routines with new ones, but the familiar patterns you start with are an important bridge over the turbulent waters of change.

Get a Life!

Resilience and adaptability are enhanced when there are several well-developed compartments in your life. What are the elements of a balanced life? Meaningful **work** is certainly part of it, whether it's a job for pay or labor within the home. But work is (or *should* be) only one part of your life. **Family** is crucial, as well. Having a spouse and/or children gives you companionship, affirmation and nourishment. But you don't have to be married or have kids to have family support. Many single people are closely connected to their parents, siblings and extended family (grandparents, aunts, uncles and cousins)—as I was until I got married. My sister and brother-in-law have no blood relatives in Minneapolis, where they live, but they developed close relationships with certain friends and *their* families. In two cases, friends' parents became like surrogate parents/grandparents for them and their children. This was especially meaningful during holidays, which are usually times for families to gather. **Friends** are the next component of a well-balanced life (and a great title for a sitcom if you're home on Thursday nights). They can be people you grew up with, college buddies, colleagues at work, neighbors or friends of friends. The wider the range of relationships the better. **Pets** provide another form of companionship that is very meaningful to people. **Community involvement** adds a rich dimension to people's lives. This can include volunteer work and/or participation in community activities. It's a great way to meet people and to feel a part of your neighborhood or town. You make a contribution, support local initiatives and usually end up feeling better about yourself. **Interests and hobbies** add great value to our lives: stimulation, pleasure, satisfaction, challenge and diversion. Recreational activities may include sports, music, reading, arts and crafts, collecting things, playing games (chess, bridge, backgammon), doing puzzles—whatever suits your fancy. **Entertainment** can include movies, concerts, theater, TV and sporting events. **New learning** is another component, whether formal courses and lessons or just learning on your own, as many people have done by exploring on their computers. Last but not least, **travel and adventure**, which can be exotic and expensive, or local and recreational.

As you cast your eye over these items, you'll realize that if your life contains aspects of even *some* of these areas, you'll not only have a richer day-to-day existence, but you'll have an invaluable cushion and security blanket to nestle into when rapid or extensive change buffets your life. And, of course, the best time to develop these other dimensions is before you really *need* them.

Pacing Yourself Through the Change Process

Managing the rate at which change occurs is one thing. Pacing *yourself* on a day-to-day basis is another. Both are important in terms of resilience and adaptability. When I got my first computer in 1989, I learned the basics about how to use the mouse, open and close files and so on. This all related to the word-processor function. It was all I needed at the time and I didn't bother with things like split screens, spreadsheets or graphics. I have always found that it's easier to learn things *as you need them* rather than in a theoretical context—and the information sticks better if you use it right away. If you try to learn *everything* at the outset of a new venture, you'll have too much to think about and you're likely to feel confused or overwhelmed.

And don't try to do too much in a single day, either. Long work hours drain you of energy (and enthusiasm), and actually don't help you to get more done, because after a certain point, performance and efficiency start to fall off. This is illustrated in the famous Yerkes-Dodson Law, related to human motivation and performance, pictured on the next page.

Notice that in the first half of the curve, increasing arousal and stress produces increased efficiency and performance. But past a certain point (the top of the inverted U) this trend reverses. In other words, *further* stress yields *decreasing* effectiveness. The message is that, past the midpoint, increased

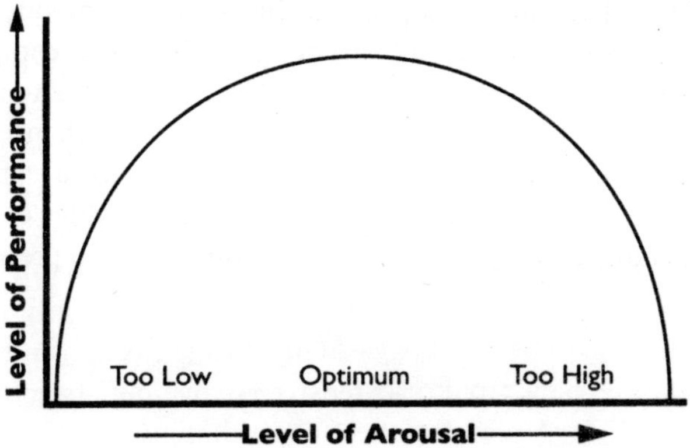

Relationship between arousal (and stress) and performance according to the Inverted-U Hypothesis and the Yerkes-Dodson Law

effort doesn't pay off. In fact, working longer and harder at that point is not only unproductive but *counterproductive*. People who work more than ten or twelve hours a day are fooling themselves if they think they're getting more done just because they're putting in the time. Productivity is not a function of time and effort; it's a function of time and *effectiveness*. You're better off to stop than to push on through your fatigue. I think very few people can work more than fifty or sixty hours a week without it hampering the quality of their efforts. They'd be better served by using some of that time to rest and recharge their batteries. If I'm reading and find that nothing's registering, or if the task I'm doing is taking longer than it should, I stop and come back to it when I'm fresh. I've urged many of my patients over the years to cut back their work hours if they're highly stressed or exhausted—and especially if they're working more than fifty hours a week. In not one case has productivity and output suffered. On the contrary, most get as much or *more* done in the fewer hours (a surprise to them but not to me—because of the lesson of the Yerkes-Dodson Law).

In summary, change is part of life. But the rate of change is accelerating, and that often makes it more stressful. Pacing is a helpful way of managing the change process. There are two aspects to this. One is to modify the speed of change whenever possible, breaking changes down into component parts that can then be dealt with sequentially. When change is too fast, slow it down. The other part is to pace *yourself* day to day, to enhance your energy and stay fresh and ready for the challenges ahead. Having a stable, balanced, well-rounded life is rewarding in itself, but it also provides extra flexibility and buffering during times when change is most rapid and pressing.

CHAPTER ELEVEN

You're Not Alone

The Need for a Support System

A NEW PATIENT CAME TO SEE ME FOR STRESS counseling. He was so agitated he could barely sit in his chair. He talked fast, non-stop, for almost an hour. It was as if a dam had ruptured and everything was rushing out at once. This chap had shared so little about himself, had kept so much in for so long, that even his wife didn't know how many siblings he had. Now it was all coming out in a torrent of words and emotions. I just sat and listened. Occasionally he'd say something like "I can't believe I'm saying all this to a total stranger," or "I've never talked this much in my life." At the end of the session he got up smiling, grabbed my hand and thanked me for all my help. I'd said almost nothing.

"No man is an Island entire of itself."
JOHN DONNE

Here's another story. A patient I'd known for years called me in early December to tell me about her depression. She was waking up in the night, not eating, isolating herself—the same symptoms she'd developed at the same time the previous year. We had an appointment already set up for the next week. At her visit nine days later she said, "I felt better almost immediately after our phone call. Acknowledging it and getting clear about what was happening made it dissipate—like 'Oh, that's what it is, I'll just ride it out.' I started talking to other people and found a lot of people have the same problem this time of year."

"No matter what accomplishments you make, somebody helps you."
ALTHEA GIBSON

There are several common themes here. One is our need to *express* emotions and the benefit we get from doing so. Another is the value of having someone to *listen* to us in an empathetic way. A third is our ability to do a lot *self-healing*. The overall message is that we all need a support system to help us cope with difficult times. **People who suffer alone suffer a lot.** There's another expression: **A problem shared is a problem halved.**

You're Not Alone

You're not the only one dealing with change. We're all in this together—in your company, your city, your country. The acceleration of change and its widening impact are being felt all over the planet. We can help one another through this period of upheaval. This is a time for people to pull together, not stay separate. We all need and benefit from the support of others—at work, at home and in our communities.

When people lose their jobs, they have a tendency to withdraw. They feel embarrassed or even ashamed. And others often avoid *them*. They feel uncomfortable, don't know what to say. Or maybe the pain is a little too close to home and they don't want to face up to the fact that this could be them sometime soon. A similar dynamic can occur when individuals become sick, especially if the illness is chronic or terminal. Or when people endure a terrible loss, such as the death of a child. The sufferers turn inward and the others turn away. This scenario of isolation and mutual discomfort is the last thing any of us needs in an emotional crisis. These are extreme examples, but they make the point: when times are tough, we need to hang together, not split apart.

Sue Johnson is a psychologist at the Ottawa Civic Hospital. She works with trauma survivors. In a radio interview she noted that when certain animals are scared, they band together for mutual protection, support and reassurance. Think of elephants, which are very intelligent animals, or puppies, or muskoxen, forming a circle, each facing outward, when they're threatened. Nature tells us there's safety—and comfort—in numbers.

In the Jewish religion there is a tradition of ritualized mourning for the dead that answers the need for people to be together in a time of grief. After the funeral, which is held as soon as possible, there is a prescribed period of deep mourning that lasts for seven days. It's called "sitting shiva" (from the Hebrew word for seven, *sheva*). During this time members of the immediate family gather together in one place, dispersing only at night to go to their respective homes to sleep. Extended family and friends come to visit and offer their sympathies. It is a *mitzvah* (Hebrew for "commandment," which has also come to mean "a good deed") to make a condolence call, to visit the mourners. So it is built into the religion that people should be with the bereaved at times of loss to pay respects to the deceased and to give support. Short religious services are held morning and evening during the week of shiva in the family's home. But services cannot begin until ten people are present. This is called a *minyan* and again reflects the communal nature of the Jewish religion. Of course, individual prayer is also a part of Judaism. But there is an understanding of the necessity and benefits of group support, as well. As a book about Jewish life in nineteenth-century Europe notes in its title, "Life Is with People."

What Can a Support System Do for You?

The benefits are numerous and often wonderful.

- **Understanding, empathy, compassion and emotional support**
  Caring arms to wrap around you, an ear to listen and a shoulder to lean on—these are all things everyone needs at times of struggle, worry, pain and loss. If you fail your exams, lose your job, go through a separation or divorce, become disabled, the nurturing presence of others helps to cushion the blow by letting you know you are not alone.

- **Encouragement and strength**
  When you face a challenge (a job interview, an important speech, a sporting event), a cheering section can give you a big boost. It builds you up to know that others have confidence in you. When I was writing my first book, I purposely told a wide array of people what I was doing. It made it more of a commitment if I announced it publicly; I knew my friends would hold me accountable by periodically asking how it was going, and keep me on track with their belief that I'd succeed. One friend said, "Good for you. Lots of people *talk* about writing a book. But you'll *do* it!" Those words came back to me many times and strengthened my resolve. Other friends sent cards, which I kept right beside my computer

throughout the five-year writing process. One from a colleague said, "Congratulations, David. You began your book! I hope it is a new beginning in a long line of happy experiences. I'm rooting for you." A *Peanuts* card from my wife said, "I know you can do it 'cause you've got the stuff, and I'm in your corner when the going gets rough!" followed by a beautiful handwritten note. And my nurse-receptionist gave me a framed cartoon of a guy sitting at a word processor. The sign on the door read, "DAVID'S BEST SELLER." It still sits on my window ledge. No one could have had a better support system.

- **Advice, suggestions, information, problem-solving**
  Having a problem with your computer? Need to find a new dentist? Looking for ideas for a surprise party? Who ya gonna call (if the *Ghostbusters'* line is busy)? We usually ask someone we know. "Didn't Roger have this problem last year?" or "Barbara's a whiz at this stuff," or "Bob built two of those things. He'll know," or "Veronica just got back from there. Give her a call."

- **Logistical support and assistance**
  Friends of mine had their lives thrown into chaos when their son was hospitalized for two weeks after a bad hockey injury. There was upset, fear, pain and long hours at the hospital. But there was also another child to attend to, and somehow the structures of their lives had to continue without too much disruption. Meals, supervision and rides to certain activities had to be arranged. The fortnight was a nightmare as it was, but it would have been a total wipeout without the support of wonderful neighbors and friends who sprang into action and kept the home front going. And the key to activating that network was *asking for help*. "I called on my support network and told them what I needed. I knew we couldn't do it alone."

- **Validation**
  Family and friends let you know you're OK, that you're normal. Parents who lose their temper with their children and feel guilty feel better when

they hear that it happens to everyone on occasion. It's helpful to know that other moms and dads can lose their cool and start yelling, and that it doesn't mean you're a bad parent. (I'm not talking here about abuse, which is a different matter.)

Your support system can show you that you're not the only one struggling. People who get panic attacks are often reluctant to admit it, but once they get past their embarrassment and actually talk about their experience, there's a payoff: invariably, my patients describe the relief they felt when they learned that many others have gone through the same thing. Close friends tell them, "Me too!" or "I used to get those," or "My brother-in-law went through that," and they feel an immediate sense of reassurance and affirmation, knowing that they're not weird or crazy or even that unusual. They're also very encouraged to know that it's a self-limited condition that people recover from. Sometimes hearing this from friends is more beneficial than if I (as a physician) give them the same information.

Another form of personal validation comes from knowing that even if you fail at something or behave badly, your family and friends love you anyway. It's wonderful to know that people care about you, faults and all, and that, overall, you're a good and worthwhile person. To feel loved and valued in that way is a huge boost to your self-esteem. In its purest form it's called "unconditional love," and it's an amazing support to be able to lean on when you feel lousy about yourself.

- **Feedback and reality checks**

  There are times when we benefit from information we don't want to hear, and who better to give you this feedback than someone you love and trust and who loves and trusts you? This is the "even your best friends won't tell you" stuff—except that your very best friends *will* tell you. This isn't just about the need for deodorant or toothpaste. It's about how you may be putting down your kids or spouse without realizing it. Or about your drinking problem that you don't want to acknowledge and think no one else has noticed. I learned about feminism in the sixties from female relatives and friends who told me when I was being chauvinistic or obtuse. Once, when I was preoccupied about some mundane issues in my bachelor life, a friend said, "What you need is to get married and have children. Then you'd have *real* problems to worry about!" (Ouch—but I sensed she was right.)

The fact that these messages are delivered with a smile by our dearest friends is very important. Another friend asked my permission before she gave me a blunt opinion. Her words were, "Can I be brutal?" Aside from my immediate curiosity, I knew I was safe with her. I said, "Yes, *you* can be brutal" (because I knew what she had to say would be important, and given with love and caring).

- **Social framework and interaction**
  You move to a new town or neighborhood. You don't know a soul. You're starting from scratch. You're not looking for someone to pour your heart out to, but it would be nice to have some company—someone to chat with, have over for tea or join you for a walk. As society becomes more fragmented and mobile, groups are forming to welcome strangers, and we need more of them. It might be the newcomers' club, an alumni chapter of your university, the brotherhood/sisterhood of your local church or synagogue, a parents' group at your child's new school, a neighborhood tennis club. If a group isn't available, you might be just the person to start one.

To Whom Do You Turn?

Most support systems start in the most fundamental unit of our society—the family. Parents, siblings, grandparents, aunts, uncles and cousins. When I was growing up, my father's brother and his family lived two houses away, and my mother's sister lived with her family across the road. It was nourishing to have so many relatives on the same block—and when tragedy struck, as it unfortunately did, the proximity of family was crucial for all of us. But changing times bring changing customs. Geographically close families are far less common, but nuclear and extended-family ties still provide the earliest and most immediate support system for most people.

Not that you can tell everything to your relatives. I heard this story of a guy in his early twenties who started staying out at night, sometimes *all* night. His mother inquired about his whereabouts but he dodged her questions.

"Tell me where you go at night," she said.

"I'd rather not."

"Tell me. I'm your parent. I want to know."

"You don't want to know."

"Yes, I do. Tell me."

"OK, Ma, I sleep with women."

"*This* you would tell your *mother*??!!"

Next come friends. Often closer than family, friends can become soulmates with whom you can share anything. And mutual trust is established because *they* share everything with *you*. Over time, a trusted teacher, older family friend, family doctor or neighbor may form part of your support system. Later, lovers and spouses are the ones we feel able to open up to. In the workplace colleagues and co-workers can also fill the role of pal and confidant. And finally, on occasion, we may need to seek out professional help—a therapist of some sort, what a colleague of mine calls "renting a friend." This is when you find a trained counselor to confide in and with whom to work out problems.

Sometimes the support comes not from individuals but from groups. Fraternities and sororities in your student days, book clubs or study groups later on. It might be a chapter of the university women's club or a baseball league. Religious institutions provide a feeling of community and common interest. So do service clubs like Rotary or the local Chamber of Commerce. If you're a musician, inquire about the town band or community orchestra.

For particular needs, there are specific groups. Alcoholics Anonymous not only provides invaluable support to people who want to stop drinking, but also generates friendship, giving and trust among its members. Al Anon does the same for families of alcoholics. There are breast cancer support groups that people can turn to for emotional help and comfort, and these seem to have a health benefit, as well. Studies show that women in these support groups live twice as long as breast cancer patients who are not in such groups. Author Joan Borysenko was quoted in a special summer issue of *Body Mind Spirit* magazine in 1997. She said, "Let's look at relationality and healing. Why do men who have heart attacks live longer if they happen to have dogs or be married? Why do social support and self-esteem make the single biggest difference to healing—a difference even larger than health habits like exercise and diet? Because love and caring affect the energy body."

Another benefit of a support system was reported in the spring 1997 issue of *The Family Therapy Networker*. Recent research shows a strong connection between resilience and a strong support system, especially during a difficult time in one's life. When we're alone and in crisis, it's easy to feel overwhelmed. If there's someone we can turn to, even a single important individual, we can draw tremendous strength—and learn important coping skills—from them. Studies done on at-risk children show that those who did well and developed into competent and confident adults shared several characteristics, one of which was the ability to find and develop a relationship with at least one caring grown-up outside their immediate families.

A sign of the times, in this post-recession period, is the emergence of networking groups for out-of-work business executives. These organizations help their members with special skills and job-seeking strategies, but they also provide a valuable forum for giving and receiving emotional and moral support: the all-important knowledge that they're not alone. People who are widowed, separated or divorced can get the same benefit from bereavement groups and support organizations.

Build Your Support System Before You Need It

When should you develop a support system? *Now.* It's not just of value when you're dealing with a crisis, it also enriches your day-to-day life. It's wonderful to have people to share *good* news with (your promotion, your child's exceptional report card, your hole-in-one). Develop a network of people you like and trust and who value and care for you. Then, if you need to draw on their support, they're there for you. Don't wait until something miserable happens and then run up to a total stranger on the street, saying, "Let me tell you about my day!" (Bartenders and taxi drivers are often recruited to fill this role, but friends are better.) As Harvey Mackay says in the title of his excellent book on networking, *Dig Your Well Before You're Thirsty*.

What should you be looking for? Surround yourself (or seek out) people who like and care about you, whom you feel good being around and with whom you feel safe. You don't need a gallery. A few close family members or friends will more than suffice. You want people you feel comfortable with and can trust. Folks that you know you can confide in and the information goes no further. Find individuals who are positive, upbeat, encouraging and fun to be around.

Don't expect a support system to come to you (unless you're incredibly charismatic). You'll probably have to take the first steps and be the initiator. This may require you to leave your comfort zone, especially if you're not naturally gregarious. But you must be willing to put yourself out there. My sister has lived in Edmonton, London (England), Boston, Calgary and Minneapolis in her adult life. And in every city she developed a marvelous network of friends. She told me one of her secrets. "When I arrived in Minneapolis, I joined every group I could find. It wasn't my preferred style and it wasn't always easy, but I made myself do it."

Her other secret was probably even more important: she is one of the most giving, warm and cheerful people you could hope to meet. She exemplifies the teaching we received from our father. His motto was **"Just keep giving and the taking will look after itself."** He not only verbalized that message but he modeled it in his everyday behavior. Simply put, **the best way to get support is to give it**. And to keep giving it. And not keep score. What goes around comes around, and not always from the original source. You might do something kind and helpful for someone—and then receive the same treatment at an important time from a totally different person. It's like spinning good vibes into the cosmos. If enough of us do it often enough, the ether's going to be brimming with positive energy, from which we'll all benefit.

A friend described what happened to his sister after she became ill—and what had preceded her illness: "From the time of her diagnosis she received an outpouring of support (from friends and acquaintances) that overwhelmed her, and it never stopped. It's like everything she ever did for people was coming back to her. Every day of her life, before she got sick, she did something for somebody else. It was part of her regular daily agenda."

We can give support to others in many ways. A phone call when someone's ill or having a tough time. A card to say, "I'm thinking of you," means a lot to people. A thoughtful gesture, such as buying them a book or CD for no particular occasion. We can offer to take care of their kids, bring over a casserole or take them for a walk.

Here's a beautiful story I heard on the radio a few years ago, showing the range of creative ways we can do things for others. It's about a ten-year-old boy in Burbank, California, who developed leukemia. Now, childhood leukemia is one of the most curable forms of cancer, but it still involves going through chemotherapy, which is not a pleasant experience. His doctors told him what to expect from the treatments: that he'd be very tired, lose his appetite, get nausea and vomiting—and that his hair would fall out. They suggested he might want to consider having all his hair shaved off at the start, instead of waiting for it to fall out bit by bit. He could get some funky hats to wear and ride out the chemo that way. He discussed it with his family and decided to take the physicians' advice. So he went to the barbershop to have his head shaved.

But he didn't go alone. His brother went with him. His teacher went with him. And thirteen of his classmates went with him. And they *all* had their heads shaved. And that's how they gave support to their friend at a difficult time in his young life. The teacher said, in a later interview, that he started to call his class "my bald eagles" because half the kids—and he himself—were bald. When it comes to ways of giving support to others, you can be very creative.

Mentors, Coaches and Teachers

Jerry White lectures and writes on issues related to money management. A couple of years ago I attended one of his presentations, entitled "What the Rich Do." It was entertaining and instructive, but for me, the big take-home of the night was that rich people all have a financial adviser. They don't try to manage their money themselves, unless that's what they do for a living. I researched and found someone to manage my assets. But that's not all he does. He has become my teacher. We meet quarterly to review my investments, discuss other options and have my questions answered. That's how I'm learning about this important and complex field.

This is another dimension to my support system. It's not just about emotional or logistical support. It's about education and personal growth. I also have a health adviser: my family doctor. And even though I'm a physician, when I get sick or injured, I seek his counsel and heed his advice. Lawyers do the same when they need legal counsel. They hire another legal eagle. They follow the adage that "a lawyer who takes his own case has a fool for a client."

Mentors and coaches are part of our support system. And not all of our teachers need to be paid professionals. When I got interested in the field of stress management in the early eighties, I had the good luck to meet Dr. Matthew Budd, a gastroenterologist who works in Cambridge, Massachusetts, and teaches at Harvard. He offered to direct my learning; I watched him work, met his colleagues in the stress field and was even invited to stay in his home. It was a remarkable gift, for which I will be forever in his debt. He did it with enthusiasm, generosity and grace, asking nothing in return, except that I apply myself, follow through on his suggestions and use the knowledge and wisdom I was acquiring to help others. This was true, altruistic mentoring. And I, in turn, have shared what I know with others in my profession.

The best advice I received before I left to do my internship was this: "Make sure you get along with the nurses and let them teach you things. They know a lot more than you do about day-to-day patient care. If you're respectful and receptive, they'll help you enormously." Truer words were never spoken. Nurses enriched my learning throughout that year and the seventeen years that followed in my general practice career.

Unofficial coaches can make a huge contribution to our work, as they can in areas like music, sports, computer skills or parenting. We all need to be lifelong learners, and it helps to seek out people who can guide and advise us. Sam Telford taught me ninth-grade English and history. He also directed our junior high play, *Toad of Toad Hall*, in which I had a small role. Mr. Telford was not only a gifted teacher but one of the most remarkable individuals I met in all my years in school. He was articulate, outspoken, funny, kind and charismatic. He also loved kids and treated them with respect. In return, his students adored him. I kept in touch with Mr. Telford all the way through high school and university. I'd go to visit him periodically, and later we'd meet for lunch a few times a year. I don't remember our specific conversations as much as the general tone of the relationship. He was interested in my development academically, socially and personally. And I was fascinated by his view of the world and the way he thought about things. He was a strong influence in my life—my mentor, ongoing teacher and cherished friend.

In med school, I learned more about the art of medicine from Dr. Tait McPhedran than from anyone else. He was a surgeon at the Toronto General Hospital and a superb teacher. I developed a warm relationship with him and would hang around with him, enjoying his company and watching how he interacted with patients. He was kind and down-to-earth with them, and had a great sense of humor—which they all appreciated. Dr. McPhedran had a profound effect on me as a doctor and as a person, and I kept in touch with him for many years after I graduated.

Whether it's a teacher or a boss you like and admire, a favorite aunt or a wise and funny neighbor, mentors are all around us if we care to find them. You don't need a contract or formal agreement ("Excuse me, will you be my mentor?"). You just need to be open to what's possible. Develop a friendship. Ask questions. Solicit advice. Let them know you value them as individuals and respect their opinion. And give something in return if you can. Depending on your age and stage, it might be mowing their lawn, helping them with their groceries, baby-sitting their kids, dropping them a line when you're away, inviting them over at Christmas, remembering their birthday. It's about relationship and friendship, as well as teaching and learning. The rewards for both parties are tremendous. And if you have a chance to mentor others, take it. It's another way of giving back—but you will also receive a lot in return.

Building a Network

Networking is a way of developing a support system of strategic contacts and allies. These are not necessarily folks you confide in, nor are they teachers per se. They are co-workers and acquaintances with whom you share common interests or pursuits, who can often supply information or advice on an ad hoc basis, and through whom you can meet other people and learn of new opportunities.

It's easy to be cynical about the idea of networking and dismiss it as a self-seeking pursuit in which people put on phony smiles, chat up others or frankly hustle them for personal gain. I used to think that way, and I'm still turned off by opportunistic or gratuitous associations, but I've changed my mind somewhat about the general concept. In his book, *How the Best Get Better,* Dan Sullivan says that successful entrepreneurs need to make a paradigm shift from "rugged individualism" to "unique teamwork." Strategic relationships are more productive than trying to do everything yourself. In this rapidly changing and increasingly complex world, we need each other more than ever. No one can be expert in everything, and if we can create constructive alliances with people who have the skills (and interests) we lack, and vice versa, why should we waste valuable energy trying to do things we're not good at, or searching for information that others can give us in five minutes? In the workplace, networking also shows up in the concept of team building. Employees leverage off one another's knowledge and skills, work collaboratively and create much greater results through synergy.

Networking can also provide business opportunities. Eighty percent of jobs are never advertised. They're filled by word of mouth. That's how I found an assistant for my office when my nurse-receptionist retired after twelve years. I drew up a job description listing skills and qualities I was looking for, and circulated it to a small group of trusted friends and associates. One day my phone rang and the following welcome news serenaded my ear: "I have found you the perfect office assistant." That's a real networking success story. I've also been introduced to speaking agents and my literary agent by friendly intermediaries. And I've returned the favor whenever possible.

So I've changed my mind about networking. I now understand its considerable value. But I have two personal rules that I live by:

- I don't network with anyone I don't genuinely like. There are too many nice and agreeable people around to bother with those who aren't. No matter how well connected or knowledgeable the person is, if it feels phony or unpleasant, I pass.

- I don't ask for anything without offering something first. Any good networker will tell you to give before you expect to get. In fact, giving *without expecting* to get is the basis of the whole structure, so just make it a part of how you function. If someone asks about something you know, share your knowledge. If someone expresses a need in your area of expertise, offer to help them. If you see an article that you know a person would find useful or interesting, send them a copy. If you know two people you think would enjoy meeting each other, introduce them. (I'm not talking about matchmaking here—unless your name happens to be Yentl!) As my dad used to say, "Just keep giving..." If the networking is not a two-way street, my guilt-meter rings loudly and I back off.

Networking's value shows up in a hundred different ways. You may draw on the wisdom and experience of relatives in matters of child-rearing or gardening. You might ask a neighbor's advice about building a deck, writing a résumé or designing a Web site. When I first decided to write a book, I called a Toronto publisher and longtime family friend to find out how to get started. When it was time to buy a new car, I consulted a friend who reads consumer reports religiously. Same with researching new stereo speakers. If I don't know who's an expert on a given topic, my network can help me there, too, guiding me to the local maven. In return I happily field calls about who's a good cardiologist, how to change careers, where to learn relaxation skills or how to find an agent. If I hear of an opportunity that will benefit someone, I'll call them or give their name to the person offering the opening. When networking is done with balance and integrity, everyone wins.

In summary, remember that you're not alone in this time of rapid change. Everyone's trying to manage and adjust. We can all help one another. Building a support system provides four major areas of benefit: emotional support, logistical help, mentoring and networking. It involves taking initiative to build relationships. Don't isolate yourself, and don't wait for people to come to you. Share yourself with others in order to build trust. Sometimes that means allowing yourself to be vulnerable. Even admitting the need for help can be difficult for some folks. But in today's turbulent world, we're all feeling the strain. It's OK to say, "This is tough. I'm struggling," or "I'm frustrated, angry, tired, frightened." It doesn't mean you're *weak*. It only means you're *human*.

So seek and accept the support of others. But give support to them in return. One of the added benefits of doing for others is that it takes our attention off ourselves and helps us see we're not the only ones having difficulty. It also tends to make us feel better about ourselves.

One More Story

A woman who had very low self-esteem told me this simple but powerful story. It's about the value of a support system, and also about how little it takes to make a profound difference to someone—sometimes just the right words at the right time. This woman bought a new and very becoming dress to cheer herself up and tried it on for some friends, saying, "This is the new me!" One of her friends, who valued her much more than she did herself, said, "No, Cynthia, that's not the *new* you. That's the *real* you!"

CHAPTER TWELVE

Living in the Question

Dealing with Uncertainty–Questions Without Answers

SOMEONE ON THE RADIO WAS LAMENTING the fact that high-school graduates are now entering a world of unprecedented uncertainty. Would they find jobs? Could they get into college or university, and if they did, would it be worth it? What courses should they take to prepare them for an unpredictable future? The questions continued to pile up. Would they have to move away from home to find work? Would they ever be able to buy their own home? Or even afford to move out of their parents' house?

"Security is mostly an illusion. It does not exist in nature. Life is either a daring adventure, or nothing."

HELEN KELLER

The commentator then asked some sobering questions of his own. Is this any worse than what faced the graduates of 1914–1918 who knew that, on graduation, they'd be entering the military and going overseas to an uncertain (and very dangerous) future? How about the graduates between 1929 and 1939 who left school during the Great Depression? Or between 1939 and 1945, when they faced the grim prospect of involvement in the Second World War?

Most eras have seen their young people enter an age of confusion, hardship and risk. When have people ever lived with certainty? Yes, there have been times when society has been relatively stable, tranquil and predictable. But perhaps they are the exception.

This is not to deny that these are difficult times in many ways. We're living in a time of transition and evolution (the so-called Information Revolution seems to be as dislocating as the Industrial Revolution ever was). This *is* an era of uncertainty and instability, and I have no panacea to offer. But I have a number of ideas on how to make this era of change easier—not necessarily *easy*, but eas*ier*. How do we "live in the question" (that is, live with questions that don't yet have answers)? How can we feel more comfortable during the interminable time we have to wait for things to clarify themselves?

We've Always Lived with Uncertainty

Can we learn to live with uncertainty? Of course we can. We've been doing it all our lives. In Chapter 4 I talked about belief in our ability to change. I made the case that, historically, we've all been change agents, but we've either overlooked that fact or not given ourselves enough credit for it. The same can be said about living with unpredictability and insecurity. It's helpful to remind ourselves that if we look closely, we'll realize that life isn't tidy, predictable and certain, and never has been. Yet we've all learned to live with that reality.

Take the area of health. None of us knows how long we are going to live, what diseases we might contract or what will ultimately cause our demise. But for the most part we don't spend a lot of time thinking about it. We accept that there are unknowns and carry on in spite of them. People with a family history of certain ailments live with more specific questions: Will I have a heart attack like my father? Get cancer like my mother? Become diabetic like my aunt Marge? Develop Alzheimer's like my grandmother? Virtually all of us have a family history of *something*, and yet few of us stay awake at night wondering if it will happen to us.

Then there are the individuals who already have a health problem. They face other uncertainties: Will I have another heart attack? Will my cancer return? These folks undoubtedly have passing thoughts about these issues, but most don't dwell on them. They either become philosophical or fatalistic about the situation—or push it from their thoughts altogether. They do the sensible things that will prevent recurrence—and then get on with their lives.

Every pregnant woman and expectant father wonders at some time during the gestation if everything will be all right. Most acknowledge the possibility of problems, without paying undue attention to that prospect. It's the same as driving on the highway. We all accept the potential for an accident. Then we usually push it out of our thoughts and get on with the trip. We've learned that dwelling on the possibilities of misfortune produces stress and anxiety, and who wants to live with that? We've taught ourselves to compartmentalize and put that stuff away, out of sight. Not that we aren't aware of it on some level; not that we don't take reasonable precautions. But at some point we realize there's only so much we can do to safeguard ourselves, and beyond that it's up to fate, God or forces we don't understand and can't control. We have learned to live quite comfortably with these uncertainties.

Relationships are another domain in which we live without certainty. "She loves me, she loves me not." How can I find out? And if she loves me now, will she love me next month—or next year? It's like the old hit songs "(Will I) See You in September" and "Will You Still Love Me Tomorrow?" These old standards are still great songs, and the former speaks to another area of concern for young lovers: Will our feelings survive periods of separation?

It is the very uncertainty of relationships that helps to make them so compelling! A friend of mine once said to me, "Romantic love is built on insecurity." I think she's right, and so do all the people with whom I've ever shared this thought. And despite the anguish of that insecurity, who would want to forgo the exquisite moments of anticipation and joy at being in love, which are the other side of the coin? Whoever said that love—or life—would be easy?

Politics are built on unknowns and unknowables. That's what makes it so fascinating. Kim Campbell took over the prime ministership of Canada from Brian Mulroney and called an election in 1993. She had a commanding lead over the Liberals' Jean Chrétien, "yesterday's man," as he was called; it was his election to lose. And yet she lost. The same thing happened to George Bush in 1992. The pundits and politicos have tried to overcome uncertainty with their constant polls. But the only thing they discover for certain is that campaigns—and voter preferences—can be volatile and unpredictable. We not only live with that uncertainty, it also adds interest to our lives. Who'd bother watching politicians' antics if the result was really "in the bag"? Then there are the unanswered questions following an election. What will this mean for *me?* Will the winners keep their election promises? Will they have to water down their ideas (for example, budgetary belt-tightening) or scrap their major programs (for example, Bill Clinton's publicly funded Medicare plan)? Questions without answers—at least for now. All we can do is stay tuned.

The economy is a huge area of uncertainty affecting every citizen. Which way will the stock market go? How long can it sustain this upward growth? What about interest rates? Unemployment? Should I buy stocks or bonds? Is there such a thing as a sure-bet investment? (Ask Donald Trump, Robert Campeau or the Reichmanns.) Should I take out a short-term mortgage or lock in for the long term? How much income will I need to retire? That depends on another unknowable: How long will I live? Will the government have enough in the treasury—or the political will—to help me in my old age? These are questions we live with all the time and make jokes about ("I just met with my accountant and she told me I have enough money to last me for the rest of my life—as long as I don't buy anything!").

And I've said nothing about some of the biggest questions of all, the ones that rivet us to our TV screens even though they have absolutely nothing to do with us! Will the movie queen marry the heartthrob hunk? Will the jailed boxer be allowed to fight again? Will the multigazillionaire ever be worth all the money the White Sox are paying him? Can the Bulls make it four in a row?

If things were certain, who would buy insurance? Who would bet on horse races? Who would bother watching the news or reading the paper? I have a friend who's a sports fan and a politics junkie; he's fascinated with both because of their unpredictability. When one team or party dominates, people start to lose interest. In fact, our lives are enriched by not knowing. Would you work as hard on a project if you knew it was destined to fail? Would you pursue a contract or a love interest if you knew you'd be rebuffed? Not only is life unpredictable, but it's better that way. I know people who go to fortune-tellers, and one of them told me about a woman in Niagara Falls who was amazing, appeared to have an uncanny skill. I said, "If I knew someone who could tell me the future with absolute precision, I wouldn't touch that person with a barge pole!" (You see, I learned *something* from that Oedipus guy!) If you could know everything in advance, would you want to? Do you read the last chapter of a book first? Would you watch the replay of a baseball game if you already knew who won?

Here's a story about a remarkable person who could have known the future but chose not to. People who live in the Arctic are often fascinating characters. This man's home was out in the bush, near a settlement that was so remote they only received four scheduled airline flights a year (this was in the sixties). He subscribed to *The Globe and Mail*, and every three months the mail and supply plane would bring him the last ninety days' worth of newspapers, each one rolled up in brown paper. The wrappers were dated so he'd know which were most recent. He'd stack them up with the newest ones on the bottom and oldest on the top. Then, each morning, he'd take the paper on the top, tear off the brown wrapping, and read it with his morning coffee as if it was that day's paper. He was always exactly three months behind on his news. (He had neither radio nor TV, so there was no other source of information.) He said the hardest part was maintaining the discipline to follow this ritual and not give in to impatience and pull out the most recent paper—to see who won the Stanley Cup, the Academy Awards or the latest election. In the north, where news travels slowly—and it doesn't seem to matter anyway—this man kept the outside world from intruding, only letting it in on his own terms and on his own schedule.

I learned about the benefits of uncertainty when I played football, which I did till I was thirty-seven (tackle football in high school and touch after that). Over time I realized that playing offense is psychologically different from playing defense. On offense, your team has the ball. You have a huddle to plan a play, then you execute the play as best as you can. Everybody has a job to do and they know what it is. Neat, clean, predictable. It's most interesting if you're the one who's going to get the pass, or at least if you're the alternate receiver. Of course, good team players try hard on every play and stay alert in case there's a busted play and they're needed as a backup option. But if you're rarely called on to be the pass-catcher, you can start to lose interest or feel you're not really in the game.

But what about defense? The defenders don't know what's going to happen, so they have to be ready for any contingency. It could be a short pass, a long bomb, the quarterback running with the ball, a reverse, pitch-out or fake. It's fun to take risks sometimes, to play your hunches (like double-teaming or blitzing the quarterback). Some people think defense is boring, because defenders rarely get to catch the ball. But not knowing what's going to happen next makes everything possible. There's a chance you'll be a key part of every play. I loved playing football, offense or defense. But I think I felt more alive on defense because I had to be more on my toes. There was always the element of mystery and surprise.

Yes, life is uncertain and unpredictable. But it's probably better that way. And learning to live with uncertainty is not only *possible*, it's what we've all been doing all our lives.

Focus on What Is Certain

Just as there are elements of uncertainty in all areas of life, so there is also an amazing number of constants you can depend on. Take pregnancy: nothing is certain until the birth (I was a twin and nobody knew there were two of us until my sister arrived thirteen minutes after me). But it does help to know that ninety-seven percent of babies are born perfectly healthy.

And think of coronary artery disease. Medical advances over the past quarter-century have led to a fifty percent decrease in mortality from heart disease and strokes: fewer people are suffering from these diseases, and those who do are having much better outcomes. Similarly, road travel has its risks, but there are many safeguards to reassure us (good highway construction, road maintenance, car safety, speed limits, conventions like passing on the left, using turn signals). If traffic were total anarchy, the feeling of peril would be acute (those eight lanes around the Arc de Triomphe in Paris, with eleven roads feeding in and out, come as close to chaos as I'll ever want).

The stock market, too, is dynamic and fluctuates daily. On a micro level (hour by hour) it can give you fits with its ups and downs. But on a macro level (year to year), there's a pretty predictable pattern of upward movement. And if you look at the record over the past hundred years, including all the depressions and recessions, bulls and bears, booms and crashes, there is an overall average gain of ten percent a year. So if you're a buy-and-hold investor, you can count on the ups exceeding the downs over time. In the short run it can be nerveracking and turbulent, but in the long run there is no better investment you can make. So, while acknowledging that uncertainties are inevitable, it's helpful to recognize that there are also many things that are predictable and on which we can depend.

Here's a story to show how the picture can change when you choose to look at the "knowns" instead of dwelling on the "unknowns." At the height of the recession a female executive lost her very stressful job when the company downsized. She received an adequate severance package but there was a bigger problem. She'd been having abdominal symptoms and was told she might require major surgery. However, with her job loss she also lost her health benefits, including disability insurance. She feared an operation would require an extended recovery period, a prospect with severe financial implications. She hired a lawyer to negotiate a larger severance payout and an extension of her medical benefits.

When we discussed the matter she related all the uncertainties she faced. What was her exact medical diagnosis? Would she require surgery? If so, when? What would her company offer in terms of money and benefits? And how soon would they agree to settle? Would she have to fight with them through her lawyer? What would her legal fees be if the matter dragged on? What kind of new job would she be able to find? How soon? Would her finances hold out if she was unemployed for a long time? These were all valid concerns and raised her stress level considerably.

It was difficult to get a handle on the situation with so many hypothetical questions. And it was further complicated because the uncertainties were all inter-related. There was nothing solid to begin with and build on. We talked in circles. It felt a bit like shadow-boxing. I suggested we stop focusing on all the unknowns and ask instead, "What do we know for sure?" Between us we came up with nine certainties:

1. She was finally out of a job that she'd found very stressful and unpleasant.
2. She got a reasonable severance package (even if they declined to increase it).
3. She was assured that there had been no serious damage in her abdomen.
4. There were treatment options for her condition that would *not* require surgery.
5. She had a good case to make with her former employers.
6. She had a good advocate working on her behalf (a well-respected lawyer).

7. Several interesting job prospects had already come to light.
8. She was highly employable (very well regarded and experienced in her field).
9. Her finances were adequate for the short run and her husband was earning a good salary.

By choosing to identify the knowns rather than the unknowns, she was able to let go of some of her worries. This story had a terrific ending. Her lawyer negotiated a good settlement with the company, she had a successful non-surgical treatment for her ailment and before long she found an excellent position that paid more than her previous post. In fact, she had overlapping incomes for a while because she started the new job before her severance ran out—a bonus windfall that strengthened her financial security.

Living in the Moment: Today's Work World

Nine out of ten new businesses fail. Deregulation is allowing more competition into every line of business. Permanent jobs are disappearing and being replaced by temporary and/or part-time positions (which usually pay less and have no benefits). Job insecurity is now a fact of life. But that's the point. Uncertainty about jobs is now a *certainty*. It's the new reality. And while it may not be viewed as good news by many people, it has left the realm of ambiguity and vagueness and become something we can—and must—count on.

Yesterday's history,
Tomorrow is a mystery,
Today is a gift,
That's why we call it
THE PRESENT
UNKNOWN

It also helps to remember that not everyone who loses a job stays unemployed. If you've got good skills and experience, there's usually a place for you somewhere. I remember when Chrysler was faced with having to shut down. (This was before Lee Iacocca stepped in and rescued them from the brink.) I commented to a friend how awful it would be if all those workers lost their jobs. He said something very interesting: "They won't lose their jobs. They'll just lose their jobs at Chrysler. If Chrysler folds, the other automakers will pick up their market share. The total number of cars being sold isn't going to change. The other companies will have to hire extra workers to produce more cars, and the Chrysler people are well trained. Where do you think the other companies will start looking first to increase their production?" I hadn't considered the redistribution of workers to meet the needs of a large buying public that loves automobiles. Even though it wasn't a certainty they'd be hired, it seemed like a strong likelihood.

There's something to be said for living spontaneously and being open to change and new possibilities, as opposed to always having a plan, following a script and knowing exactly where you're going. I have friends who often travel without an itinerary or even a map, just playing it by ear and going by weather and inclination on a day-by-day basis. Instead of predictability and certainty, we should learn to be more reactive and light on our feet. It's like sailing or doing comedy improvisation or playing jazz without sheet music. You learn to go with the flow, change directions comfortably and explore unknown terrain. It can be an exhilarating and liberating experience.

Have a Contingency Plan

While it's helpful to define both the ambiguities and the certainties in your life, it's also useful to have a plan to fall back on if the worst-case scenario occurs. We have fire drills, fire extinguishers, escape routes and procedures for two reasons. One is for psychological preparation so that, in the unlikely event of a fire, people won't panic. The other is that if the real thing happens, folks will have a clear idea of what to do and will follow an efficient and orderly plan of escape. It's a good idea for your peace of mind to do the same thing with any situation about which you feel insecure.

Worry is not a helpful emotion. It is stressful and unpleasant. But when I urge patients to stop worrying, many feel I'm suggesting a laissez-faire, laid-back, who-cares approach to life. But this is not the case; I'm not advocating complacency or denial (where problems are ignored). I'm suggesting that "concern" be the middle ground between these two attitudes, as diagrammed below.

Denial ← Complacency ← CONCERN → Worry → Anguish

I make a distinction between "worry" and "concern" as noted in these two columns:

WORRY	CONCERN
Involves emotion	Involves the mind, is rational
Creates fear, fretting, anxiety	Creates interest, involvement
Problem-oriented (reactive)	Solution-oriented (proactive)
Stressful, draining	Appropriate, constructive
Hurtful	Helpful

There's an exercise I advocate that's useful for developing a contingency plan. I've heard it called "creative worrying," but to me it's an exercise in "prudent concern." It's best done in writing and consists of answering the following questions:

1. What's the worst that can happen? (What's your greatest fear?)
2. How likely is it to happen? (It's important to keep things in perspective.)
3. What would you do to handle it? (This is the contingency-plan portion.)
4. What can you do about it right now (to prevent or prepare for it)?

Let's see how this works with some real issues that people fret about, all of which involve change and elements of uncertainty.

Fear of Illness

You have a family history of cancer and the worry about developing a malignancy is never far from your mind.

What's your greatest fear? "Getting cancer. And having it kill me." (There, you've said it.)

How likely is it to happen? It depends on the statistics for that type of cancer and any other risk factors you may have. It's helpful here to look at your own past history and see how much unnecessary worrying you've done in the past. I had a patient with cancer phobia who was anxious about her long history of headaches; later she developed a breast cyst, then a second breast cyst, then an ovarian cyst. With all of these, her worry had reached extremely high levels, and yet everything worked out well: the headaches disappeared and the cysts were benign. Although I can't guarantee that she'll never develop cancer someday, I always remind her that her worry in the past turned out to be unnecessary, and it would be helpful for her if she could avoid the fears that occupy her mind, upset her emotions and sometimes plague her sleep. And I point out that she's in excellent overall health, has a good support network and is financially able to get whatever help or extra resources she might need.

What would you do to handle it? You'd see your family doctor, have the appropriate tests, see the appropriate specialists and receive the treatment recommended.

What can you do about it right now? Eat a healthy diet, stay physically active, have regular checkups (including self-examinations), learn to manage stress and keep as positive an outlook as possible. It would help if you got involved in fun activities and stimulating pursuits, things you can be passionate about and get absorbed in.

Fear of Job Loss

This has been a biggie since the recession began in the late eighties. Downsizing, restructuring, merger, automation, companies going bankrupt—there are many reasons people are losing their jobs these days.

What's the worst that can happen? "I'll be unemployed," "I won't be able to find another job," and "I'll lose my house."

How likely is it? This question can't be answered without specific details. But a realistic assessment of the situation puts you on solid ground, and you can eliminate *unnecessary* worry.

What would you do to handle it? Write a résumé, watch the want ads for job opportunities, apply for jobs with companies in your field (even if they're not advertising), get help with interview skills, go to interviews, network with as many people as possible, seek out a headhunter, take some upgrading courses (in computer skills, accounting, managing), go for career counseling, possibly go back to school or maybe start your own business. Spend more time with your family and friends, start a regular exercise program, kick back, relax and enjoy yourself, maybe take a trip you've been putting off. And you might do some volunteer work (to keep active, meet people, possibly learn new skills, give something back to the community and feel good about yourself). You might apply for unemployment insurance, watch your spending to conserve money, moonlight at some odd jobs, remortgage the house if you need extra funds. As a last resort, you could take money out of your retirement savings or sell your house.

What can you do right now to prevent or prepare for it? Do the best you can at your job, make yourself as valuable to the company as possible. Prepare (or update) your résumé, even get some coaching in how to do that, so it's always ready. Start networking, and keep your eyes and ears open for possible job openings. You can take some upgrading courses now, possibly even through your present company. The skills you learn will help you do your present job better—but would also be portable if you do lose your job. You should start managing your money more wisely and be more frugal in your spending. And you could start putting some money into savings. Then it's there if you need it.

Fear of Marriage Breakdown

There are two ways a marriage can end. Separation and divorce, or the death of a spouse. Both can happen unpredictably and both can be devastating.

What's the worst that can happen? "My marriage could end and I could be left on my own."

How likely is it to happen? The answer here varies with your age, health, state of the marriage and so on.

What would you do to handle it? Again this varies with age, gender and circumstances, but let's consider a woman who is widowed, which is, regrettably, the more common scenario in our society. She would deal with the immediate events of the funeral and period of mourning. Then she'd have to deal with legal and financial matters, winding up affairs and so on, following the guidance of her lawyer and accountant. She'd have to decide whether to enter the paid workforce. She would spend time with her family and friends and maybe do some traveling. She would continue her present activities (bowling, volunteer work) and probably join some other groups (for example, badminton, bridge, book club). She'd have to learn to manage the household accounts and investments that her husband always took care of. If she's having trouble getting on her feet again, she might consider getting some counseling.

What can you do to prevent or prepare for it now? It would be a good idea for her to develop some other interests and friendships so she's not so dependent on her husband for entertainment and companionship. For example, she might go out herself when he goes to play golf. She could ask him to show her how he keeps the household accounts, maybe take over some of it from him. She could learn more about his investments and even go with him when he visits his financial counselor a few times a year. It would help to know their affairs are up to date, and that they're both properly covered with life insurance, wills and powers of attorney.

Worry Doesn't Help

In cases like the three above, going through this exercise allows you to address your fears, work through some of the issues involved and develop a game plan to follow if your greatest fear comes to pass. Then let the exercise help you set aside your feelings of worry and uncertainty and get on with living your day-to-day life—not oblivious to possible upheavals in the future, but prepared to deal with them if they do occur. Worrying will add absolutely nothing to your preparation. So now you can sit back and get on with your life, knowing you have a backup plan, a parachute and a safety net if you need them.

When people are faced with uncertainty, they often start to think negatively, looking at the downside and focusing on their biggest fears. They listen to rumors and exaggerate the negatives. It's as if they put on dark glasses that make everything look gloomier and more suspect than it really is. If you want to see these dynamics in action, just watch how the stock market reacts to the subtlest of rumors. The antidotes to these stress producers are factual information, clear objective thinking, an open mind and patience. Easy to say, hard to do. But those who can do it are best able to handle the insecurity.

So don't be an alarmist. I have often found myself reserving judgment about some issue until I read or hear it from an authoritative source. The medical profession has ongoing struggles with government, and sometimes it seems that the rules, regulations and agreements are all up for grabs. I've learned to dismiss rumors and gossip and wait for a definitive statement from the politicians or our own medical officials before I react. When you hear news that doesn't make sense to you, wait until it's confirmed and save yourself a lot of emotional buffeting. Pretend you're a news reporter who has learned to clarify and verify before believing—or speaking. Don't just swallow what you hear. And don't pass on such information to others.

Some questions don't yet have final answers. In a sense, you have to make an educated guess, pick a premise and make it *your certainty* until evidence to the contrary comes along. For example, I've been following the cholesterol debate (and its relationship to cardiovascular disease) since I entered the field of medicine. Is cholesterol a risk factor in the hardening of arteries or not? And if so, how great a risk is it? Experts have made conflicting statements, studies have shown that it is and shown that it isn't. I made up my mind in the seventies that it *was* a risk factor and started to modify my own diet—and my advice to my patients—accordingly. That view was heavily reinforced when I heard Dr. William Castelli speak in 1979 about the findings of the ongoing Framingham Study. My logic was partly predicated on my inclination to err on the side of caution. If I eat more carefully now and find out later it wasn't a major risk, what have I lost, other than all that greasy butter on movie theater popcorn? But if I eat a fat-rich diet until I find out it *is* a problem, then what? I'd be stuck with clogged arteries and self-recrimination. Perhaps more people should have followed their hunches or early suspicions about the dangers of cigarette smoking when the first evidence was floating around in the early sixties. My wife and I have taken the same tack with microwave ovens (we don't have one) and vitamin supplements (we take them), even though all the evidence isn't in yet. Sometimes you have to go with your gut feeling in uncertain and confusing times.

Control What You Can, Accept What You Can't

At a time of uncertainty and insecurity, it's easy (and normal) to feel a loss of control. But there are areas in which we still have control: the way we think about what's going on, the action we take to deal with the situation and the lifestyle choices we make (around issues like sleep, exercise, time with family, leisure, managing finances). We should focus our attention and efforts on those areas, make things as good as they can be in the circumstances and feel more positive about ourselves overall. The message is this: Control what you can control and either learn to handle and live with the rest—or let it go altogether.

In summary, we're living in a time of rapid change, which leads to uncertainty and insecurity. No one knows where we're headed, and a lot of questions will only be answered by the passage of time and unfolding of events. In the meantime there are things we can do to help us adjust to the unpredictabilities of our time. One is to recognize and acknowledge that we already live with a great deal of uncertainty—and most of us do it rather well. Another is to have contingency plans for the various possibilities that might occur. It's also important to focus on the positive, not the negative, and on what is present and certain around you.

Dr. Sherwin Nuland wrote a book with the arresting title *How We Die*, which became a major bestseller. One of his reasons for writing the book, he said, was to urge people to live life as fully as possible while they're here, because we all have only a finite amount of time allotted to us (and none of us knows what that is). In a time of uncertainty, focus on what you *do* know. Anticipate and plan for the future—but not at the total expense of enjoying the pleasures of living one day at a time.

CHAPTER THIRTEEN

How the Masters Do It

The Ingredients of Change-Hardiness

THE AFRICAN QUEEN WAS A TERRIFIC 1952 movie starring Katharine Hepburn and Humphrey Bogart, with John Huston as director. All these names are legends, and Bogart won an Oscar for his role. You can still catch this classic on late-night TV or rent the video. Great story and acting.

> ***"The individuals who will succeed and flourish will also be masters of change."***
> ROSABETH MOSS KANTER

The movie was filmed on location in what was then the Belgian Congo and plagued by all kinds of problems, from weather to food to insects. What I remember best from reading about this saga was that Bogart apparently spent a lot of time grumbling about the hardships and oppressive conditions on the shoot. (Good thing he had his wife, the young and glamorous Lauren Bacall, along to cheer him up.) But what particularly stuck in his craw was Katharine Hepburn's cheerful outlook about the adverse conditions. According to him, Kate found everything just wonderful. The heat was thrilling, the humidity was divine, the leeches were splendid, and so on. It sounded as though her sunny outlook drove Bogey crazy.

Now, Katharine Hepburn grew up in a well-to-do family in Hartford, Connecticut, where her father was a noted surgeon. From this comfortable background, what made her reaction to the steamy heat of equatorial Africa so upbeat? Why did she view the whole thing as a big adventure when others couldn't wait to get out of there? To broaden the question, what makes some people able to deal with adversity better than others? And whatever they've got, can it be learned or acquired by others? Or are you just born with it if you're lucky?

This type of resilience is sometimes called "hardiness." The phrase "stress-hardy" has been used to describe individuals who are able to handle a lot of stress—and not just survive, but thrive on it. The same qualities, which I might call "change-hardiness," can help people deal with change, and I believe they can be learned, practiced and developed as skills. You can learn a lot from resilient people if you use them as models or teachers, rather than as a standard to judge or measure yourself by. Use these folks as a picture of what's possible for *you*—and then learn all you can from them.

Characteristics of Change-Hardiness

What are the factors that contribute to resilience? What attributes do these individuals possess that strengthen them in new situations or times of change?

1. Commitment

Twice a year my family and I volunteer at our local food bank. We spend a few hours sorting, boxing and stacking nonperishable items donated during the Thanksgiving and Easter food drives. It's interesting to work with a cross-section of people from the community who give their time to this worthy project. There's a nice feeling of teamwork and cooperation that quickly develops among people who mostly don't know each other but who are gathered together in a good cause. What always impresses me is the way these individuals get into this activity. They're more than just conscientious or hard workers. They get totally involved. They jump in with both feet. They're not just making a gesture—many of them come back day after day until the food drive is over. They don't merely participate. They demonstrate commitment.

There's an old joke about the distinction between participation and commitment. To illustrate the difference, think of a breakfast of ham and eggs: the hen is a participant—but the pig is committed! Commitment is about giving yourself to what you're doing, investing energy, caring about the process and the outcome. It's not about going through the motions, paying lip service or standing on the sidelines. In a stronger form, commitment develops into passion, an excitement that generates its own energy. There's a fervor, a zest, a joyfulness. It's a wonderful state to be in.

Some people confuse commitment with passion and think that you either have it or you don't. I make a distinction between the two. I think of passion as a feeling and commitment as an attitude, although the latter can lead to the former.

I think of these two entities on a spectrum:

Disinterest → Interest → Involvement → Commitment → Passion

My son used to have a passion for Lego, playing with it constantly and in a state of total absorption. Lately he's developed the same feeling for musical theater. He's now thirteen and has seen a host of musicals, including *Cats, The Phantom of the Opera, Joseph and the Amazing Technicolor Dreamcoat, Grease, Damn Yankees* and *Ragtime*. He loves them all. He has all the programs, CDs and sheet music. He knows the stories, the songs and the words, and has taught himself to play them beautifully on the piano. That's passion. There are teenagers who have a similar passion for basketball. They'll shoot hoops till midnight if there's even a glimmer of light. I know people who adore their new computers. They're transfixed, spending hours with their CD-ROMs or surfing the Internet. That's passion, too. It's an exciting state to be in. It's engaging, pleasurable, often challenging—like the "flow state." The activity feels effortless. There's total focus and endless motivation. Most people would love to have that feeling, and while you can't *make* it happen, you *can* create the circumstances that encourage it to appear.

Commitment, on the other hand, is an attitude and a choice, a decision. And therefore it's available to anyone. And whether it leads to passion or not, it's still a good space to be in. Where passion reflects animation and eagerness, commitment entails dedication and devotion. Commitment could be seen as rational, passion as emotional; but in fact they're simply at different points on the continuum, as depicted in the figure above. The outcome is positive in both instances.

Here's an example of a change situation that illustrates the different stages from "disinterest" to "passion": a reorganization at work or a merger with another company. But let's consider how different attitudes produce different personal outcomes.

You can react to the new situation with **disinterest** ("I don't really care and I'm not going to participate.") or **interest** ("I'm going to watch what happens; I'm kinda curious."). Or you can get **involved** in the situation, but without enthusiasm ("Yeah, I'll go along with this. It'll probably be OK."). The last is slightly positive but it's flat. In these cases your involvement will probably be minimal and your work uninspired. An alternative would be to embrace the situation and make the best of it ("If this is the new reality, I'm going to give it my best shot. I'm going to dig in and make it work."). This is a statement of **commitment**. It's not a divine inspiration or a feeling that washes over you. It's a *choice*. The last type of reaction along the spectrum might be outright **enthusiasm** ("Hey, this is great. I can't wait to get at it!"). This is what I call **passion**. It's a visceral reaction, not something you can program. It's either genuinely there or it's not. But if it's really how you feel, you'll work with great eagerness and energy and enjoy the whole experience.

When you see people greet change situations with commitment, you probably admire or even envy them. Maybe you say, "Gee, I wish I could be like that." The fact is you can. You have to *find* passion, but you can *choose* commitment.

What are the advantages of commitment? If you show yourself willing to be a stakeholder in the change process, it gives you a seat at the table of planning and decision-making. You can have some input and possibly some influence on what's being proposed or what eventually happens. That also increases your feelings of control. Pretty good payoffs for throwing your hat into the ring!

In change situations that are difficult, choosing commitment can be especially helpful. For example, if a spouse or parent becomes sick, or a special-needs child is born, people often respond by deciding that "if this is the way it's going to be, I'm going to devote my time and effort to his/her well-being." They make a project out of learning everything they can about the condition or illness. They search out treatment options and the leading specialists; they give special care and dedicated support. A friend of mine had coronary bypass surgery about ten years ago. From the moment high cholesterol was identified as his major risk factor, his wife sprang into action and made the management of his diet her focus and concern. She learned all she could about dietary sources of cholesterol and fat. She found tasty recipes for low-fat, nutritious meals and began cooking that way for the whole family, so her husband wouldn't have to eat differently than everyone else. This is a story about love and concern and caring—but also of commitment. In for a penny, in for a pound. Her involvement was total—and it was a choice.

2. Challenge

Resilient people see change as a challenge. When things get difficult they don't say, "Oh no, now what?" or "This is impossible. I can't handle this." Instead they roll up their sleeves and say, "Ah, this is where it starts to get interesting," or "I wonder how much of this I can get done *before* the deadline." Some people seem to do this instinctively: they find difficulties stimulating, a challenge to their problem-solving ability. But even if this reaction doesn't come naturally, you can learn to think this way through intention and practice. It's like the entertainment-unit story in Chapter 4. What I saw as insurmountable, my wife saw as exciting. From that experience I changed not only my beliefs about myself but the way I looked at problems in general.

One of the best surgeons I ever worked with was an orthopedist who had a wonderful approach to difficult cases in the operating room. I never saw him rattled, but occasionally, when something wasn't working out or an unexpected problem arose, he'd ask everyone to stop talking and let him think. You could almost see the wheels turning in his head as he weighed the options and decided on the next step. But he wasn't shaking or sweating. He was summoning his knowledge, ingenuity and determination; then he dealt with the problem and resolved it. Afterward he'd be exhilarated and elated by the experience, like an athlete who had struggled fiercely against a worthy opponent. It was awesome to watch him rise to the challenge and prevail.

Looking at difficulties as challenges is a mind-set, not a skill. It's a point of view, a perspective. And it can be learned. And choosing to take that approach contributes to resilience.

Viewing things as a challenge is also helpful when something is considered routine or uninteresting. Let's return to the food bank. Sorting, boxing and stacking donated food is a repetitive task that doesn't require much training;

it could even be seen as dull. But resilient, change-hardy people find ways to make any task interesting. They turn it into a game or a contest; they experiment to find ways of doing the job more efficiently, maybe by grouping things together as they put them in the boxes. They'll try different ways of packing the cartons, as if they were solving a puzzle in which you had to combine neatness with getting the most stuff in. Then there is the challenge of speed. How many boxes can I fill in an hour? That sort of thing. They have a knack of making even the humblest tasks interesting, challenging and fun.

3. Confidence

"Parents treat their first child like china—and their second like rubber." That's an expression I once heard about raising kids. With a first child it's all new. You're not sure how to do it, so you're overcautious. But with time you realize how sturdy and supple children are. They fall and get back up. They hurt themselves, cry, and two minutes later they're laughing. Once you appreciate that they're not so fragile, you relax and become more confident in yourself as a parent.

Self-doubt gets in the way of dealing with new situations and change. Resilient people believe in themselves. They know they can learn to do things well, that they can succeed. Whether it's built on past successes or an innate feeling of competence, confidence is a beacon that lights the way forward. Can you *choose* to be confident? It's not as easy or as simple as some of the other choices we've discussed. But you can build up your confidence by the way you talk to yourself. Remind yourself of all the things you've handled well in the past. No matter who you are, you've got a lifetime of achievements behind you—big and small. Build yourself up, the way you would someone else if you were in their cheering section: "Come on, you can do this. I know you can. Go for it."

4. Context

This refers to the ability to put things in perspective, to see the big picture. I was counseling a man who'd been unemployed for almost a year. He was discouraged, down on himself and worried about the future. Without a job he felt his life was without meaning. One day we made a list of all the other aspects of his life: his roles, relationships and activities. It turned out to be a very long list, including husband, father, son, brother, friend, neighbor, coach, hobbyist and volunteer. I drew a big circle on my presentation board and wrote in all the items he listed, creating a sort of mosaic to illustrate that he was a multifaceted person and that the only thing different about him from the year before was that the part of his life called "job" was empty for the moment. In that context, he could see that the unchanged part of his life was much fuller than he'd acknowledged. And the "job" space in the circle was not really empty. First, he was doing some part-time tasks he enjoyed and earning a little money that way. Second, he currently had a job to do, even though it didn't bring him a wage—yet. The "job" was to find employment. He was approaching it in an organized, systematic way and spending several hours a day at it. In a sense it was like prospecting for gold. He hadn't had a payoff yet, but he was certainly working at it like a job.

I urged him to keep things in perspective; he'd been caught in the numbers crunch, just like thousands of other well-qualified people with excellent work records. And he was having trouble finding a new job, not because he was deficient, but because the economy was still sluggish and companies weren't hiring yet. In other words, none of this had a lot to do with *him* (his capabilities or his worth as a person).

Then there was the financial picture to put in context. He was thinking doom and gloom. I reminded him that he'd received a one-year severance package so that, in a sense, he was still on a twelve-month vacation with full pay! Furthermore, he had sensibly curtailed a lot of his discretionary spending, and his fifty-two-week severance package was probably going to stretch to another ten or twenty weeks. That was an achievement for which he'd neglected to give himself any credit.

We did another exercise to put his finances into perspective. We constructed a chart on my presentation board, looking at his assets and liabilities. It turned out he had more money than he realized (including savings and equity in his house) and a manageable amount of debt. In addition, his wife was still working and bringing in a reasonable paycheck. By the end of our discussion, he felt a lot better about his situation and about himself. Nothing in his situation had changed. He still didn't have a job. But what had shifted considerably was the perspective in which he viewed his position. (PS: Within months he had found a new, challenging, well-paying job in his field of expertise.)

Another way of seeing things in context is to see where your small part of an enterprise fits into the bigger picture. For example, the bullpen coach on a baseball team usually doesn't see what's happening on the field. He's in the background, warming up relief pitchers and letting the manager know when they're ready to be sent into the game. It's not a glamorous job or even a visible one most of the time, but these guys are crucial to the fortunes of the team as a whole. I often wonder what goes through their minds, being sequestered from the action like that. Do they feel left out at times? If so, that's when they should remind themselves how essential their job is to the overall functioning of the club.

5. Humor

Change-hardy people usually have a wonderful sense of humor. The ability to see the funny side of uncomfortable, new or difficult situations, to laugh easily and often, to be cheerful and laugh at yourself even in tense moments, has an energizing, healing effect when struggling with change. (See Chapter 5 for a more detailed discussion—and some good jokes.)

6. Flexibility

There's an old song called "When I'm Not Near the Girl I Love, I Love the Girl I'm Near." The title conveys the idea that if things aren't the way I want or like them, I'll adapt to the way they are. Flexibility involves the willingness to try new things, to be open to new ways of doing things, to take on different roles. In the theater actors who can play only one kind of role get typecast—if you want a villain, call Murray; Harriet's your perennial girl-next-door. They're like round pegs that can only fit into round holes. But performers who can play many roles are much handier to have around. In sports you want players who can play more than one position—and are agreeable to a switch when required. Flexibility is about attitude, as well as ability. It's about being ready, willing and able to adjust. These folks have a sense of variety and adventure, and when the situation changes, they make the necessary adjustments and fit right in.

Here's an example of flexibility. A few years ago Mike Wallace interviewed a group of street cleaners in a suburb of Tel Aviv. He told his "60 Minutes" viewing audience that they were probably the most unusual street sweepers in the world. They were hard at work, but took a break when he called them over for a chat. As they spoke, it emerged that they were all Russian immigrants, recently arrived from the Soviet Union, and that the group included a surgeon, a physicist, a biologist, a mathematician and a violinist. Why were such bright, accomplished professionals wielding brooms? Because that was the only work they could get when they arrived. Israel already had the highest number of PhDs per capita of any country in the world, even before the influx of highly educated Soviet scholars. These men might have been forgiven for disdaining such menial work and choosing to wait until jobs befitting their talents and status came along. But instead they were willing to do whatever was necessary to keep busy, earn a wage and make a contribution. When Wallace asked why they were so cheerful, they all replied that they were extremely grateful to be in a free country where they could live and practice their religion without government interference. Besides, the sun was shining, the weather was warm and they were getting good exercise. What was there to complain about?

7. Optimism

Resilience and optimism seem to go hand in hand. There's an old joke about the *pessimistic* child who hates all his expensive presents, and his incurably *optimistic* brother, who, given no presents at all except a huge load of horse manure, immediately sets to work digging through the pile of manure, because, he says, "There's got to be a pony in here somewhere!"

Are there really such people in our midst? People who keep bouncing back, for whom hope springs eternal? Yes, there are, although probably not many at this extreme end of the spectrum (which you could call "Pollyanna meets the Unsinkable Molly Brown"). However, there are countless people who tend to see the positive side of things and expect that things will usually work out well. This character trait serves them well when they confront change or difficult situations.

Are they born this way? Is this an inherent quality, or one you can acquire? It's probably both. Your background will undoubtedly shape your point of view. If your past has been filled with positive and life-affirming events, you'll be more likely to believe that the world is a good and friendly place. If your experience has been marked by adversity, abuse and tragedy, it follows that you'll be doubtful and wary about the future.

Psychologist Dr. Martin Seligman has written an exciting book called *Learned Optimism* in which he shows that optimism is a way of thinking that can be learned and developed as a positive habit. He uses the phrase "explanatory style" to describe "the manner, learned in childhood and adolescence, in which we explain our setbacks to ourselves." Some people acquire an assumption that their problems are their own fault and can't be solved. Others base their "style" on a belief that they are generally good, capable people, and that difficulties can always be overcome. Because our "explanatory style" is learned and not innate, it can be unlearned and replaced by a new way of talking to ourselves. This is the basis of cognitive therapy, in which you learn to choose different ways of looking at things and thinking about situations, which then leads you to *feel* better. The benefits of optimism are considerable, so it's a skill worth developing.

There are two kinds of optimism. One relates to yourself and things you can influence (and is related to self-confidence). The other pertains to events beyond your control. When he was three years old, my younger son was learning to hit a plastic baseball with a plastic bat. Initially he missed the ball most of the time. We'd encourage him with comments like "Oh, that was close" or "You almost had it" after each pitch. But then he developed a little pattern of his own. Before each pitch, he'd get set and say, "This time I'll *hit* it!" No matter how many times he whiffed, he began each new encounter with a positive statement that he really believed. He *expected* that the next pitch was the one he would hit. That was an optimistic self-belief relating to something he could govern. It kept him motivated, focused, hopeful—and had the added possibility of creating a self-fulfilling prophecy.

What about situations where you *can't* affect the results? We can be optimistic that our team will win the pennant, that our political party will carry the election, that the stock market will go up, that our children will do well in school. Our high hopes and our positive outlook will reduce stress, relieve worry and make us feel comfortable, but there is no possibility of self-fulfilling prophecies here. Yet an optimistic attitude can influence our behavior. We'll be more inclined to go to the games and cheer our team, help out our local candidate, invest money with our broker and encourage or help our children with their homework. And if things *don't* work out, there's another optimistic reaction: no matter what happens, I'll find a way to handle it. I'll still be okay.

When it comes to dealing with change, optimistic people are more resilient because they believe that most things will work out for the best. For example, if there is a major reorganization in your company and you're pretty sure the change will make things better for everybody concerned—yourself included—you're more likely to get involved, do your best, cooperate with others, maybe even make sacrifices for the greater good of the project. You'll reach more deeply into yourself, draw on your inner resolve and resources. The result is you'll probably perform to your full potential, be a good team player and a happy, positive influence others will want to be around. Pessimists, on the other hand, tend to stop trying and give up, figuring there's no point. They won't do good work, they'll pollute the atmosphere and possibly drag other people down. These are not folks who will adjust and adapt.

Being optimistic may be something that comes naturally and easily to you, or it may be a pattern of thinking you have to adopt and then practice until it becomes a habit. You can base it on religion or spiritual faith, or learn it as a skill. Either way, it will be an indispensable part of your resiliency repertoire.

8. Action

Resilient people are action-oriented. Their style is toward doing rather than reflecting. This doesn't mean action without thought—which leads to impulsive and often disorganized behavior (like the man described by Mark Twain, who "jumped on his horse and rode off in all directions"). It means making things happen; it involves movement and momentum, as opposed to sitting on the sidelines and waiting for others to do something.

Here's a story that illustrates what action can do. A man had started a business, and things were going OK—but then the phone stopped ringing. New orders, which had been flowing in, now came in dribs and drabs. He sat down, looked at the books and became extremely discouraged. He lamented his sorry situation to his wife, which only made it all the more real and alarming for him. He went to bed that night and slept fitfully, tossing and turning, and finally woke up at 5:00 a.m. His mind was actively wrestling with the problem, but instead of doom and gloom, he was hatching ideas to turn things around. When he realized he wasn't going to get back to sleep, he got up and went down to the kitchen. Grabbing a pad and pen, he sat down and wrote out his solutions. They included new services he could provide, marketing ideas, a different office schedule. He started to feel mobilized. After a shower and breakfast, he greeted his amazed wife with a smile and an air of enthusiasm. She wondered what he'd been up to that had him looking so perky. The answer was that he'd *taken action*. He had devised a strategy to deal with his problem, and instead of feeling lost and powerless, he was now directed and energized. This is a story about *resilience* (which comes from the Latin word *resilire,* "to bounce back"). Note that he hadn't even implemented his ideas yet; just drawing up the plan was a form of action that got him going. He quickly took the steps to put the program into operation and turned his business around. He's been successful ever since.

9. Risk-Taking

Resilient people are risk-takers. Not daredevils, just folks who are prepared to take a chance rather than always play it safe. Risk-taking involves both an attitude and a behavior. It's about saying, "Let's go for it," and then following through. Some people practice this mind-set and behavior by purposely stepping our of their comfort zone periodically to stretch their risk-taking muscles. Exotic activities are emerging for the truly adventurous. Whitewater rafting, rock-climbing, bungee jumping, skydiving and the myriad new roller coasters are all ways individuals can challenge themselves; and wilderness experiences and programs like Outward Bound allow folks to test their mettle but also to make the *idea* of risk-taking more comfortable. On a more modest level (but no less significant for her) is a stretch one of my patients told me about. She was swimming in a lake and decided to swim to a nearby island. "I wanted to see if I could *do* it. It was a way of conquering my own fear." She made it—and grew from the experience.

"You miss 100 percent of the shots you don't take."
WAYNE GRETZKY

Another woman I know has a terrific outlook on risk-taking. She was asked to give a short speech by a local group she belongs to. She told me, "Part of me wants to do it—to push myself to a new level. It'll be a great thing to conquer; I'll be stepping over a new threshold. And part of me is scared to death." (She did it and it went well.) Many weeks later she told me she'd gone even further: she did a short interview for our local cable TV station, which she described as a nerveracking experience. "I'm continuing to stretch myself," she said. "Then after, I say to myself, 'YEAH! I *did* that!' A new experience under your belt."

A friend who sustained a broken neck in a ski accident, which rendered her a quadriplegic, astonished me with the activities she undertook in the ensuing years. She tried sled-skiing in Colorado, wheelchair-racing in Minnesota, even horseback riding. I said to her, "Horseback riding? Wasn't that dangerous?" I've never forgotten her answer: "I had to try it to find out if I could do it. And I learned that I can't, because I don't have the balance. But at least now I know. It was a bit scary, but I'm glad I did it." By taking those kinds of chances, she was pushing the envelope, but it helped her discover and define her boundaries, which were much broader than she—or any of us—ever imagined. It also made other activities, like swimming and driving her own van, seem much easier by comparison. When I called her last fall, she'd just come back from a month in Africa—on safari! She regularly goes to her family's cottage on an island in Lake Superior. She is by far the most resilient person I know. And risk-taking is simply part of her tool kit for dealing with the change that so suddenly altered her life many years ago.

"I recommend that the Statue of Liberty on the East Coast be supplemented by a Statue of Responsibility on the West Coast."

DR. VIKTOR E. FRANKL

10. Responsibility

Change-hardy people take responsibility for outcomes and results. They don't blame others for what happens. They hold themselves accountable. If they make a mistake or miss a deadline, they acknowledge it without making excuses. In a time when complaint and feelings of entitlement are so common, these folks are very refreshing to be around. Here's a true story about a farmer who was moving some cattle to market. His workers had loaded the cows onto a large flatbed truck while he was doing other chores. At some point the animals discovered that the gate on the back of the truck wasn't secured. They pushed it open and all of them got out, dispersing themselves across the countryside. When a worker saw what had happened, he yelled to alert the others, and everyone who was available ran to help. The farmer came blustering up and demanded, "What happened? Who left the gate open? How could you let this happen?" to which someone else sensibly replied, "I don't think this is the time to assign blame. What do you say we just go out and round up the cows?"

This story illustrates two points. First, that rectifying a mistake is much more important than affixing blame. Second, that asking what you *yourself* did or didn't do to create a situation is more useful than looking for a scapegoat. Before our final examinations one year in med school, a teacher made what sounded like a cheeky remark. "Enjoy your exams," he said. "Yeah, right!" everybody scoffed. (As in, "Easy for you to say. We're sweatin' and frettin'. We don't see any pressure on *you*.") The teacher made a profound statement in reply: "Actually, *we're* being tested as much as you are. If you don't do well, it means we either selected the wrong students or we didn't teach you very well. We're all on the line here." What stayed with me was the idea that this teacher felt responsible for the performance of his pupils. It wasn't just "I did *my* job, so if they screw up, it's *their* fault."

When faced with a new situation, don't wait for others to lead. Take the initiative. And don't do only what's required of you. Do whatever needs to be done, whether it's technically your job or not, to get the best outcome. When everyone on a team is willing to carry more than his or her own load, the results can be amazing. And if something goes wrong, don't duck or point fingers—fix it!

Illness makes some people very passive. They want others to make them well, whether it be doctors, nurses, therapists or family members. But this is a situation in which taking responsibility can be very important. Fortunately patients are now realizing how much they can contribute to their own recovery. Diabetics are learning to test their urine or blood for sugar and to give themselves insulin; they're learning how to manage their diet, exercise, foot care and so on. It used to be that if you had a heart attack, you were in hospital for three weeks, the first of which was spent lying in bed. About twenty-five years ago that all changed. Now cardiac patients are in a chair on the second day, up walking on day three or four and out the door after a week. Some of the inpatient time is spent in educational classes or one-to-one teaching—about what happened, how the heart works and the role of cholesterol, high blood pressure and stress. Patients are also taught about diet, exercise and stress management. They become partners in their own treatment. Most join a cardiac rehabilitation program of supervised exercise and continuing education. And by taking responsibility, they're getting much better outcomes and feeling more in control of themselves and their lives.

11. Determination and Persistence

People sometimes give up too easily. Here's an example. The first 3-D movie was shown at the World's Fair in New York in 1939. A movie mogul from Hollywood saw it and was unimpressed. "Big deal!" he said. The inventors became discouraged after that and put the project on a back burner. Only ten years later did they learn that the skeptical California producer had a glass eye.

Resilient people are fighters. They don't give up. They display a dogged persistence in dealing with problems and challenges. It's a wonderful quality to have—and an important one to develop if it doesn't come naturally. I remember flying a kite with my kids and one of their friends several years ago. I was a novice at this activity, and even though we were on a huge, open field, I managed to get the kite caught in a tree on the edge of the park. (Charlie Brown was right—there really are kite-eating trees!) The more I tried to dislodge it, the more tangled it got. I was growing increasingly frustrated and discouraged. My older son (then about eight) had always been a persistent problem-solver. He rose to challenges and showed both patience and creativity well beyond his years. He was getting annoyed at my impatience. When I said we might as well forget it (it was now hopelessly snarled), he wanted no part of my surrender. He and his buddy kept working away at it. Then his friend's father came by and gave us a hand. Having two tall people made it easier to untangle the mess and slowly but surely we liberated the kite from the jaws of this tree. I was surprised and pleased with the outcome as we made our way back to the car. It was in that moment that my son walked past me and in a low voice bordering on disdain said, "Never give up!" I didn't know whether to laugh or apologize, but I knew this philosophy would serve him well in the future.

12. Creativity and Resourcefulness

When conventional wisdom isn't sufficient, some people become creative and resourceful, drawing on their ability for lateral thinking to see new ways of approaching a problem. Change produces problems but also opportunities. Who ever thought that an entire industry could be created around recycling garbage? We need to keep our eyes and ears open, and our imagination in gear. The story of Charles Darrow is a case in point. Darrow was a salesman of heat and engineering equipment in Germantown, Pennsylvania, until he lost his job during the Great Depression. As many folks probably did during that harrowing time, he started to think back to better times and imagined himself living well in Atlantic City, where he'd vacationed in the past with his family. Like many others, he escaped the desolation of his circumstances through fantasy. Then one day in the early thirties, he drew up a grid with street names from Atlantic City and printed up some play money, creating a game he could play with his friends and family. It was a diversion, a way of escaping, of dreaming that he was a rich property-owner walking on the boardwalk. Only, Charles Darrow went one step further. His depression fantasy became a national institution, which it remains to this day—the board game Monopoly (the best-selling game of all time).

"Imagination is better than knowledge."
ALBERT EINSTEIN

Interestingly the second-most popular game of all time was also invented during the Depression by an unemployed man, an architect in Poughkeepsie, New York, named Alfred Mosher Butts. It wasn't patented until 1948, but 100 million games were sold in its first fifty years. The game is Scrabble.

When massive layoffs began in the early nineties, resourceful people explored every option for finding employment. The conventional process involved job-hunting, but the creative folks were using phrases like "I bought myself a job" and "I decided to hire *myself*." Translation: "I bought a business that I'm going to run" and "I'm starting my own business (consulting, desktop printing, making birdhouses and so on). Entrepreneurism has become the fastest-growing segment of the economy and will be the prime source of new jobs in the next century (according to the "Strategic Coach," Dan Sullivan).

Look around you. Start noticing what needs there are that aren't being met. Anticipate future needs. Then figure out how you can meet those needs. Voilà! A new job or business for you. When people got too busy to walk their dogs, dog-walkers emerged to fill the void. There are people who will shop for you if you don't have time, be it for gifts or groceries. A man I know noticed how many people were affected by the problem of snoring and how disruptive it was for their bed-partners. So he set about designing an antisnoring pillow and created a nice little business for himself, providing an inexpensive item that was a great boon to others. Having trouble with clutter? There are now professional consultants who will come and de-clutter your life and get you organized. Others will analyze your skin and hair color and help you choose clothes, makeup and jewelry that complement your natural appearance. Artistic people are making personalized videos for birthday parties, designing Web sites and putting graphics and artwork on mundane things like mouse pads.

Once these enterprises are up and running, we take them for granted, forgetting that some resourceful person had to come up with the concept in the first place. And the next idea could be yours. There's a great *Far Side* cartoon that shows an innovative caveman carving a rudimentary wheel out of stone. Beside him is an equally busy caveman who is even more creative and forward-thinking. This guy is carving a parking meter!

In summary, change-hardy people are masters of resilience and adaptability. The characteristics that serve them so well include the following:

1. **Commitment** to what you're doing
2. Seeing change as a **challenge**
3. **Confidence** that you will succeed

4. Ability to see things in **context**

5. Ability to see **humor** in new situations and to laugh easily

6. **Flexibility** and willingness to try new things or do things in a new way

7. **Optimism** that things will work out well—and that in any case *you'll* be OK

8. Inclination to take **action** rather than wait for improvement

9. Willingness to be a **risk-taker** instead of "playing it safe"

10. Taking **responsibility** for outcomes and results

11. **Determination** and **persistence**

12. **Creativity** and **resourcefulness**

While it may appear that these qualities are inborn, and that having them is a matter of luck, the fact is they can all be learned, practiced and developed. We can *choose* to acquire these traits. But whether they come with ease or with effort, one thing is sure. These characteristics will be very helpful as we navigate the rough waters of rapid change.

CHAPTER FOURTEEN

You Have More Control than You Think

You Can Do This!–Conclusion

IT'S 1968 AND I'M FRESH OUT OF MY INTERNSHIP. I move to Inuvik in the Canadian Arctic, population 2800. Twice a year a guy comes up to give flying lessons. I discover that many government employees (nurses, teachers, policemen) have pilot's licenses: flying is one of the great Northern recreational activities. One day a couple of Mounties (RCMP officers) try to talk *me* into taking lessons, but I'm worried. "What if the engine quits in midair? It's not like your car running out of gas on the highway. You can't exactly pull over to the curb and wait for the Motor League to show up!" They assure me that the ground-school classes teach all about such situations. They smile and encourage me. I agree to enroll.

> ***"Change is the law of life. And those who look only to the past or present are certain to miss the future."***
> **JOHN F. KENNEDY**

Flash forward. I'm several weeks into the course. On a crisp sunny day in September I'm in my eighth solo hour, practicing stalls over the Mackenzie Delta. There are six things you're supposed to check before you put the plane into a stall. On this day I remember five but forget to turn on the carburetor heater. I go into a stall and the engine sputters slightly. I pull out of the stall and it continues to make a coughing noise. I realize what's happened (we discussed this very problem the night before in ground school): my engine has iced up. I turn on the carburetor heater to melt the ice—but that floods the mixture with water, diluting the gas. The engine starts missing. I give the throttle a forceful thrust (to kick off pieces of ice) and the engine misses completely. I quickly ease back the throttle and get a little more power again. And then *KFLOOF, KFLOOF*... and silence. My engine has quit—and it's a single-engine plane. And, just as I feared, there's no curb for me to pull over to. It's very quiet up there. The only sound is my knees knocking together. I'm 2000 feet in the air and there's nothing below me but trees and water—nowhere to land (not that I know how to do a forced landing anyway). Just then I realize something amazing. My plane is not falling like a stone. I seem to be floating up there. I'm astonished, but enormously relieved; I've got some time to think. Fortunately my medical training has taught me to think clearly in a crisis. I reset the controls as if I was on the tarmac and turn the key. The engine turns over and starts humming like nothing has happened. The ice must have melted. I've never heard a sweeter sound. I fly straight to the airport and touch down. My knees are still knocking, but I force myself to take off again and make one more circuit (like getting back up on the horse you fell off of). I land again, get out and, on still-wobbly legs, walk over to the terminal building. I sit down, tell my instructor what happened and happily endure his angry outburst about my carelessness.

What does all this have to with managing change? One of the lessons I came away with that day was that, even though my worst fear had occurred, I didn't fall out of the sky. I'd thought that if your engine died, you would, too. I had no idea that a plane could stay aloft without power. (I'd obviously never thought about what keeps gliders up so long.) And that story became a metaphor for me. Even if the worst happens, I now trust that I won't fall out of the sky. That I'll figure out what strategies are needed to deal with it. And that's an important message when it comes to handling change. I've seen patients survive lost jobs, disabling injury, bankruptcy, spousal infidelity, marriage breakdown and death of loved ones. It's never easy, but they get through it. And often they come out stronger for the experience. So remember, you won't fall out of the sky. You'll figure out what you have to do, what support or resources you'll need, and you'll deal with it.

The Best of Times, the Worst of Times

We're living in a time of turbulence and difficulty, of rapid and extensive change. Yet it's also, I believe, the most exciting time in human history. The Internet is transforming world communication. There are more democracies on the planet today than ever before, and international cooperation has improved significantly since the end of the Cold War. Western countries are reversing decades of national deficit and becoming more fiscally responsible, which bodes well for the years after the present belt-tightening is over. Progress is being made in reversing air and water pollution. Biotechnology offers exciting prospects for preventing and controlling disease.

Government and business leaders are doing their best to figure out how to manage all the change that's happening and to lead us into the twenty-first century. But it's all new territory, and things are happening fast. It's a collective learning curve for all of us, whether we like it or not. I'm convinced we're up to the challenge. I don't want to sugarcoat the dislocation and sometimes devastating effects that change can bring. Some things will be hard no matter *what* we do. But I believe we have the ability not just to get by, but to thrive and flourish in a climate of change.

We Can't Always Write the Script, but We Can Always Write Our Part

We don't always get a vote in the changes that occur. But we *do* have a choice in how we respond.

We can **reject** the change.
We can **resist** the change.
We can **accept** the change.
Or we can **embrace** the change.

I'm not suggesting that we endorse every change that comes along. We need to evaluate each situation on its own merits. There are times when fighting against a change will be appropriate, but generally speaking, if change is inevitable, we serve ourselves better by finding ways to accept and welcome the change than by opposing it. To borrow a phrase from Dr. Hans Selye:

Strive for your highest attainable aim;
But don't put up resistance in vain.

Our reaction to change is really a choice and a series of decisions. If change occurs in your workplace, you have a set of options to consider: you can **stay** or **leave**. For example, if you object to the changes, leaving the job *is* a possibility. Alternatively you can **fight** or **fit**. You can oppose and resist the change or you can decide to accept what's happening and work to make it a success. You have another choice, too, although you may not see it as one at first: you can **suffer** or **not suffer**. You can complain, lament, get angry, become bitter and pessimistic or feel helpless. Suffering *is* an option, even though it won't change anything and will likely make you miserable. Or you can choose to make the best of it. To reduce your stress and increase your comfort by being flexible and resilient.

This book is about staying in the game, deciding to fit and finding ways to *minimize the discomfort* and *maximize the opportunity*. The ideas I've been discussing are intended to make change easier and more comfortable. We've looked at ways to think about change and how to act in the face of change. In short, it's about attitude and action. There are tools we can learn to use that will make us more change-hardy—more able to deal with new situations and handle the consequences of change. The scope of the book has not just dealt with obvious areas of change such as the workplace, economics and politics. The messages apply to other kinds of change, as well: graduation, leaving home, marriage, parenthood, moving to a new city, separation or divorce, retirement, illness and disability. These all represent changes in our circumstances, some chosen voluntarily, many uninvited and unwanted. But in all cases, they are situations in which we need to make individual adjustments.

Your Mind Is Your Greatest Asset

Dr. Christine Padesky is an internationally known expert in cognitive therapy, a superb therapist and teacher. One of the concepts I learned from her is a simple equation developed by her colleague, Dr. Kathleen Mooney. It summarizes the source of our anxiety about change:

$$\textbf{Anxiety} = \frac{\textbf{Overestimation of Danger}}{\textbf{Underestimation of Coping/Resources}}$$

Source: Anxiety equation developed by Kathleen A. Mooney, PhD (1990) at the Center for Cognitive Therapy, Newport Beach, CA.

The equation shows that anxiety increases with the amount of danger or threat you attach to a situation. There's no surprise there. If you're afraid of flying, it's because you think you are at serious risk in the air. But there's another side to the equation. Your anxiety will also increase if you feel you can't handle the danger. However, both of these variables are subjective. They exist in your mind and attitude, not in objective reality. Some people love roller coasters because they feel confident they won't get hurt. Others are petrified of these rides because they're sure they are dangerous. In neither case do they have much objective information on which to base their opinion. But how they *think* about the experience determines their level of anxiety. Similarly, if they are convinced that they can't handle the ride, their level of fear will rise. But if they *believe* they can deal with it on a day when there's no wind or if they're with people who have done it before, then they probably will be less anxious. Anything you can do to diminish your fear of danger or increase your confidence in your ability to cope will decrease your feeling of anxiety.

A friend of mine was afraid of highway driving. Not just the Los Angeles freeways or the twelve-lane Highway 401 across Toronto. *Any* highway! The high speeds made her nervous, aggressive drivers scared her, impatient tailgaters intimidated her and switching lanes felt perilous. In addition, she felt she lacked the skills to cope. She was afraid she wouldn't react fast enough if someone stopped quickly. She doubted she could swerve to miss an obstacle. She feared she'd miss her exit. She didn't know what lane to be in when traffic merged. The whole thing filled her with angst and tension. Her bottom-line assessment was that (a) highways were dangerous, and (b) she was inept.

The problem with this fear of expressways was that it took her twice as long to get places. She decided to confront the issue. First she reassessed her feeling of danger. She acknowledged that, despite the occasional erratic driver, most cars stuck to their lanes, drove near the speed limit, signaled their lane changes in advance and kept a safe distance between vehicles. She rarely saw an accident and any she did see were minor. She began to question the level of danger she'd conjured up in her mind. She also realized she didn't feel at all unsafe if someone else was driving. All these reflections neutralized the top half of the equation: **overestimation of danger.**

Next she looked at *herself* and her ability to cope with highway driving. She thought of some timid souls she knew who had mastered this skill and thought, "If *they* can do it, *I* should be able to do it." She reflected on aspects of driving that she *had* mastered (such as rush hour) and reminded herself that she handled most other situations well. Then she started a gradual program of skill- and comfort-building. First she tried Sunday mornings when traffic was light, then slowly moved to other low-volume hours. She got someone to show her the ropes and talk her through various scenarios. She stayed in the right-hand lane for a year, never exceeding the speed limit. She left lots of room between her car and the one ahead of her. If aggressive drivers came along, she slowed to let them pass. Bit by bit, with practice and patience, she grew more comfortable and confident. This attitude addressed the bottom half of the equation: **underestimation of coping and resources**. She understood that she actually did have the skills to handle it. After that, it wasn't long before she was tooling along highways as if they were quiet country roads.

Attitude Is Everything

This leads to another important concept. Change-hardiness is not only a set of tools and strategies. It's also a **mind-set**. It's not just *thinking* you can do it, but *knowing* you can. When the plumber comes to your house to deal with a flooded basement, he doesn't arrive thinking, "Gee, I hope this is something easy. Otherwise, I'm cooked!" He shows up knowing that, whatever he discovers, he'll be able to handle it. He doesn't know which tools he'll have to use, but knows he has them, if not in his truck, then back at the shop. **That's what mastery is. It's skill plus attitude.** And both are important. When a surgeon does an operation, he doesn't open an abdomen saying to himself, "Gosh, I hope this is appendicitis. I'm really good at that." He makes the incision knowing that, whatever he finds when he gets in there, he will have the skill, tools and judgment to deal with it. We meet many things in life for which we have no direct previous experience. But indirectly, *all* of our previous experiences have contributed to preparing us to handle new situations. In this century we in Canada have dealt with two world wars and a Great Depression. Americans had two more wars (Korea and Vietnam), the

McCarthy Era, nuclear threats, the Cold War, a Civil Rights revolution, a presidential assassination and other traumas. We're all amazingly resourceful and resilient when we have to be.

Sue Bender wrote a lovely book called *Everyday Sacred*, in which she used a wonderful analogy for dealing with uninvited change: the story of the begging bowl. "Each day a Zen monk goes out with an empty bowl in his hands. Whatever is placed in the bowl will be his nourishment for the day. The essential practice of a monk is to *accept* what is placed in the bowl—and be grateful." In a similar way we all encounter situations in life we did not choose, but must live with. If we can go one step farther and make the *best* of whatever happens, we can not only *cope* with change, but find ways to *flourish* in it. The question we need to ask is not "How will this work out?" but "What can *I* do to make this work out the *best* way possible?"

In summary, we are living in a time of rapid change—a time of flux, dislocation and experimentation.

The pace of change is going to continue or even accelerate.

No one knows for certain what's going to happen next or how to handle it.

Change is difficult and stressful for most people.

You're not alone. Most of us are struggling in one way or another.

There are things you can do to make change easier and more comfortable (**thinking** strategies, **doing** strategies and **self-care** strategies).

We're all capable of handling change. You *can* do this.

We all have the ability not to just *survive* in a climate of change, but to *thrive* in it.

Resilience and *adaptability* are skills that can be developed.

Believe in yourself and have faith in your future.

And finally, a useful piece of philosophy I received from a meeting planner, when I asked her what message she wanted me to convey to her group: **Change is what life is about. So to enjoy life, we have to learn to enjoy change.**

We can all learn to "take more kindly to change." I did. And so can you.

APPENDIX

We Have More Control than We Think

There are many things we can do to make change an easier and more positive experience. Here they are in summary:

1. Understand the need for change, even if you don't necessarily agree with the reasons.
2. Look for and focus on the benefits of change. There's good and bad in almost every situation. Think positively as much as possible.
3. Believe in yourself and your ability to deal with change. We've all been through tough times before. We're all change agents.
4. Keep your sense of humor. It not only reduces stress and relieves tension, but it makes situations easier—sometimes even enjoyable. And it can enhance your creativity and innovative thinking, which are useful in times of change.
5. Know where you are in the change process. It will help to keep you grounded and to feel less confused or overwhelmed.
6. Get strategic. Work smart, get organized, break the situation into manageable parts, acquire new skills and be a lifelong learner. Anticipate the future and plan for it. Manage your finances and your health. Ask for help and be a team player.
7. Practice change so you get more comfortable with it and less threatened by it. Prepare and plan for change. Be proactive. Don't let change take you by surprise. Assume it's coming and plan accordingly.
8. Keep up your energy. Change requires adaptation energy. It's hard to be resilient when you're tired. Good health habits will reward you.

9. Pace the rate of change. Take things gradually and incrementally as much as you can. And pace yourself. Know when to extend yourself and when to ease off. Take time-outs to rejuvenate yourself,
10. Build a support system and use it. And don't forget to be a support to others.
11. Learn to live with uncertainty. Some questions don't have answers yet, and we have to carry on without all the information. This is not only necessary but also makes life more interesting. Develop contingency plans as part of "creative worrying."
12. Develop the characteristics of change hardiness: commitment, seeing change as a challenge, confidence, seeing events in context, flexibility, optimism, taking action, taking risks, accepting responsibility, determination and persistence, creativity and resourcefulness.

Suggested Readings

Everyday Sacred	Sue Bender HarperCollins, 1995
Transitions	William Bridges Addison Wesley, 1980
Managing Transitions	William Bridges Addison Wesley, 1991
Jobshift	William Bridges Addison Wesley, 1994
From Chaos to Confidence	Susan M. Campbell Simon & Schuster, 1995
Sleep Thieves	Stanley Coren Free Press, 1996
Flow	Mihaly Csikszentmihaly Harper & Row, 1990
Your Money or Your Life	Joe Dominguez and Vicki Robin Viking, 1992
Resilience	Frederic Flach, MD Fawcett Columbine, 1988
Rethinking the Future	Edited by Rowan Gibson Nicholas Brealey Publishing, 1997
The Age of Unreason	Charles Handy Harvard Business School Press, 1989

The Empty Raincoat (The Age of Paradox)	Charles Handy Arrow Business Books, 1994
The Learning Paradox	Jim Harris Macmillan Canada, 1998
Crisis & Renewal	David K. Hurst Harvard Business School Press, 1995
On Death and Dying	Elisabeth Kübler-Ross The Macmillan Company, 1969
Dig Your Well Before You're Thirsty	Harvey Mackay Doubleday, 1997
Beyond the Wall of Resistance	Rick Maurer Bard Books, 1996
12 Steps to Mastering the Winds of Change	Erik Oleson Macmillan, 1993
The 20 Minute Break	Ernest L. Rossi, PhD Tarcher/Putnam, 1991
The Overworked American	Juliet B. Schor Basic Books, 1991
Learned Optimism	Martin E.P. Seligman, PhD Alfred A. Knopf, 1990
The 10 Natural Laws of Successful Time and Life Management	Hyrum W. Smith Warner Books, 1994
The Great Crossover	Dan Sullivan The Strategic Coach, 1994
How the Best Get Better	Dan Sullivan The Strategic Coach, 1996

Index

acceptance, 90–92
action, 207–208
actors, 113, 134, 197
adaptability, 20
adaptation energy, 137
advancement, 58
adventure, 133, 164
advice, 170
advisers, 176–178
African Queen, 197
The Age of Unreason, 27–28
aging, 82–84
airline travel, 47–48
Anger (book), 100
anger (emotion), 90–93, 99–100
anxiety, 218–219
appearance, 84
attitude, 52–54, 199–200, 220–221
Auschwitz, 66–67
authority, 38
automobile industry, 26, 189–190
automobiles, 50

balanced lifestyle, 163–164
  See also health
baldness, 84
bargaining, 90–92
baseball, 26
  See also professional sports
basketball, 64
  See also professional sports
beginning, 88, 96–97
belief, 68–76
Bender, Sue, 221
benefits of change, 47–67
Benson, Herbert, 150
Beyond the Wall of Resistance, 75
blame, 210
blended families, 45
board games, 212
Bogart, Humphrey, 197
breaks, 147–152
breast cancer, 80–81, 98, 173
Brecher, Harold, 153
Bridges, William, 87–88, 90
Budd, Matthew, 177
business
  change in, 18
  corporate mergers, 79
  opportunities in, 179
  reorganizing of, 25–26, 44
  See also workplace
Butts, Alfred Mosher, 212

caffeine, 144–147
Campbell, Kim, 184
Campbell, Susan M., 95–96
Canadian Intern Placement Service (CIPS), 34–35
career change, 95
Carrey, Jim, 113
cash flow statement, 119–121
certainties, 187–189
challenges, 60–61, 132, 201–202
change
  and belief, 68–76
  difficulty with, 34–46
  and energy, 136–155
  and humor, 77–86
  levels of, 21

  message of, 21–22
  need for, 24–33
  and perspective, 47–67, 49–50
  preparing for, 125–135
  process of, 30–32, 87–101
  rate of, 17–18, 48, 156–166
  and resilience, 197–214
  and strategy, 104–124
  summary of techniques, 223–224
  and support systems, 167–181
  types of, 16
  and uncertainty, 182–196
change agents, 68–76
change-hardiness, 197–214
choice, 51, 217
Chrysler, 26, 189–190
clock exercise, 153–155
clutter, 107
coaches, 176–178
collective learning curve, 19
comforts, 121
comfort zone, 36–37, 131–134
commitment, 198–201
community involvement, 163
competence, 37
concern, 190–191
confidence, 37, 202
constants, 187–189
context, 202–204
contingency plans, 130–131, 190–194
control, 36, 42, 109–110, 196
coping strategies, 100, 218–220
Coren, Stanley, 140
corporate mergers, 79
creativity, 86, 112–113, 212–213
crisis, 58–59, 59–60
Csikszentmihaly, Mihaly, 61
customs, 162–163

danger, 218–219
Darrow, Charles, 212
deadlines, 108
death, 32, 90–93, 98–99, 168–169
debt, 121
  See also personal finance
delegating, 108
denial, 90–92
depression, 90–92
determination, 211–212
Diana, Princess of Wales, 32
Dig Your Well Before You're Thirsty, 174
Dominguez, Joe, 121–122
Douglas, Tommy, 74
Do What You Love, the Money Will Follow, 114
downsizing. *See* job loss
dream, loss of, 39–40
driving, 96, 129–130, 219–220

economic insecurity, 121
economy, the, 185
embarrassment, 43
emotions
  anger, 90–93, 99–100
  dealing with, 98–100
  emotional support, 169
  expressing of, 167
employment status, 25–26
encouragement, 169–170
ending, 88
energy cycles, 148
energy management, 136–155
entertainment, 164
entrepreneurism, 25–26, 114, 213
events, 98
Everyday Sacred, 221
exercise, 142–144
  See also sports
experiencing events, 98
external change, 16

failure, 42, 65
family, 45, 163, 172–173
fear, 40–44, 82, 191–194, 219
feedback, 171–172
fifties, the, 29–30
financial insecurity, 121, 203
financial management, 118–121, 176
financial statements, 118–119
First, You Cry, 98
flexibility, 129, 204
flex-trade, 25
Flow, 61
flow state, 61–62

flying lessons, 215–216
football, 186
  See also sports
Ford, Henry, 76
Frankl, Victor, 67
friends, 84, 163, 173
From Chaos to Confidence, 95–96
fulfillment curve, 122–123
fun, 85

Gillick, Pat, 26
  See also professional sports
global change, 21
golf, 21, 82–83
  See also sports
Gordon, Sol, 153
government, 18, 24–25
government debt, 121
graduation, 89
Great Depression, 212
grieving process, 90–93
groups, 173
growth, 58

Handy, Charles, 27–28, 65, 115
hardiness, 197–214
Harris, Jim, 43
health
  and contingency planning, 130
  health care system, 74
  healthy lifestyle, 137–155
  and uncertainty, 183
  See also illness; medicine
help, asking for, 117
Hepburn, Katherine, 197
high school, 89, 177–178
hobbies, 163
Holmes-Rahe scale, 158–161
Holocaust literature, 66–67
hospitals, 24–25, 45, 115
How We Die, 196
humor, 77–86, 204

identity, 37–38
illness
benefits of, 51–52
contingency plans for, 191–192
and emotions, 91, 98
and humor, 80–82
and responsibility, 210–211
See also health; medicine
immigrant women, 49–50
imposed change, 157
improvement, 62
information, 170
insecurity, 121
interests, 163
internal change, 16
internship (medical), 34–35, 79
interruptions, 107
isolation, 168

job hunting, 179, 203
job loss
  and certainties, 187–189
  contingency plans for, 130, 192–193
  and control, 36
  and creativity, 212
  and grieving process, 92, 97–98
job-sharing, 113
Johnson, Sue, 168
Jordan, Michael, 133–134
Judaism, 168–169

kangaroos, 21
knowledge, 111
Kübler-Ross, Elisabeth, 90–93

laugh therapy, 81
  See also humor
learning
  and balanced lifestyle, 164
  benefit of, 58
  learning curves, 20, 60–61
  learning experiences, 63–64
  lifelong learning, 112, 128–129
  and new skills, 111–112
The Learning Paradox, 43
leisure, 152–155
life events, 158–161
Life is Uncertain, Eat Dessert First!, 153
listening, 167–168
literature, 66–67
local change, 21

logistical planning, 126
logistical support, 170
loss, 36–40, 90–93
luxuries, 121

Mackay, Harvey, 174
major life events, 158–161
Malone, Brendan, 64
  See also professional sports
Managing as a Performance Art, 43
Maple Leaf Gardens, 32
  See also professional sports
marriage, 88–89, 92, 193–194
  See also relationships
Marshall Plan, 74–75
maturational readiness, 33
Maurer, Rick, 75
McPhedran, Tait, 178
meaning, 66
medicine
  health care system, 74
  hospitals, 24–25, 45, 115
  medical school, 34–35, 72–73, 178
  obstetrics, 127
  pregnancy, 41–42, 127
  trends in, 114–115
memory loss, 83–84
mentors, 176–178
metric system, 156
mind-set, 220–221
mistakes, 65
monarchy, 32
money, 118–121, 176
Monopoly, 212
monthly cash flow statement, 119–121
Mooney, Katherine, 218–219
Moore, Gordon, 19
Moore's Law, 19
  See also technology
mourning, 168–169

napping, 150–152
national change, 21
natural cycles, 29
need for change, 24–33
needs, 121–122
negative thinking, 52–54, 64, 194–195

networking, 178–180
neutralizing situations, 64
neutral zone, 88, 93–96
1950s, 29–30
no, saying no, 109–110
Nuland, Sherwin, 196
nutrition, 137–138

Oakville, 30–31
obstetrics, 127
  See also medicine
On Death and Dying, 90
Ontario government, 24–25
opportunity, 58–60
optimism, 205–207
optimizing situations, 64
organization, 105–110
oxygen, 142–143

pacing yourself, 164–165
Padesky, Christine, 218
passion, 114, 198–200
Pearson, Lester B., 38
people
  connections between, 163
  fear of, 44
  interaction with, 59, 172
  loss of, 39
perfectionism, 108
persistence, 211–212
personal change, 21
personal finance
  financial insecurity, 121
  financial management, 118–121, 176
  financial statements, 118–119
  perspective on, 203
personal time, 152–155
perspective, 49–57, 202–204
pets, 163
phasing in change, 157–158
physical appearance, 84
physical faculties, 40, 82–84
places, 39
planning, 125–135, 190–194
play, 85
politics, 58, 184
positive thinking, 52–54, 64

power, 38
pregnancy, 41–42, 127
  See also medicine
prejudging outcomes, 73–76
preparedness, 125–135
problem-solving, 170
productivity, 106–110, 164–165
professional sports
  change in, 19
  Maple Leaf Gardens, 32
  Sea Gals, 43
  tennis, 93
  Toronto Blue Jays, 26
  Toronto Raptors, 64
  trading athletes, 54–55
  See also sports
promises, unrealistic, 108
public speaking, 132
psychological preparation, 126–127

rate of change, 17–18, 48, 156–166
reaction to change, 90–93, 217
reframing, 54–57, 64–65
regional change, 21
relationships
  and change, 59
  loss of, 38–39, 39–40
  marriage, 88–89, 92, 193–194
  and neutral zone, 94–95
  and preparedness, 131
  and S-curve, 28–29
  and uncertainty, 184
relaxation, 150
reorganizing businesses, 25–26, 44
resilience, 20, 197–214
resources, 218–220
response, 217
responsibility, 209–211
rest, 149–150
retraining programs, 25
risk-taking, 62, 208–209
rituals, 162–163
Robbins, Anthony, 65
Robin, Vicki, 121–122
roles, shift in, 37–38, 42
Rollin, Betty, 98
Rossi, Ernest J., 148–149
routines, 162–163
Rusting Out, Burning Out, Bowing Out, 159

San Francisco, 72
Saskatchewan, 74
saying no, 109–110
scheduling time, 153–155
Scrabble, 212
Sea Gals, 43
  See also professional sports
self-care, 117–118
self-discovery, 93–96
self-doubt, 202
self-employment, 25–26, 114, 213
self-esteem, 37, 181
self-fulfilling prophecies, 74
Selye, Hans, 48–49
Sigmoid curve, 27–29
Sinetar, Marsha, 114
sitting shiva, 168–169
"60 Minutes," 205
skills, 58, 111
sleep, 138–142, 145–146, 150–152
social frameworks, 172
speed of change, 17–18, 48, 156–166
sports
  exercise, 142–144
  football, 186
  golf, 21, 82–83
  tennis, 61, 93–94
  track-and-field, 69–70
  See also professional sports
sports teams, 19
  See also professional sports
stability, 161–162
status, 38
The Strategic Coach, 60
strategy, 104–124
street sweepers, 205
strength, 169–170
stress
  and Holmes-Rahe scale, 158–161
  and humor, 77–78
  and perspective, 48–49
  stress-hardiness, 197–214
  successes, 71–72
Sullivan, Dan, 60

support groups, 173–174
support systems, 167–181
survival needs, 121

tasks, prioritizing, 106–107
Tavris, Carol, 100
teachers, 176–178
team players, 116–117
technology
  and change, 31–32, 43
  and learning, 58, 128
  and Moore's Law, 19
  and S-curve, 28
  and Sea Gals, 43
Telford, Sam, 177
tennis, 61, 93–94
  See also professional sports; sports
thoughts, 52–54, 64
time, 44
time management, 107, 152–155
time-outs, 108, 147–152
Toronto, 24–25
Toronto Blue Jays, 26
  See also professional sports
Toronto Raptors, 64
  See also professional sports
track-and-field, 69–70
  See also sports
tradition, 32, 162–163
training courses, 111
transitions, 66, 82–84
Transitions, 87–88
travel, 133, 164
trends, 114–116
trial-and-error phase, 20, 62
Truman, Harry, 74–75
The 20 Minute Break, 148

ultraradian rhythms, 148
uncertainty, 41–42, 182–196
understanding, 169
unemployment, 202–204
university, 89–90
unknown, the, 41–42, 128
Unlimited Power, 65
unrealistic promises, 108

Vaill, Peter, 43
validation, 170–171
value conflicts, 45
variety, 57

wake-up call, 63
Wallace, Mike, 205
wants, 121–122
Wheatley, Margaret, 75
White, Jerry, 176
Wiesel, Elie, 66–67
work, 163
working smarter, 106–110
workplace
  change in, 18
  and creativity, 112–113
  and humor, 78–80
  retraining programs, 25
  and team players, 116–117
  and uncertainty, 189–190
  See also business
worry, 190–191, 194–195

Yerkes-Dodson Law, 164–165
Your Money or Your Life, 121–123

To contact Dr. Posen for speaking engagements or seminars, please call or write to:

Dr. David B. Posen
1235 Trafalgar Road
Suite 406
Oakville, Ontario
Canada L6H 3P1
Telephone: (905) 844-0744
Fax: (905) 844-4540
E-mail: **davidposen@globalserve.net**
Website: **www.davidposen.com**